Birding North Carolina

Help Us Keep This Guide Up to Date

Every effort has been made by the authors and editors to make this guide as accurate and useful as possible. However, many things can change after a guide is published—trails are rerouted, regulations change, techniques evolve, facilities come under new management, etc.

We would love to hear from you concerning your experiences with this guide and how you feel it could be improved and kept up to date. While we may not be able to respond to all comments and suggestions, we'll take them to heart and we'll also make certain to share them with the authors. Please send your comments and suggestions to the following address:

The Globe Pequot Press
Reader Response/Editorial Department
P.O. Box 480
Guilford, CT 06437

Or you may e-mail us at:

editorial@GlobePequot.com

Thanks for your input, and happy travels!

Birding North Carolina

Carolina Bird Club

Edited by Marshall Brooks and Mark Johns, with contributions from the Carolina Bird Club

FALCONGUIDE®

GUILFORD, CONNECTICUT
HELENA, MONTANA
AN IMPRINT OF THE GLOBE PEQUOT PRESS

Text design by Eileen Hine
Maps by XNR Productions, Inc. © The Globe Pequot Press

Library of Congress Cataloging-in-Publication Data
Birding North Carolina/the Carolina Bird Club;
  edited by Marshall Brooks and Mark Johns;
  with contributions from the Carolina Bird Club.—
1st ed.
        p. cm. —(A FalconGuide)
  Includes bibliographical references.
  ISBN 0-7627-3134-6
  1. Bird watching—North Carolina—Guidebooks.
2. North Carolina—Guidebooks. I. Brooks,
Marshall, 1942–II. Johns, Mark, 1958–III. Carolina
Bird Club. IV. Series.

QL684.N8B57 2005
598'.07'234756—dc22

                                    2005045973

Manufactured in the United States of America
First Edition/First Printing

For North Carolina's birds—present and future

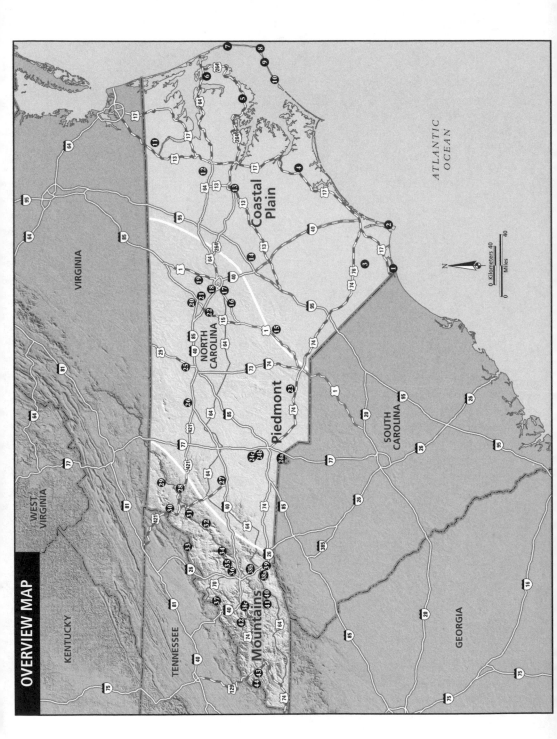

OVERVIEW MAP

Contents

Acknowledgments ix
Foreword xi
Introduction 1
   How to Use This Guide 2
   When to Go Birding 3
   What to Wear 4
   Essentials for a Successful Birding Trip 4
   Where to Stay 6
   Field Hazards 6
   Birding Ethics 7
North Carolina's Varied Environments 8
   Topography 8
   Climate 10
   Habitats 10
   Birds of North Carolina's Varied Environments 17
   Seasons 18
   Migration 18

Coastal Plain

  1. Sunset Beach 23
  2. Fort Fisher State Recreation Area 26
  3. Green Swamp Preserve and Lake Waccamaw State Park 29
  4. Croatan National Forest 32
  5. Mattamuskeet National Wildlife Refuge 36
  6. Alligator River National Wildlife Refuge 41
  7. Pea Island National Wildlife Refuge 46
  8. Cape Hatteras National Seashore 50
  9. Gulf Stream Pelagic Birding 55
10. Ocracoke Island 57
11. Merchants Millpond State Park 61
12. Roanoke River 64
13. Greenville Area 68
14. Howell Woods Environmental Learning Center 71
15. Weymouth Woods Sandhills Nature Preserve 74

Piedmont

16. Jordan Lake State Recreation Area 79
17. Hemlock Bluffs Nature Preserve, Ritter Park, and Swift Creek Bluffs . . 84
18. William B. Umstead State Park 88
19. Falls Lake State Recreation Area 91
20. Eno River State Park 95

21. Duke Forest 97
22. Mason Farm Biological Reserve 100
23. Pee Dee National Wildlife Refuge 103
24. Charlotte-Mecklenburg Area 107
25. Greensboro Municipal Reservoirs 111
26. Salem Lake 114
27. Riverbend Park and Lower Lake Hickory 116

Mountains

28. Blue Ridge Parkway North 121
29. New River 124
30. Amphibolite Mountains and Elk Knob Game Land and State
        Natural Area 127
31. Moses Cone and Julian Price Memorial Parks 132
32. Linville Gorge and Surrounding Area 135
33. Roan Mountain 139
34. Mount Mitchell State Park 142
35. Big Ivy, Craggy Gardens, and Balsam Gap 145
36. Blue Ridge Parkway from Craven Gap to Lane Pinnacle 149
37. Max Patch Road and Environs 152
38. Lakes of the Southern Mountains 155
39. Jackson Park 159
40. Davidson River and Pink Beds 163
41. Devil's Courthouse and Black Balsam 167
42. Heintooga Spur Road and Nearby Parkway Locations 170
43. Stecoah Gap 174
44. Joyce Kilmer Memorial Forest and Cherohala Skyway 176

Appendix A: North Carolina Specialty Birds 179
Appendix B: Official North Carolina State Bird List 192
Appendix C: American Birding Association's Code of Birding Ethics 198
Appendix D: North Carolina Birding, Bird Conservation Organizations,
        and Programs 200
Appendix E: Rare Bird Alerts 201
Appendix F: Additional Resources for Birding in North Carolina 202
Index 204
About the Editors 210

Acknowledgments

Birding North Carolina is the result of the vision of Len Pardue who, during his presidency of the Carolina Bird Club, began working on making it become a reality. Len asked us to coordinate the development of the guide and to serve as the coeditors. Many individuals have generously shared their time, energy, and knowledge of birds and birding sites with this guide.

Birding North Carolina would not be a reality if had not been for the untiring efforts and dedication of our two associate editors, Karen Bearden and Marilyn Westphal. Each served as a regional coordinator in recruiting the authors of site descriptions, Karen for the coastal and piedmont regions and Marilyn for the mountains. Each edited the original site descriptions and then reviewed and commented on the descriptions that were ultimately included in this guide. We are greatly indebted to them for their guidance and contributions throughout the development of the guide.

In the process of developing *Birding North Carolina* we solicited site descriptions from individuals throughout the state. We want to thank the following authors for submitting one or more site descriptions for the guide: Ron Anundson, Louise Barden, Karen Bearden, Brian Bockhahn, Colleen Bockhahn, Dennis Burnette, John Connors, Will Cook, Sam Cooper, Sudie Daves, Kelly Davis, Doug DeNeve, Jeff Esely, Wayne Forsythe, Lena Gallitano, John Gerwin, Charlotte Goedsche, Jeff Hall, Elizabeth Hanrahan, Scott Hartley, Mark Johns, Jeff Lewis, Sidney Maddock, Jeff Marcus, Ernie Marshall, Dwayne Martin, Lori Martin, Mary McDavit, Reece Mitchell, Pat Moore, Bob Olthoff, Len Pardue, Brian Patteson, Taylor Piephoff, Jeff Pippen, Liz Pullman, Jean Richter, Josh Rose, Linda Rudd, Jamie Sasser, Melody Scott, Don Seriff, Steve Shultz, Norma Siebenheller, Curtis Smalling, Clyde Smith, Clyde Sorenson, Bert Speicher, Mary Stevens, Erik Thomas, Simon Thompson, Howard Vainright, Judy Walker, Linda Ward, and Marilyn Westphal.

We are very appreciative of the work of the following individuals for their time and effort in checking site descriptions by driving the routes, walking the trails, and birding the sites: Joe Bearden, Karen Bearden, Karen Beck, Susan Campbell, Kent Fiala, Anita Gerling, Stephen Harris, Gail Lankford, Janie Owens, Lisa Richman, Kerry Sadler, Bob Wood, and Rachel Wood. We also appreciate the following individuals for their willingness to submit photos for inclusion in the guide: Kate deGategno, Edward Dombrofski, Bill Duyck, Nikki Landry, Jeff Pippen, Jeremy Poirier, Jamie Sasser, and Harry Sell.

We thank Dr. Marcus Simpson, author of *Birds of the Blue Ridge Mountains,* for his guidance in identifying sites along the Blue Ridge Parkway, and Curtis Smalling of Audubon, North Carolina, for single-handedly writing the descriptions for sites in the northern mountains. We also want to acknowledge the support and assistance that we received from the Carolina Bird Club Executive Committee and Bob Wood, the club's current president; the North Carolina Partners in Flight

Education and Outreach Committee; the North Carolina Wildlife Resources Commission; and North Carolina Wesleyan College. We are very grateful for the support and advice from Erin Turner, Gillian Belnap, and staff of The Globe Pequot Press in bringing the guide to fruition.

Harry LeGrand of the North Carolina Natural Heritage Program and Ricky Davis, the Southern Atlantic editor for *North American Birds,* provided invaluable expertise throughout the development of the guide. In addition to kindly accepting our invitation for writing the foreword, helping with site sections, and insuring that we had the most up-to-date list of North Carolina birds, Harry provided us with advice and guidance throughout the process. We are very grateful to Ricky for giving generously of his time when we most needed it by reviewing site descriptions and species accounts of North Carolina bird specialties. His knowledge of birds and of the birding sites in North Carolina contributed significantly in improving the accuracy of the seasonal abundance and distribution of the specialty birds and of the site descriptions.

A special thanks goes to Marshall's wife, Susan Brooks, and Mark's parents, Robert and Tillie Tingen, for their patience and support throughout the entire process of developing this guide.

Thus, *Birding North Carolina* is the result of a collaborative effort. It has been a pleasure and privilege to work with more than eighty birders and naturalists in this endeavor. We are delighted that on behalf of all the volunteers, the Carolina Bird Club, North Carolina Partners in Flight, and the North Carolina Wildlife Resources Commission that the royalties from this guide go to a special fund, managed by the Carolina Bird Club, dedicated to promoting research and conservation of the birds of the Carolinas.

Foreword

North Carolina is one of the premier birding destinations in the United States. With an Official Bird List of 443 species and 17 more on the Provisional List, the state's 460 bird species (as of August 2004) that have been reliably reported rank higher than all states east of the Mississippi except for Florida, Massachusetts, New Jersey, and New York. Florida's total can be explained by its proximity to the West Indies, with dozens of strays from that region, not to mention receiving strays from the western United States that erroneously migrated to the Southeast. For the other three states, their list is simply due to extremely high density and coverage by birders.

North Carolina's extensive bird list is a combination of factors. First, because North Carolina lies at the confluence of the cold waters of the Labrador Current and the warm waters of the Gulf Stream, pelagic (offshore) birding can be excellent and is the state's best claim to fame. No other Atlantic Coast state has a higher seabird list, and several first continental records have been made off our state. Birders from across the continent travel to Manteo or Hatteras to visit our offshore waters, because a handful of regularly occurring species can, for all intents and purposes, be seen nowhere else in North America. Second, the state has the greatest elevation range (sea level to 6,684 feet) of any state in the eastern half of the country. Third, the state has a fairly high density of birders, though that density is centered in the Piedmont, well away from the coast. If more of the North Carolina density of birders lived along, or close to, the coast—as in Massachusetts, New York, New Jersey, and Florida—then that state total likely would be closer to 470 or 480 species. Why is that? The majority of strays and first state records show up along the coast, where birds wandering far off course, such as from the western United States, are stopped by coastlines. Of course, birders inland have contributed their share of first state records.

Despite the state's great diversity of birds, not only on the total list but also on the breeding list (around 200 species), there has never been a statewide bird-finding guide for North Carolina. True, the mountain region has an excellent guide—*Birds of the Blue Ridge Mountains* (1992), written by Marcus (Mark) Simpson. And, two years later, an even more valuable book was published—*A Birder's Guide to Coastal North Carolina*. This book, by John Fussell, is a birder's bible, in that most out-of-state birders who travel to North Carolina visit our coast and offshore waters.

Birding North Carolina is not the first attempt at a statewide bird-finding guide. I am aware of at least three other attempts from publishers to have such a book in their portfolio. After all, most of the fifty states already have statewide guides, some written by a "committee" approach and some by mostly a single author. But for one reason or another, such efforts failed, mainly because no one took charge to crack the whip and force deadlines for authors of accounts. Thankfully, Marshall Brooks and Mark Johns were successful in rounding up authors, in part because of their partnership with North Carolina Partners in Flight. Marshall has also developed the NC PIF Web site, and Mark is the state Breeding Bird Survey coordinator. Thus, these two editors have contacts with large numbers of birders in the state and have the expertise necessary in getting contributions from them.

So, now we have the question: Why is a statewide bird-finding guide necessary? First, North Carolina has not had a statewide annotated bird book describing the status, abundance, seasonal occurrence, habitat, and distribution of its birds since *Birds of the Carolinas* (1980), by Eloise Potter, James Parnell, and Robert Teulings. Their book provided only general species accounts, without providing details of individual reports, for both North and South Carolina. The last state book, detailing rarity reports, was *Birds of North Carolina,* written way back in 1942 and updated with new records in 1959. Second, many birders, both in-state and out-of-state, need bird-finding information for sites *between* the mountains and the coast. Most birders live in the Piedmont and inner-central Coastal Plain. Out-of-state birders who attend meetings or visit friends for brief periods often request bird-finding information about sites around Raleigh, Durham, Chapel Hill, Greensboro, Winston-Salem, Charlotte, and other populated areas. There is a dire need to have bird-finding information for sites all across the state.

Birding North Carolina will fill both of the gaps mentioned in the preceding paragraph, as well as updating information presented in the previous guides that might now be out-of-date. First, the annotated list of North Carolina Specialty Birds in the back of the book provides a quick summary of the birds of the state, regions where they occur, their abundances there, and the best times to see them. Second, at long last the important birding sites in North Carolina will be presented in a single reference. And, because the sections were written collectively by some of the most experienced birders in the state, as opposed to a single person who might not be familiar with all of the sites, one can expect that each section was written by someone intimately familiar with the birds, other features of interest, and—perhaps most important—how to reach the sites!

I hope you enjoy the book and use it frequently. Most of all, I hope everyone adds many bird species to his or her own state list, or life list, with help from the book. As a longtime birder in the state and chair of the North Carolina Bird Records Committee for many years, who just recently hit 420 birds for my personal state list, I sure wish I had had a statewide bird-finding guide at my disposal all those years ago. Thanks to Marshall and Mark, and all of the contributors to *Birding North Carolina.*

Harry E. LeGrand Jr.
North Carolina Natural Heritage Program
Department of Environment and Natural Resources

Introduction

North Carolina has as impressive diversity of habitats, vegetation features, and climate that yield one of the richest collections of birdlife in North America. From some of the highest mountain peaks in the eastern United States to isolated coastal barrier islands that are constantly shifting in response to weather and tides, North Carolina is truly a birder's paradise throughout the year. There are birds in the spruce fir forests of the mountains that are typical of similar habitats in Canada to go along with some of the largest wintering waterfowl concentrations in the East in this state.

Some of the rarest birds in the Southeast can be seen in North Carolina, like the Red-cockaded Woodpecker and the Wood Stork. Southern specialties such as Swainson's Warbler can be found at both the coast and western regions of the state, and the reclusive Black Rail and fire-dependent Bachman's Sparrow are present. Impressive counts of migrating raptors can be seen with ease along sections of the Blue Ridge Parkway, or you can search for a huge assortment of shorebirds and colonial waterbirds at the coast.

This book contains a selection of many of the best birding areas in the state, described by the top birders in North Carolina. Obviously they are not the only good areas to bird in North Carolina but are a compilation of outstanding sites across the state. Most any species found annually in North Carolina can be found at one or more of these sites. Often top birding sites are lost to development, urban sprawl, or habitat alteration over time, but sites in this book should remain important for some time to come.

Anyone who is birding on a regular basis understands that important habitat for a wide variety of birds is lost or altered daily in North Carolina and other areas in the United States. Birders are some of the most conservation-minded individuals you will ever meet, often spending large amounts of money to support organizations involved with bird conservation in their home state, in their region, nationally, or around the world. In North Carolina, an active Partners in Flight program seeks to increase communication, cooperation, and collaboration among concerned government agencies, conservation organizations, private industry, academia, and concerned individuals to further bird conservation throughout the state, region, and the Americas. There are Partners in Flight programs in every region of the United States and Canada. North Carolina Partners in Flight is coordinated by the North Carolina Wildlife Resources Commission.

There are volunteer opportunities for birders of all abilities, as well as a plethora of information about birds and bird conservation efforts throughout the state and the Americas on the North Carolina Partners in Flight Web site, www.faculty .ncwc.edu/mbrooks/pif/. You can also reach the NC Partners in Flight Web site via www.ncwildlife.org.

How to Use This Guide

There are an astounding number of quality places to bird in North Carolina at all seasons, and the sites featured in this guide should produce some great birding experiences. Although this guide won't help you with identifying birds in the field, it should help you get to places that regularly allow for good viewing opportunities.

The state has been divided into three regions: Coastal Plain, Piedmont, and Mountains. The next chapter provides information on how to plan your birding trip, as well as descriptions of the regions and habitats of the state. Each of the three regional chapters includes site descriptions and directions, as well as suggestions on how and when to bird each area. There is also information about key species and where and when to find them in North Carolina, as well as an official state bird list, in the first two appendixes at the end of the book.

Each site description follows a similar format, and it is best to read the entire description before making decisions about a visit. Keep in mind that there may be logistical considerations and advanced planning required for visits to some of the sites. There will be a site contact in most cases and also the county location. Each site is formatted to give the following at-a-glance information.

County: This section names the county or counties where the site is located.

Habitats: This section lists the major habitat types found at each birding site. To most effectively use this section, you should read the next chapter, which contains habitat descriptions.

Key birds: This section features a list of some specialty birds as well as birds typical of each site at various times of the year.

Best times to bird: This section suggests the best times to bird each site, focusing on the seasons.

About this site: This is the most detailed and important part of each site description. It tells you where to look to find what species and in some cases provides details on conservation issues associated with specific species or habitats. This section contains general information on the site and in some cases an orientation on what to expect regarding facilities, trails, and overall access.

Other key birds: This section provides a list of many of the other birds that are present at the site.

Nearby opportunities: This section points out areas that provide interesting birding opportunities that are relatively near the site. Additional information for many of these opportunities is available online at the Carolina Bird Club's Web site, www.carolinabirdclub.org.

Directions: This section will provide enough travel information and direction to assure that you can find the site. This information should be used in conjunction with a state highway map, state roadway atlas, or local map with greater detail.

Access: This section provides information about any areas of the site that are accessible for persons with disabilities. Some sites are such that visitors may bird from the car, while others are reachable only by a footpath. Some have a wheelchair-accessible viewing platform or observation deck.

Bathrooms: This section explains whether there are restrooms available and if so, where they are located on the site.

Hazards: This section identifies hazards that are more pronounced than those normally encountered in the field.

Nearest food, gas, and lodging: This section lists services most convenient or closest to the site.

Nearest camping: For public campgrounds the name and number of available sites is provided. If a public campground is not available, the name of a nearby town that has private campgrounds is listed.

DeLorme map grid: This section provides the page number and grid location for the site.

North Carolina Travel Map grid: This section provides the grid location for the site.

For more information: This section includes phone number, address, and Internet Web site (where available) for the site.

The information in this guide will get you to the sites and help you bird efficiently at the best times of the year. With this guide you can simply pick the sites you want to visit that sound interesting, or cross check in Appendixes A and B for the specific species and their distribution and status within the state to concentrate on target birds. The book concludes with four more appendixes (C through F) to help guide you through reporting rare birds or find birding organizations and wildlife management agencies in North Carolina.

When to Go Birding

Because of the state's diverse landscape, birding in North Carolina is a year round activity throughout the state, from the mountains to the coast. Each season of the year has birds that will excite even the most experienced birders. Given the location of the state and the variety of the habitats, the best time for birding depends on what one wants to see. The late spring and summer months, April through July, are an excellent time to experience the song and sights of breeding birds, particularly in the deciduous woods of the Piedmont and mountains of North Carolina. During this same period shorebirds and waterbirds are migrating along the coast. If it's sheer variety of land and shorebirds that you are wanting to see, then the period of March through May, when spring migration is in full swing, is an excellent time to be in the field. The Outer Banks can be a natural funnel for fall migrating land birds. Fall also provides an excellent opportunity to catch the southward march of migrating hawks above the ridges of the Blue Ridge Mountains. Pelagic birding off the coast of Cape Hatteras National Seashore Recreational Area generally reaches a high point during the last two weeks of May, when the species count is increased as the result of migrants passing through and the arrival of the summer resident species. In addition to the viewing of sparrows, the winter months are excellent for viewing a multitude of waterfowl along the coastal and inland waters of the eastern part of the state.

What to Wear

What you wear in the field depends, of course, on your own taste in clothing, the time of year, location, and level of activity. Yet, with any foray into the field, perhaps with exceptions of ocean beaches or summer pelagic trips, the birder should wear long pants and the field-appropriate footwear, which includes socks and walking shoes or hiking boots. Wearing a hat is also important for protecting oneself from the sun and insects in the warmer months and for maintaining body heat in the winter. Baseball caps with a moderate to long bill are good for shading eyes from the sun and reducing glare. With daytime temperatures in North Carolina changing greatly from the early morning hours to midday, it is also important to layer clothing that can be removed or added as needed. Sudden afternoon showers are common in the state during the hot summer months, so having a lightweight rain jacket or disposable poncho is recommended when in the field and away from shelter.

Essentials for a Successful Birding Trip

Binoculars

Having the right equipment when heading into the field will enhance your likelihood of having an enjoyable and rewarding birding experience. The birder's primary tool is a pair of binoculars. Binoculars come in all shapes, sizes, and price ranges. If you do not already have a pair, it would pay to spend a little time researching a variety of makes and styles in your price range. Information about how to select binoculars can be found at online sites as well in various birding magazines. There are numerous online sellers of binoculars as well as specialty stores that feature birding supplies, sporting goods, and outdoor equipment and clothing. Large discount stores usually have a limited selection of inexpensive models.

Bird Guides

Just as there are a variety of binoculars, the same can be said about field guides for birds. Some guides have photos of birds while others use images that are painted or drawn. A list of field guides is provided in Appendix F.

Maps

We consider two maps essential to have on hand for birding in unfamiliar locations in North Carolina: the *Official State Transportation Map for North Carolina* and the DeLorme *North Carolina Atlas & Gazetteer*. All sites in this book reference both of these sources.

The *Official State Transportation Map for North Carolina* is available as one enters the state by car at North Carolina Welcome Centers on Interstates 26, 40, 77, 85, and 95. To order a map inside North Carolina or for general information, call (800) DOT–4YOU, or (800) 368–4968. To order maps from outside the state, call (800) VISIT NC, or (800) 847–4862. If calling from within the state, the number is (919) 715–3097. If you are birding coastal areas which have access only by ferry, call (800) BY-FERRY, or (800) 293–3779, for information and reservations. For real-time information on incidents, such as weather and construction, affecting highway travel across North Carolina, visit the Web site www.ncsmartlink.org.

The DeLorme *North Carolina Atlas & Gazetteer,* 4th edition, which is copyrighted 2003, is the most current version. You may find it in bookstores, outdoor equipment stores, and discount stores throughout North Carolina, or from online booksellers if you are ordering from outside the region. You can also order direct from DeLorme at (207) 846–7000 or www.delorme.com. The combined atlas and gazetteer contains road listings from major highways to county roads, along with the topography of the area. The gazetteer categories include bike routes, boat launch sites, campgrounds, ferry locations, major hiking trails, state game lands, and state designated wildlife viewing areas.

Parks and Wildlife Management Areas

Most of the sites described in this guide are located on land that is managed by either a governmental agency or a nongovernmental organization such as the Nature Conservancy or Audubon. A few of the sites are located in areas that are designated as game lands or waterfowl management areas which are set aside for hunting and/or fishing. It is important to avoid dates when hunting is allowed. Local numbers for these areas are provided in the site description. Additional information for the National Wildlife Refuges located in North Carolina can be found by visiting the U.S. Fish and Wildlife Southeastern Region Web site at http://southeast.fws.gov. Information regarding North Carolina State Parks is available at Welcome Centers, the Division of Tourism, and on the Web at www.ils.unc.edu/parkproject/ncparks.html.

Checklist of Essentials
- ☐ Binoculars
- ☐ Field guide
- ☐ Insect repellant
- ☐ Sunscreen
- ☐ Note pad
- ☐ Appropriate clothing and hat
- ☐ DeLorme and North Carolina Highway Maps

Optional items include a spotting scope, particularly for coastal, lake, and reservoir birding; portable CD or tape player for playing recordings to help in identification (a tape player could also be used for recording unfamiliar birds); and a camera for taking scenic or bird shots.

Where to Stay

Most of the sites in this guide are within an hour of a town or community with restaurants and accommodations. The North Carolina Division of Tourism has a number of excellent publications that highlight visitor attractions and accommodations throughout the state. Guides that we have found to particularly informative include *North Carolina: The Official Travel Guide; North Carolina RV & Camping Guide Directory;* and the *North Carolina Outdoor Recreation Guide: With Lodging and Outfitters Directory.* These guides are available at North Carolina Welcome Centers or from the Division of Tourism: (800) VISIT NC, or (800) 847–4862, if calling from outside North Carolina, or (919) 715–3097 if calling from within the state. Information for camping in a state park is available through the Division of State Parks Web site, www.ils.unc.edu/parkproject/ncparks.html.

Field Hazards

Because biting insects such as mosquitoes, "no-see-ums," and flies can be present beginning in spring and lasting until late fall, it is important to carry insect repellant into the field. Ticks and chiggers generally tend to be a problem primarily during the warmer months. The best protection from ticks and chiggers is to wear long pants and long-sleeved shirts. By tucking your shirt into your pants and your pant legs into your socks, you can help prevent insect pests from gaining access.

The type of clothing that you wear for protection against ticks and chiggers is also effective in avoiding an allergic reaction to poison ivy, poison oak, and poison sumac, all of which are found in the varied habitats throughout North Carolina. Direct or indirect contact with any part of these plants can result in severe inflammation and blistering of the skin. A good habit to develop is to use a good soap and wash well your hands, arms, and legs (if wearing shorts or short sleeves) the very first thing when coming in from being in the field.

North Carolina is one of the fastest-growing states in the country. It is also a favored vacation area throughout the year. As a result you are very likely to encounter other vehicles on most roads throughout the state, paved or not. In addition, many of the sites described in this guide are accessible only from the road. It is very important that when stopping along a road, you are sure to park in a safe area off the road. Do not stop or park in a traffic lane regardless of the condition of the road and even if it appears to have no other traffic. Also, take care in watching for traffic when you are out of the car along a roadside. An additional road hazard throughout the state, particularly from dusk until dawn, is a white-tailed deer that may suddenly dash across the road. Hitting a deer with a car can result in "totaling" the vehicle as well as causing serious or fatal injury to the occupants.

Six species of venomous snakes are found in North Carolina. Three species are rattlesnakes (eastern diamondback, timber, pigmy), and then there are copperhead, cottonmouth, and coral snakes. While you will not find all of these species throughout North Carolina, there are only a few areas in the state that do not have at least one species present and active during warm weather. The best way to avoid snakes is to be alert when in likely habitat by watching where you walk and by not reaching into areas where you cannot see. If you see a snake, quickly walk away; you can be out of its reach in three steps.

Black bears are native to North Carolina and found mainly in the mountains and coastal plain. A black bear is normally shy and nonaggressive unless it is a female with cubs. If you are birding in areas where bears are known to be present, then exercise caution about leaving food out, and never attempt to approach or feed a bear.

During the summer months particularly, there is the possibility of lightning strikes. It is best not to start an excursion into the field if a thunderstorm is likely. If caught in a storm, take shelter immediately in a hardtop vehicle or building if possible.

Birding Ethics

Everyone who enjoys birds and birding must always respect wildlife, its environment, and the rights of others. In any conflict of interest between birds and birders, the welfare of the birds and their environment comes first. Not all the birding sites listed in this guide are open to public access. For these sites it is very important that you make arrangements with the associations or private landowners before visiting. In all cases birders should be respectful of the rights and regulations of the landowners. See Appendix C: American Birding Association's Code of Birding Ethics.

North Carolina's Varied Environments

North Carolina boasts a natural landscape of great richness and diversity. This landscape is a result of long and continued interactions among the land, climate, and living things, including people. The state has an abundance of habitat types, variable topography, and many interesting plant communities. All of this variety helps yield a plethora of avian species throughout the year for birding enjoyment and also presents many opportunities for avian conservation actions by birders.

Topography

The state's varied landscape extends from the mighty Atlantic Ocean to the majestic Great Smoky Mountains National Park. From the western end of the state in Murphy to the Outer Banks community of Manteo on Roanoke Island is a journey of about 543 miles. There are three recognized physiographic provinces: Coastal Plain, Piedmont, and Mountains.

Almost one-half of the state is within the Coastal Plain, which varies in width between 100 and 140 miles between the ocean and the fall line at its boundary with the Piedmont. The Coastal Plain can be divided into tidewater and inner Coastal Plain sections. The tidewater section contains the Outer Banks, capes and areas that border the coastal sounds. Elevation is typically 20 feet or less. The inner Coastal Plain extends west to the fall line and reaches elevations of about 600 feet above sea level.

A view of salt marsh and estuarine waters at Cape Hatteras National Seashore.
PHOTO: KAREN BEARDEN

Spruce fir forest and rhododendron balds on Round Bald at Carver's Gap. PHOTO: KAREN BEARDEN

The Piedmont is about the same size in area as the Coastal Plain and lies between the fall line and the escarpment of the Southern Blue Ridge Mountains. With its rolling hills, it reaches elevations of around 2,000 feet above sea level. There are also some isolated peaks and ridges such as the Uwharrie Mountains, Sauratown Mountains, Kings Mountain range, and outliers from the Blue Ridge province such as the Brushy and South Mountains.

The Mountains physiographic region is about 15 to 50 miles in width, lies along the western boundary of North Carolina, and contains a little over 10 percent of the state's land area. It includes two very dissected chains of mountain ranges, including the Blue Ridge Mountains along the east and another range that contains the Unaka, Great Smoky, and Unicoi Mountains which basically parallel the Blue Ridge to the west. Elevations range from about 3,000 feet to 6,000 feet above sea level. There are several cross-ridge connections of the two main chains of mountains, including the Black Mountains and the Pisgah, Balsam, and Nantahala Mountains. The eastern continental divide follows along the crest of the Blue Ridge Mountains. The Black Mountains feature a dozen peaks in excess of 6,000 feet, including Mount Mitchell at 6,684 feet, which is the highest point of land east of the Black Hills of South Dakota.

Climate

Climate and weather have influenced the landscapes of the state since there have been landscapes to affect. A broad range of climatic conditions exist in North Carolina due to three distinct physiographic areas: the Southern Appalachians, Piedmont, and the Coastal Plain. The topographic structure of the state and the presence of the Gulf Stream off the coast combine to give North Carolina impressive climate variability in both rainfall and temperature.

In general, the Piedmont is warmer in the summer and drier throughout the year than either the Coastal Plain or Mountains due to the coolness of the higher elevations of the mountains and to the coast's proximity to the ocean and sounds. Obviously the Mountains region temperatures can be quite cold during winter (below freezing), especially at higher elevation, and the eastern half of the state can commonly have temperatures above ninety degrees in summer. Snowfall is unusual in the Piedmont but can be quite common some years in the Mountains. Afternoon thunderstorms can produce torrential rainfall for short periods of time in any region of the state during summer.

In sum, the state is characterized by warm summers and mild to moderate winters, with 40 to 60 inches of rainfall spread fairly evenly across the year. Weather conditions in the short term can change quite rapidly, however, as fronts or low-pressure systems pass through the state. It's best to be prepared by layering clothes and carrying rain gear at all times.

Habitats

There are many diverse habitat types in North Carolina. The North Carolina Natural Heritage Program recognizes dozens of natural communities in its book *Classification of the Natural Communities of North Carolina* by Michael Schafale and Alan Weakley. Within each community there are often dozens more sample plant communities listed. For example, the Fraser Fir Forest community type lists more than twenty sample plant communities. To simplify matters regarding habitat types for this guide, habitat areas are combined into major categories to increase ease of use for birders.

Fraser Fir–Red Spruce Forest

The highest mountain areas of North Carolina are mostly Fraser fir forests, generally at elevations above 6,000 feet but extending lower in exposed places or more mesic coves. The climate in these areas is like boreal Canada. At other high mountain areas above 5,500 feet (although locally lower), there are forests dominated by Red Spruce with or without Fraser fir components.

These forests have been highly disturbed in almost all areas by an introduced insect pest that attacks and kills Fraser fir, the balsam woolly adelgid. In addition, there are other concerns related to air pollution that apparently affects growth and

Counting birds on a Breeding Bird Survey route in Madison County. PHOTO. MARSHALL BROOKS

survival of spruce and has added to past damage in these high-elevation forests caused by logging and associated fires in the early parts of the twentieth century. Changes that have resulted from death of adult firs or spruce have led to an increase in the shrub component of these forests, many more gaps and dead trees, and declines in moss and herbaceous plants. These changes have in turn greatly affected and changed the bird community (and other wildlife) present in these sites. There are several bird species of high conservation concern in this habitat type, one of the most endangered in North America.

Hardwood Forest

This is a common habitat type in North Carolina that is dominated by a variety of broad-leaved tree species, with occasional needle-leaved trees (e.g., pine, hemlock, or cypress) present in small amounts. In the mountains, cove forests and northern hardwood forests are common and dominated by mesophytic trees, including occasional needle-leaved trees. There are oak or oak-hickory-dominated forests in all parts of the state, ranging from the high elevations in the mountains to the Coastal Plain, that are well-drained. Historically these upland forests burned infrequently but with consistency over time, but natural fire has been all but eliminated from these communities for many years, leading to a lack of understory diversity.

Mesic hardwood forests of various types are found mainly in the Piedmont and

A wooded swamp is a likely spot for Wood Ducks. PHOTO: MARSHALL BROOKS

Coastal Plain. Floodplains as well as bottomland hardwood or swamp forest systems of various widths and size with decent hardwood components are also common, with much more extensive bottomlands found in the Piedmont and especially Coastal Plain regions. Some of these lowland forests can be seasonally or almost constantly flooded. Several bird species of high conservation concern are in lowland habitats, especially at the coast.

Mixed Conifer Hardwood Forest

These forests occur in a variety of age classes and sizes throughout the state. Basically any woodland that is made up of mostly pines (or hemlocks in the mountains and cypress in the Coastal Plain) and hardwoods falls in this category. Some of these areas may succeed to mostly hardwoods of some type over several years.

Many birds historically typical of hardwood areas (like Scarlet Tanager, Ovenbird, Red-eyed Vireo, and Black-and-white Warbler) are also found in this type of habitat, although midstory and understory development and tree species diversity are often lacking due to fire suppression. In many parts of the state, red maple, sweet gum, and tulip tree are common hardwoods in these stands more so than they were historically due to disturbance or fire suppression, which has led to a decline in oaks and hickories.

Pine Forest

Several types of pine-dominated forests in of various ages and sizes occur through-out the state, including loblolly pine forests of industrial timber companies in the Coastal Plain. In the mountains there are forests with successional white pine, as well as xeric pine-dominated ridges with Virginia pine, pitch pine, and table mountain pine. In the Coastal Plain and Sandhills of the state, there are longleaf pine forests of various sizes and soil types. Some of them, like pine flatwoods and savannas, are rather moist. The Sandhills region also has some very sandy, dry pine-dominated habitats with a variety of midstory and understory conditions, depend-ing on past fire history.

Pocosin

A variety of peatland community types exist in the Coastal Plain of the state. Some are dominated by dense shrubs (low pocosin and high pocosin) and are sea-sonally flooded or saturated. These habitats include poorly drained interstream flats, as well as peat-filled Carolina bays and swales. Pond pine woodlands have an open to nearly closed canopy of pond pine and some other trees along with a very dense shrub layer. There are also within a mosaic of these peatland communities some forests with decent components of Atlantic white cedar and other wetland trees, as well as bay forests dominated by evergreen woody vegetation.

There are also stream-head pocosin habitats in the headwater areas of small streams in the Sandhills that have dense shrub layers. Some of these habitats have significant amounts of Atlantic white cedar in the canopy. Many pocosin habitats were subjected historically to periodic intense fires, and these fires played a major role in shaping the plant and animal species diversity of these communities. Rarely now is fire of any kind a part of the dynamics of pocosins in the state, much to the detriment of bird species diversity.

Early Successional

This habitat category contains shrub and scrub-dominated areas (as well as regen-erating young-forested habitats) and assorted grasslands, pastures, hayfields, and assorted old field habitats. Some of these shrubby habitats at the coast are adjacent to or transition into marshy habitat.

At the immediate coast, there are also some maritime shrub habitats with asso-ciated dense shrub layers. Some of these maritime areas have some tree compo-nents featuring live oak and loblolly pine. Painted Buntings occur in these maritime habitats in parts of the lower coast of North Carolina. This bird is one of the highest conservation priorities in the Coastal Plain of North Carolina. Grass and shrub areas of high elevations in the mountains include grassy and heath balds. Human actions likely played a role historically with keeping some of these areas in an early successional state along with a variety of other factors.

Fields, pastures, and hayfields occur throughout the state in a variety of shapes and sizes, although most of these patches are small and not of high quality and are

Grassy balds near top of Round Bald at Carver's Gap. PHOTO: KAREN BEARDEN

somewhat ephemeral over time. Of all bird species, grassland birds have suffered some of the highest population declines continent-wide and in North Carolina.

Early successional species like Eastern Meadowlark and Grasshopper Sparrow occur in the grass-dominated systems, while shrubland has the Indigo Bunting, Yellow-breasted Chat, Eastern Towhee, Common Yellowthroat, and Gray Catbird. Plowed fields can attract open country birds such as the Horned Lark and concentrations of shorebirds, especially if there is standing water present. Farm fields with any amount of field borders present can hold impressive numbers of sparrows in winter.

Marshland

Marshes are dominated by dense herbaceous vegetation often growing in the water, including grasses, rushes, sedges, cattails, and other wetland plants. Most of these areas have ground that is quite moist and often underwater. Fresh, brackish, and saltwater marshlands almost always hold birds. Several birds common to marshes of some kind are of high conservation concern, especially rails.

Typical freshwater marsh habitat includes margins of estuaries, edges of rivers and creeks flooded with freshwater tides, and beaver ponds and edges or shorelines of artificially created ponds and reservoirs. Brackish marshland is found where fresh and salt water mix near the mouths of rivers that flow to the ocean. Salt marsh areas include the margins of sounds and estuaries, backs of barrier islands, and old flood tide deltas near closed inlets that have regular saltwater tides. These areas are typically dominated by cordgrass and are the home of salt marsh sparrows such as Nelson's Sharp-tailed Sparrow, Saltmarsh Sharp-tailed Sparrow, and Seaside Sparrow. Rails and bitterns are other species of marshland birds in North Carolina.

A marshy area provides excellent opportunities for seeing a variety of sparrows during the winter. PHOTO: MARSHALL BROOKS

Impoundments throughout the state provide gathering spots for winter waterfowl.
PHOTO: MARSHALL BROOKS

Beach

This habitat type includes tidal flats that are flooded by the tide twice each day and upper beaches composed of sand and shell contents (including the dunes adjacent to the upper beach) above the high-tide line. Tidal flats are great places to see many types of shorebirds, terns, gulls, and wading birds, and the upper beach holds nesting waterbirds such as American Oystercatchers.

Water

This category includes open water areas, including the Atlantic Ocean, where many waterfowl species can be found by scanning from the beach. In some cases even pelagic birds may be seen from the shoreline after intense storms. Other open water habitats to visit are the increasing numbers of man-made reservoirs (often called lakes although they are created by dams), which are good places for waterfowl, Bald Eagle (a federally threatened species), and Osprey.

Ponds are smaller bodies of water that can be quite productive for a variety of waterbirds. With low water conditions in lakes and ponds, the mudflats that are exposed are great for shorebirds and wading birds. Managed diked bodies of water such as wastewater treatment plants and aquacultural farms are worth inspecting.

The open water of rivers and large streams can yield interesting finds at all times of the year. Bridges that have safe access and boat launch ramps are good spots to use to check out moving open water systems. Small streams are included in other previously discussed habitat types, because birds found in them are often really components of those habitats.

Birds of North Carolina's Varied Environments

Some birds can exploit a variety of habitats at various times of the year during different parts of their life cycle. However, some birds are more likely to be found in association with specific habitats, and the following list suggests the best (but not necessarily only) places to find these species in some region of the state, during the breeding season unless otherwise indicated.

Fraser Fir–Red Spruce Forest
Black-capped Chickadee
Blue-headed Vireo
Brown Creeper
Canada Warbler
Common Raven
Northern Saw-whet Owl
Pine Siskin
Red Crossbill
Red-breasted Nuthatch
Winter Wren

Hardwood Forest
Acadian Flycatcher
American Redstart
Black-throated Blue Warbler (mountains)
Canada Warbler (mountains)
Cerulean Warbler (mountains/Roanoke River)
Hooded Warbler
Kentucky Warbler
Mississippi Kite (coastal)
Prothonotary Warbler
Rose-breasted Warbler (mountains)
Scarlet Tanager
Swainson's Warbler
Veery (mountains)

Warbling Vireo
Wood Thrush
Worm-eating Warbler
Yellow Warbler
Yellow-bellied Sapsucker (mountains)

Mixed Conifer Hardwood Forest
Blackburnian Warbler (mountains)
Blue-headed Vireo
Broad-winged Hawk
Pileated Woodpecker
Red-headed Woodpecker
Ruffed Grouse (mountains)
Scarlet Tanager
Summer Tanager
Whip-poor-will
Wood Thrush
Worm-eating Warbler
Yellow-throated Warbler

Pine Forest
Bachman's Sparrow (longleaf)
Brown-headed Nuthatch
Chuck-will's-widow
Red-cockaded Woodpecker

Pocosin
Black-throated Green Warbler (w/conifers)
Common Yellowthroat
Indigo Bunting
Red-cockaded Woodpecker (w/pond pine)
White-eyed Vireo
Yellow-breasted Chat

Early Successional
Alder Flycatcher (mountains)
American Pipit (winter)
Blue Grosbeak
Blue-winged Warbler (mountains)
Bobolink
Chestnut-sided Warbler (mountains)
Eastern Kingbird
Golden-winged Warbler (mountains)
Grasshopper Sparrow
Henslow's Sparrow (coast)
Horned Lark
Indigo Bunting
Loggerhead Shrike
Painted Bunting (immediate lower coast)

Ruffed Grouse
 (mountains)
Vesper Sparrow
Willow Flycatcher
Yellow-breasted Chat

Marshland
American Bittern
Black Rail
Glossy Ibis
Least Bittern
Little Blue Heron
Long-billed Dowitcher
 (winter)
Marsh Wren
Nelson's Sharp-tailed
 Sparrow (winter)
Saltmarsh Sharp-tailed
 Sparrow
Seaside Sparrow
Sedge Wren (winter)

Snowy Egret
White Ibis

Beach
American Avocet
American Oystercatcher
Black Skimmer
Black-necked Stilt
Bridled Tern (vagrant)
Brown Pelican
Curlew Sandpiper
 (vagrant)
Gull-billed Tern
Least Tern
Lesser Black-backed Gull
Marbled Godwit (winter)
Piping Plover
Purple Sandpiper (rock
 jetties)
Roseate Tern
Sandwich Tern

Short-billed Dowitcher
 (winter)
Sooty Tern (vagrant)
Wilson's Plover

Water
Bald Eagle
Canvasback (winter)
Cliff Swallow (dams and
 bridges)
Common Merganser
 (winter)
Greater Scaup (winter)
Harlequin Duck
Hooded Merganser
Long-tailed Duck (winter)
Osprey
Purple Gallinule
Snow Goose
 (also cropland)
Tundra Swan (winter)

Seasons

North Carolina has distinct seasons, but which physiographic region of the state you are birding in can make a big difference regarding weather conditions. Snow may occur during any month of the year in the high elevations of the Mountains, and the Piedmont and Coastal Plain can be dangerously hot during summer. Travel during poor weather conditions is rarely worth the potential risks.

Birding in extreme weather (especially in winter) can yield good finds, but birders need to go afield prepared for the weather. Temperatures that are quite warm on a sunny day (even in winter) can drop dramatically at night. Dress in layers, and always bring along extra water and a change of clothes.

Spring is a great time to look for migrants of all types, and although fall migration is not as intense, in most spots it can still produce good finds, especially with migrant raptors. Winter brings outstanding numbers and types of waterfowl into North Carolina, especially at the coast and inland reservoirs.

Migration

Predicting migration for specific bird species can be tricky. Weather fronts and systems greatly influence the timing and intensity of pulses of migrants. Spring migration can depend on latitude and altitude but generally occurs from March into May. Fall migration starts as early as August and continues into October and early November. In North Carolina, April is a great time to find many spring migrants, and September into at least mid–October is a good time to search for fall migrant land birds and raptors. November and December bring most of the winter residents into North Carolina, especially waterfowl at the coast.

Most of North Carolina experiences latitudinal migration, but the mountains also have altitudinal migration. Latitudinal migrants include the colorful neotropical migrants like tanagers, vireos, and most warblers and flycatchers, while altitudinal migrants like the Dark-eyed Junco, Black-capped Chickadee, and Winter Wren move to lower elevations (in fall and winter) from higher-elevation breeding areas. Fall migration brings impressive numbers of migrating raptors such as Broad-winged Hawks. The migration periods are unique in that certain species, for example, shorebirds, are easier to see and more likely to be located.

Coastal Plain

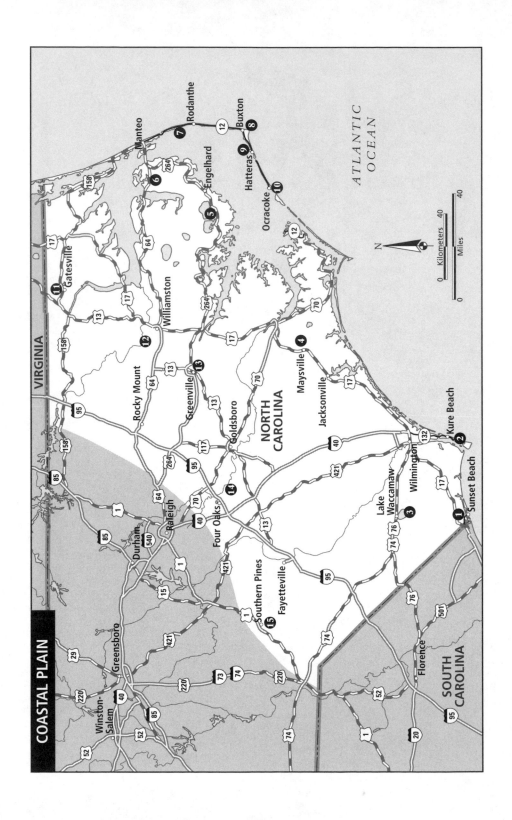

1 Sunset Beach

by Mary McDavit

County: Brunswick.

Habitats: Ocean, coastal inlets, coastal flats, salt marsh, Intracoastal Waterway, floodplain forest, cypress swamp, creek, freshwater lakes, Calabash River, sewage lagoons.

Key birds: *Summer:* Least Tern; American Oystercatcher; Black Skimmer; Anhinga; Wood Stork; Little Blue Heron; Wilson's Plover; Chuck-will's-widow; Great Crested Flycatcher; Eastern Kingbird; Summer Tanager; Blue Grosbeak; Indigo and Painted Bunting. *Winter:* Red-throated Loon; Horned Grebe; Hooded Merganser; Greater Scaup; Canvasback; Marbled Godwit; Nelson's Sharp-tailed Sparrow. *Year-round:* Snowy Egret; Brown Pelican; Red-headed Woodpecker; Brown-headed Nuthatch; White Ibis.

Best times to bird: Any time of the year.

The marsh at Sunset Beach. PHOTO: KAREN BEARDEN

About this site:

The Sunset Beach area includes both mainland and island habitats. The island itself is approximately 3 miles long, with ocean beaches and a network of salt marshes and tidal flats. While a favorite summer vacation spot, the developed areas consist mostly of single-family homes.

Begin birding as you cross the causeway. Watch for Wood Storks, which often show up, from late spring to midfall along the Intracoastal Waterway. Look for wading birds and, at low tide, for shorebirds on the flats. After crossing onto the causeway, there is a boat launch on the right, and about 0.2 mile beyond that is a place on the right where you can pull over. Watch out for soft sand. Look for Seaside and Sharp-tailed Sparrows in the marsh grass in the fall.

The causeway ends at a T-junction. Go straight into the town's free parking lot, where you will see a gazebo marking the way to the beach. You can search the ocean from either the beach or the pier. There is an admission fee for the pier, and it is closed in winter. Late in winter and early in spring, rafts of hundreds of scoters, mostly Surf, are common. In winter look for Common and Red-throated Loons, Horned Grebes, Northern Gannets, Hooded and Red-breasted Mergansers, scaup, Buffleheads, American Wigeons, and Brown Pelicans. *Note:* You are not allowed to climb even the smallest dune in Sunset Beach. There is a marker denoting the legal limit of Sunset Beach.

Continue by turning right out of the parking lot and driving 1 mile on Canal Drive to where the road ends in a private parking lot. If you park along the road, use only the designated parking areas, being sure not to block driveways or beach accesses. Walk on the path from the private parking lot to get views of the marshes, sandbars, and beaches. Check the marsh edges for Reddish Egrets from mid-July through summer. Look east for Black Skimmers on the beach or a sandbar nearest to Ocean Isle.

Return on Canal Drive for 0.5 mile, turn right on Cobia Street, and then go right again in 0.2 mile on North Shore Drive East. Watch for Painted Buntings in trees and on wires. Between Seventeenth and Eighteenth Streets, there is a place to pull over where you can park. Be sure to avoid parking or driving off into the soft sand. Walk to the end of North Shore Drive and turn onto Nineteenth Street to look north across the inlet. Look for shorebirds on the beach and on the sandbars in the inlet. From mid-July through summer Reddish Egrets may be seen along the marsh edges. Also look for Black Skimmers on the beach or a sandbar nearest to the other side of the inlet.

Return to where you parked and backtrack on Cobia Street to Canal Drive. Turn right on Sixth Street, then left on North Shore Drive, cross Sunset Boulevard, and drive to the west end of Sunset Beach and Bird Island, and then turn right onto Fortieth Street. Immediately on your right is a marshy tidal area in which Clapper Rails are found at times. From here to Bay Street check out the flats for wading birds and shorebirds at low tide. The marsh grasses are full of both species of Sharp-tailed Sparrows in the fall.

Return to Fortieth Street and drive to Main Street. There is a small public parking lot on the right at the end of West Main Street. Check out the marsh directly in front of you. Follow the boardwalk path to the beach. Go right about a half mile to an area where the dunes are smaller and roped off. During the summer look for Wilson's Plovers and Least Terns. This is also a good area to look for a variety of terns year-round. There will be the typical sandpipers and plovers. Lesser Black-backed Gulls are possible in addition to the expected Laughing, Ring-billed, Great Black-backed, Herring, and Bonaparte's Gulls.

Other key birds: *Summer:* Green Heron; Reddish Egret; Orchard Oriole. *Winter:* Black and Surf Scoter; Common Loon; Red-breasted Merganser; Bufflehead; Redhead; Northern Gannet; Long-billed Dowitcher; Sanderling. *Year-round:* Pileated Woodpecker; Yellow-crowned Night-Heron.

Nearby opportunities: There are several areas on the mainland, across the causeway from the beach, that offer a variety of waterfowl, shorebirds, and land birds. East Lake of Twin Lakes is good for Wood Storks, Green Herons, White Ibises, and Great and Snowy Egrets; Black-crowned Night-Herons are seasonal residents along the lake. Sunset Lakes is comprised of two lakes that are impounded cypress swamps and good for winter waterfowl. The best bet to see Painted Buntings may be a short side trip to the east end of Ocean Isle Beach. Additional details for these sites are available online at the Carolina Bird Club's Web site: www.carolinabirdclub.org.

Directions: From the junction of U.S. Highway 17 and Highway 904, go east on Highway 904 for 3.5 miles to the second light. Turn right on Sunset Boulevard. At 5.3 miles stay straight where Highway 179 Business turns right and proceed across the single-lane bridge. This historic swing bridge is expected to be replaced sometime in the near future.

Access: All sites are accessible by car.

Bathrooms: Located in service stations and restaurants.

Hazards: Soft sand and highway traffic in some locations.

Nearest food, gas, and lodging: There is a restaurant on the pier, and there is a deli in one of the stores that is open in late spring, summer, and early fall. A restaurant next to the swing bridge on the mainland is open most of the year. There are motels open year-round on US 17 Bypass.

Nearest camping: Privately owned campgrounds in Sunset Beach.

DeLorme map grid: Page 86, B2.

North Carolina Travel Map grid: H5.

For more information: South Brunswick Islands Chamber of Commerce, (910) 754-6644; www.sbichamber.com.

Fort Fisher State Recreation Area

by Sam Cooper

County: New Hanover.

Habitats: Beach, salt marshes, mudflats, maritime communities.

Key birds: *Summer:* Brown Pelican; Least Tern; Wilson's Plover; Painted Bunting. *Fall:* Peregrine Falcon. *Winter:* Red-throated Loon; Great Cormorant; Long-tailed Duck; Marbled Godwit; Purple Sandpiper; Short-billed Dowitcher; Nelson's and Saltmarsh Sharp-tailed Sparrow. *Year-round:* White Ibis; Little Blue Heron; Snowy Egret; Black Skimmer; American Oystercatcher; Seaside Sparrow.

Best times to bird: Fall and winter months.

About this site:

Several birding hot spots near the recreation area provide a variety of diverse habitats and birds. Carolina Beach State Park is best during the fall when large mixed flocks of migrant land birds can be common. The best locations within the park include the woodlands along Campground Loop 2 and the woods along Snow's Cut between the campground and the picnic area. The trail to Sugarloaf, which begins from the boat ramp parking lot, offers nice views of the Cape Fear River. It crosses several marshy creeks where Marsh Wrens and Clapper Rail are often found. Brown-headed Nuthatches are common throughout the park. From the park you follow Dow Road south toward Fort Fisher, or return to U.S. Highway 421 and proceed south through highly developed beach areas.

Carolina Lake, a town park off US 421 in Carolina Beach, is often worth a stop. In the winter there are often various waterfowl present. The summer is often quiet, but the nesting Common Moorhen, or Least Bittern, usually is found in the surrounding scattered marsh.

The next stop to the south is Fort Fisher State Historic Site. The trail around the fort ruins is worth the walk during the fall. The land between the ocean and Cape Fear River is very narrow here, which concentrates southbound migrating species. This is one of the best locations to view migrating raptors. Check the shrubs on both sides of the power lines south of the fort ruins for Painted Buntings during the summer and migrants during the fall. The oceanfront parking area across from the historic site offers great opportunities for ocean watching. Large flocks of Red-throated Loons and scoters are often seen during the winter. Rarities occasionally viewed from this area include jaegers and alcids. A natural rock outcropping just north of this site often attracts sea ducks and an occasional Purple Sandpiper during the winter.

Just prior to the end of US 421, park alongside the road just north of the entrance to the ferry landing. Check the grassy areas around the ferry landing, and walk down the sandy road just north of the landing. Regular fall rarities often found in this area include Western Kingbirds, Lark Sparrows, Clay-colored Sparrows, and Dickcissels. The salt marsh between the parking lot and along the "rocks" often has good numbers of Seaside Sparrows and wintering Nelson's and Saltmarsh Sharp-tailed Sparrows. The rocks lead to Zeke's Island and often attract large flocks of shorebirds, including Marbled Godwits and Short-billed Dowitchers. During high tide in the fall and winter months are especially good. The range markers in the river, especially those near Zeke's Island, often attract Great Cormorants. The "basin" east of the rocks is a popular windsurfing location, but the shallow waters and mudflats also attract large flocks of birds, especially during the winter. The off-road path along the beach offers better access to some areas of the basin but requires a long walk or four-wheel-drive vehicle.

Other sites to visit include areas around the ferry terminal and boat ramp for migrant birds and waterbirds, the North Carolina Aquarium for migrant land birds, and the "spit," or four-wheel-drive path, south of the aquarium for waterbirds. Access to the off-road path requires a fee for vehicles or a long hike for others. A colony of nesting waterbirds composed of primarily Black Skimmers, Least Terns, and Wilson's Plovers are often present within posted, roped-off areas south of the aquarium.

The Long-tailed Duck is a rare to uncommon visitor to offshore coastal North Carolina.
PHOTO: HARRY SELL

Other key birds: *Summer:* Common Tern. *Winter:* Common Loon; Black and Surf Scoter. *Year-round:* Tricolored Heron; Great Egret; Royal Tern; Willet.

Nearby opportunities: Wrightsville Beach is a highly developed barrier island about 7 miles long. Rock jetties are found on both sides of Masonboro inlet and extend approximately a half mile into the ocean. The jetties offer some of the best habitat for attracting sea ducks and Purple Sandpipers.

Greenfield Lake is a birding oasis within busy downtown Wilmington. The lake is within a city park and is fringed by mature cypress trees and a variety of mixed upland woods. Birding can be good year-round for those willing to walk the path around the lake. The lake supports a wide diversity of land birds and waterbirds. Anhingas are often present on the lake but difficult to see.

Additional details for these sites are available online at the Carolina Bird Club Web site, www.carolinabirdclub.org.

Directions: Follow signs from Wilmington to the North Carolina Aquarium, located near the south end of US 421. The aquarium and a visitor center for Fort Fisher State Recreation Area are found off Loggerhead Road about 5 miles south of Carolina Beach. The site may also be accessed from Southport via a state ferry (fee) across the Cape Fear River. Carolina Beach State Park is located off Dow Road, which is accessed from the north by turning right after crossing the Intracoastal Waterway.

Access: There are wheelchair-accessible public restrooms and showers during the summer at the Fort Fisher State Recreation Area visitor center.

Bathrooms: At Fort Fisher State Historic Site, the ferry landing, and Carolina Beach State Park.

Hazards: Extreme care must be taken while driving in soft sand. Walking the "rocks" is extremely dangerous. Rocks that are wet and algae-covered are very slippery.

Nearest food, gas, and lodging: Carolina and Kure Beach.

Nearest camping: Carolina Beach State Park has eighty-three campsites in the family campground area, with two of the sites wheelchair-accessible.

DeLorme map grid: Page 87, A7 and B7.

North Carolina Travel Map grid: I5.

For more information: Fort Fisher State Recreation Area, (910) 458–5798; www.ils.unc.edu/parkproject/visit/fofi/safety.html. Carolina Beach State Park, (910) 458–8206; www.ils.unc.edu/parkprojectvisit/cabe/do.html.

Green Swamp Preserve and Lake Waccamaw State Park

by Joshua S. Rose

Counties: Brunswick and Columbus.

Habitats: Longleaf pine savanna, pocosin, bay forest, Carolina Bays.

Key birds: *Summer:* Bald Eagle; Swainson's and Prothonotary Warbler; Bachman's and Henslow's Sparrow. *Year-round:* Red-cockaded Woodpecker; Brown-headed Nuthatch. *Migration:* Mississippi and Swallow-tailed Kite.

Best times to bird: Spring and summer for the Green Swamp, winter and migration times for Lake Waccamaw.

About this site:

The Green Swamp Preserve is of national significance in botanical circles. It lies within the highly restricted native range of the Venus flytrap and hosts the highest diversity of carnivorous plant genera in the world. Within the greater Green Swamp ecosystem is Lake Waccamaw. It is the largest of the Carolina Bays, a cluster of round and shallow oblong lakes in the coastal plain of North and South Carolina with mysterious origins. The lake is unusual also because a nearby limestone outcrop gives it near-neutral water, which is in contrast to the acidic conditions of other Carolina Bays. As a result, the lake has endemic species of snails, mussels, and fish.

The federally endangered Red-cockaded Woodpecker and the Bachman's Sparrow are found in the longleaf pine and wiregrass savanna that once dominated the landscape of the Green Swamp Preserve. Pine Warblers and Brown-headed Nuthatches are common. The early successional habitats offer opportunities for Henslow's Sparrows and Prairie Warblers. Look for Swainson's Warblers and White-eyed Vireos in the broad-leaved evergreen shrubs that grow in lower wetter areas.

The pond by the parking area sometimes has a few ducks or wading birds. A trail leads east away from Highway 211. Go right where it forks by the far corner of the pond. Follow the boardwalk, watching, in the summer, for Swainson's Warblers, White-eyed Vireos, and Acadian Flycatchers. The trail emerges from the pocosin entering the Shoestring Savannah, a longleaf pine habitat. *Note:* This trail is sometimes underwater after a rain. As you enter the savanna, be careful not to step on Venus flytraps, other rare plant species, and other wildflowers. Also, be aware that the wiregrass off the trail can conceal venomous snakes and holes from rotted-out pine stumps. In spring and summer Bachman's Sparrows should readily be seen, and Red-cockaded Woodpeckers may be sighted year-round. Look for nest trees marked with white bands of paint near the base. The nest holes will be visible higher up, surrounded by oozing pine resin that helps defend the nests from rat snakes and other predators. The woodpeckers visit the holes mainly in the early morning and late evening, except when they are feeding young. Retrace your steps to return to the parking area.

Lake Waccamaw State Park has large populations of Ospreys, Belted Kingfishers, and herons and egrets. Access to the lakeshore is by the boardwalk that leads to the fishing pier. Migrant and wintering warblers, vireos, and thrushes can often be detected along the boardwalk. On the pier a spotting scope is helpful for surveying the water and shoreline. Various waterfowl spend the winter or drop in during migration. Ospreys and Bald Eagles nest nearby, and Forster's, Black, and other terns visit in late summer and fall. A variety of wading birds can be found in any season. In spring watch for migrating Mississippi and Swallow-tailed Kites. Many species of migrant, breeding, and wintering land birds can be along the lake margins. Pine Warblers and Brown-headed Nuthatches are common in pines accessed by Sand Ridge, Pine Woods, or Loblolly Trails.

Evening falls in the Green Swamp Preserve. PHOTO: JEREMY POIRIER

Other key birds: *Summer:* Forster's and Black Tern; Osprey; Acadian Flycatcher; White-eyed Vireo; Yellow-throated and Prairie Warbler. *Winter:* Red-breasted Merganser. *Year-round:* Pine Warbler; Red-bellied Woodpecker.

Nearby opportunities: Jones Lake State Park, located near Elizabethtown and adjacent to Bladen Lakes State Forest, includes two lakes that are part of the Carolina Bays ecosystem. Carolina Bays, a series of elliptical or oval depressions, are found only in the coastal plain of southeastern United States. The depressions were given the name "bays" for the sweet bay, loblolly bay, and red bay trees found growing around them. The park is designated as an Audubon Important Bird Area with many varieties of birds, including Red-cockaded and Red-head Woodpeckers. For additional information call the park office at (910) 588-4550 or visit www.edu/parkproject/ncparks.html.

Directions: Take U.S. Highway 701 south, exit 90 off Interstate 95, or exit 343 off Interstate 40. Continue past the towns of Clinton, White Lake, and Elizabethtown. Turn left on Highway 211 and go approximately 20 miles south of Elizabethtown. For Lake Waccamaw State Park, turn right on Highway 214 in the town of Bolton and drive approximately 7 miles. Watch for the LAKE WACCAMAW STATE PARK sign indicating a left turn onto Bartram Lane. Take another left onto Bella Coola Road just before reaching the lake. The park driveway is several miles farther down on the left. To visit the Green Swamp Preserve, continue on Highway 211 through Bolton. Drive approximately 20 miles, cross Driving Creek, and look for a large pond on the left just beyond a thin strip of pine trees. An unpaved parking lot is just south of the pond.

Access: At Lake Waccamaw State Park, the picnic area, restrooms, and some picnic tables are accessible for persons with disabilities.

Bathrooms: Green Swamp Preserve has no facilities. Lake Waccamaw State Park has restrooms located at the visitor center and the picnic area.

Hazards: Common field hazards.

Nearest food, gas, and lodging: The nearest food and gas are at the highway crossings in Supply, about 7 miles south, and Bolton, about 18 miles north. Bed-and-breakfast and Dale's, a seafood restaurant, are located in the town of Lake Waccamaw.

Nearest camping: Primitive campsites at Lake Waccamaw State Park.

DeLorme map grid: Page 82, C3 and 4; page 86, A4.

North Carolina Travel Map grid: H5.

For more information: For Green Swamp, contact the Nature Conservancy, (910) 762-6277; http://nature.org/wherewework/northamerica/states/northcarolina. For Lake Waccamaw State Park, contact North Carolina State Parks, (910) 646-4748; www.ils.unc.edu/parkproject/ncparks.html.

④ Croatan National Forest

by Bert Speicher

Counties: Carteret, Craven, and Jones.

Habitats: Pine forest, mixed pine-hardwood forest, pine savannas, several lakes, streams, drainage basins, marshland, and pocosins, bounded by the Neuse and White Oak Rivers and Bogue Sound.

Key birds: *Spring and early summer:* Mississippi Kite; Bald Eagle; Chuck-will's-widow; Whip-poor-will; Great Crested Flycatcher; Eastern Kingbird; Yellow, Worm-eating, Prothonotary, Swainson's, Black-throated Blue, and Black-throated Green Warbler; American Redstart; Bachman's Sparrow; Blue Grosbeak; Summer Tanager; Painted and Indigo Bunting. *August:* Wood Stork. *Year-round:* White Ibis; Red-cockaded and Red-headed Woodpecker; Brown-headed Nuthatch.

Best times to bird: Spring and early summer.

About this site:

These 160,000 acres are administered by the U.S. Forest Service. In addition to extensive birding opportunities, visitors can enjoy a diversity of wildlife and plant life.

The best birding is in the central, southern, and western portions of the forest. Catfish Lake and the waterfowl impoundment are in the northern section, but the impoundment is productive only in the fall and winter, and the other lakes provide the same or better sightings. In the southern portion of the forest, the best opportunity to see both Red-cockaded Woodpeckers and Bachman's Sparrows is Millis Road Savannah. It can be reached from Highway 24 about 8 to 9 miles east of Cape Carteret between Broad and Gayles Creeks. Turn north on Nine Mile Road at the stoplight, continue 3 miles to Millis Road, and then turn west onto a road that is not named for just over a mile. The savanna begins on the left and extends intermittently for about another mile. Red-cockaded Woodpeckers are present all year but best seen early or late in the day. Bachman's Sparrows are generally heard and seen from late March through August. While seeking those rarities, Brown-headed Nuthatches, Carolina Chickadees, Eastern Bluebirds, Great Crested Flycatchers, Eastern Wood-Pewees, and various woodpeckers also can be seen.

Continue on this road and stop at creeks and drains to look for Swainson's, Worm-eating, Prothonotary, and Hooded Warblers, Acadian Flycatchers, and Blue-gray Gnatcatchers. For another opportunity to see Red-cockaded Woodpecker, continue 5.1 miles to Forest Service Road 123, also called Pringle Road, and turn left and go for 3.6 miles to Highway 24. Turn left onto Highway 24 and continue 1 mile to Patsy Pond Nature Trail. Walk the short or long loop trails that are directly across from the North Carolina Coastal Federation office.

Retrace your route to where you turned left on FSR 123/Pringle Road, turn left, and continue 2.8 miles to Whitehorse Fork Lane and then left 1.6 miles to Highway 58 at Coastal Marine & Sports. Turn left toward Cape Carteret for another mile, watching for signs to the National Forest Recreation Area and Wildlife Viewing Area, which lead to Cedar Point Campground and Tideland Trail. This area is best visited from April through early June. The marsh area will produce egrets, herons, White Ibises, and Ospreys, as well as Painted Buntings and Red-headed Woodpeckers. The upland portion will have a variety of warblers and vireos, Brown-headed Nuthatches, Blue-gray Gnatcatchers, Great Crested Fly-catchers, Eastern Kingbirds, and Yellow-billed Cuckoos.

To visit another site for Red-cockaded Woodpeckers, return to Highway 58 and go north almost 4 miles to Old Church Road on the right. There are Red-cockaded Woodpecker colonies starting at about 2 miles and continuing until rejoining Highway 58.

Return to Highway 58 there and continue north. There are several roads that to explore on the west side of Highway 58 that lead to the White Oak River. The

The Painted Bunting, in this case a female, is an uncommon summer resident along the central-to-south coast of North Carolina. PHOTO: HARRY SELL

first of these is just 0.1 mile on the left. The next is at 1.4 miles, which goes to Stella, and then Hillfield Road at 3.0 miles and Haywood and Long Point Landings at 3.9 miles. Stops along these roads should yield Yellow, Prothonotary, and Worm-eating Warblers, Summer Tanagers, Wild Turkeys, Ospreys, Great Blue and Green Herons, and an occasional Bald Eagle or Mississippi Kite as you near the river.

On the east side of Highway 24, there are two roads that lead to Great Lake, Catfish Lake, and the central part of the National Forest. The first of these is 0.4 mile just before the railroad crossing. The second, Hunter's Creek Road at 1.4 miles, is directly across from Stella Road, between two convenience stores, which leads to Great Lake. These roads take you through a variety of habitats, managed for birds. These areas can all be covered by car, with stops as the habitat changes and at the drains. If present at the site early in the morning, listen for Eastern Screech-Owls. The drains frequently produce Ovenbirds, Swainson's and Prothonotary Warblers, Wood Thrushes, and Red-eyed Vireos. In the pine savannas look for Summer Tanagers, Hairy and Pileated Woodpeckers, and Brown-headed Nuthatches. Brown Creepers are present in winter. Where the vegetation thickens listen for Gray Catbirds, Northern Bobwhites, and Eastern Towhees. Open areas allow sightings of Red-tailed and Red-shouldered Hawks, Ospreys, Turkey and Black Vultures, and Bald Eagles. In August a few Wood Storks are sometimes present on the lakes, and the swampy edges contain large numbers of Swainson's and Prothonotary Warblers, plus a consistent population of American Redstarts. Watch for venomous snakes and alligators along the edges.

Other key birds: *Summer:* Green Heron; Eastern Wood-Pewee; Wood Thrush; Red-eyed Vireo; Ovenbird; Northern Parula. *Year-round:* Great Blue Heron; Eastern Screech-Owl; Red-tailed and Red-shouldered Hawk; Osprey; Turkey and Black Vulture; Eastern Bluebird; Pileated Woodpecker.

Nearby opportunities: Weyerhaeuser's Cool Springs Environmental Education Center is approximately 1,700 acres of forestland owned by Weyerhaeuser Company along the Neuse River about 6 miles upriver from New Bern. Virtually every forest ecotype of eastern North Carolina is represented on the tract. A 3-mile trail including a 700-foot boardwalk loops through the swamp, and additional trails are located on the longleaf ridge area. Additional details are available online at the Car-olina Bird Club Web site, www.carolinabird club.org.

Directions: Croatan National Forest is south of New Bern, bounded roughly by U.S. Highway 70, Highway 24, Highway 58, and U.S. Highway 17.

Access: Many of the areas can be birded from the road.

Bathrooms: At campgrounds and picnic areas.

Hazards: Mosquitoes, snakes, ticks, venomous snakes, alligators, black bears with cubs, and unmarked forest roads, which are very muddy after heavy rains.

Nearest food, gas, and lodging: New Bern, Havelock, Morehead City, Atlantic Beach, Emerald Isle.

Nearest camping: A total of seventy-four camping sites are located in the National Forest at Fisher's Landing, Neuse River Campground, and Cedar Point.

DeLorme map grid: Pages 77, A/C7, and 78, B1/2–D1/2.

North Carolina Travel Map grid: J3/4.

For more information: Contact Croatan National Forest District Office, on US 70 about 8 to 9 miles south of New Bern; (919) 638–5628. Maps and information are available at the district office.

Mattamuskeet National Wildlife Refuge

by Kelly Davis

County: Hyde.

Habitats: Freshwater lake and marsh, mixed pine-hardwood forest, bald cypress swamp, cropland.

Key birds: *Spring and summer:* Least Bittern; Eastern Kingbird; Blue Grosbeak; Indigo Bunting. *Fall and winter:* Tundra Swan; Snow Goose; Eurasian Wigeon; Canvasback; Peregrine Falcon; Bald Eagle; Sedge Wren; Baltimore Oriole; American Pipit. *Year-round:* Snowy Egret; White and Glossy Ibis; Hooded Merganser; Red-headed Woodpecker; Brown-headed Nuthatch.

Best times to bird: Excellent opportunities are available year-round, with spectacular waterfowl sightings during the fall and winter.

About this site:

Mattamuskeet National Wildlife Refuge (NWR) is renowned for its fall and winter populations of migratory swans, geese, and ducks. The refuge includes most of the 40,000-acre Lake Mattamuskeet, 6,000 acres of forested and shrub-scrub wetland, 3,500 acres of natural and managed marshes, and 400 acres of cropland. The lake bed's submerged aquatic vegetation, shoreline vegetation, managed impoundments, cropland, and nearby private impoundments draw tens of thousands of Tundra Swans, Snow Geese, and ducks during the fall and winter. Marshes and lake shoreline attract fall and spring migrating shorebirds; shallowly flooded areas and canal banks host wading birds. This site offers outstanding lake and marsh vistas and forested drives from which to seek more than 235 species of birds. Checklists are stocked at the headquarters, the entrance road kiosk, and the observation platform.

The lake is easily viewed from the 6-mile Highway 94 causeway that includes an observation platform located 2.5 miles north of U.S. Highway 264. Managed marsh impoundments, natural marsh, and forested wetlands are accessible from the 2-mile entrance road, the 4-mile Wildlife Drive, and the quarter-mile New Holland Trail boardwalk.

Prime viewing is from mid-November through the end of January, when thousands of Tundra Swans, Northern Pintails, and American Wigeons can usually be viewed from Highway 94 and the entrance road. Scan the open water for Eurasian Wigeons, Green-winged and Blue-winged Teals, Canvasbacks, Redheads, Lesser Scaup, and Tree Swallows. Inspect the five culverts for Pied-billed Grebes, Double-crested Cormorants, Buffleheads, Ruddy and Ring-necked Ducks, Laughing and Bonaparte's Gulls, and Forster's Terns. Watch for Cooper's and Sharp-shinned Hawks, Northern Harriers, and occasionally Peregrine Falcons. Bald Eagles often perch in the bald cypress east and west of the southernmost culvert. Examine

An adult Snow Goose with characteristic black wing tips. PHOTO: HARRY SELL

exposed shoreline and shallowly flooded areas for Great Blue Herons, Great and Snowy Egrets, Glossy and White Ibises, Great Black-backed and Ring-billed Gulls, Royal Terns, Western, Semipalmated, and Least Sandpipers, Dunlins, and Long-billed Dowitchers. Check the tree islands along the entrance road for Black-crowned Night-Herons and Great Egrets. In the canals adjacent to the entrance road and along the south canal, look for Pied-billed Grebes and Double-crested Cormorants. Watch the more concealed north canal for Gadwalls, Wood Ducks, and Hooded Mergansers. Look and listen in the brush along these drives for passerines including House Wrens, Blue-gray Gnatcatchers, Blue-headed and White-eyed Vireos, Orange-crowned, Palm, and Yellow-rumped Warblers, and Common Yellowthroats. Anything is possible, including vagrant warblers, flycatchers, and buntings. Watch marsh edges and cattails for Marsh and Sedge Wrens.

During late winter and spring, check Highway 94 and the entrance road for Ospreys and late-migrating Blue-winged Teals and Northern Shovelers. From the open and marshy portions of the entrance road and Wildlife Drive, watch for resident Canada Geese, American Black and Wood Ducks, and Red-tailed Hawks. Look along the woody edges of the drives for migrating or breeding passerines such as Yellow-billed Cuckoos, Northern Parulas, Black-throated Blue, Yellow, Pine, Prairie, and Yellow-throated Warblers, and Baltimore and Orchard Orioles. Walk the Marsh Impoundment 3 (MI-3) dike in spring to look for breeding Wood Ducks, Eastern Kingbirds, and Prothonotary Warblers. During mid- to late

THE NORTH CAROLINA BIRDING TRAIL

North Carolina's Coastal Plain has an abundance of natural resources and attracts millions of birds to the area. Therefore, the North Carolina Wildlife Resources Commission, North Carolina Sea Grant, North Carolina State University Cooperative Extension, and Audubon North Carolina are now seeking support to plan and implement a North Carolina Birding Trail (NCBT) beginning with the coast that will utilize these resources for the benefit of the local Coastal Plain communities as the first section of the NCBT. For more information visit www.ncbirdingtrail.org.

Objectives for the North Carolina Birding Trail

- To plan and develop a coastal birding trail first to unify existing and potential birding sites into a single cohesive and marketable unit
- To develop public access, provide interpretative information, and enhance viewing opportunities at individual birding sites along the trail
- To publicize the trail in order to provide maximum opportunity for public recreation and education and to facilitate sustainable tourism

Anticipated Outcomes for the Coastal Birding Trail

1. Increased economic development within the coastal region of North Carolina
   A. The entire coastal region of North Carolina will become a destination for birding.
   B. Rural coastal communities can partner with adjacent destinations and enhance the appeal of the entire region as a tourism destination.
   C. New entrepreneurial opportunities will arise to accommodate the increasing number of wildlife viewers who will travel to the region.
2. Increased awareness among North Carolina rural coastal communities of the value of natural resources and the need to conserve them as assets for the future
   A. Support will be gained from trail users and surrounding communities for additional conservation practices that would benefit wildlife.
   B. Increased public support will encourage sustainable and effective management practices to support wildlife.
   C. Understanding the economic value of the natural resources will enhance long-range planning that will support the conservation of natural undeveloped areas.

spring and late summer to early fall migrations, scan the shallow flooded or muddy marsh edges of Highway 94 and the entrance road for foraging Greater and Lesser Yellowlegs, Western and Semipalmated Sandpipers, Black-bellied Plovers, Dunlins, Long-billed Dowitchers, and Forster's and Caspian Terns.

The mature pine-hardwood forest along the southern stretch of Highway 94, the eastern portions of the entrance road, and the Wildlife Drive are great places to view or hear resident or breeding birds. Early morning birding along the Wildlife Drive might yield the calls of Great Horned, Barred, and Eastern Screech-Owls. Examine cattail stands and other shoreline vegetation along all drives for American and Least Bitterns, King and Virginia Rails, Marsh Wrens, Common Yellowthroats, and Red-Winged Blackbirds.

The quarter-mile New Holland Trail boardwalk, accessible from the Wildlife Drive, is an easy walk that traverses a shrubby edge, a bald cypress swamp, and a cattail marsh. In spring and summer listen for Wood Ducks, Eastern Towhees, Carolina Wrens, Prothonotary Warblers, Eastern Wood-Pewees, and Pileated Woodpeckers. In fall and winter watch for Wood Ducks, Mallards, woodpeckers, Carolina and Winter Wrens, Hermit Thrushes, Ruby-crowned and Golden-crowned Kinglets, as well as Yellow-rumped, Yellow-throated, and Black-and-white Warblers.

During fall and winter examine refuge marshes and fields (including the East and West Ends) and cropland adjacent to public highways for Tundra Swans, Canada and Snow Geese, Northern Pintails, Mallards, American Wigeons, Green-winged Teals, Wilson's Snipes, American Woodcocks, Killdeers, Tree Swallows, American Pipits, Rusty Blackbirds, and Eastern Meadowlarks. Watch roadsides, ditch banks, and brushy edges for sparrows.

Other key birds: *Spring and summer:* Osprey; Green Heron; Caspian Tern; Yellow-billed Cuckoo; Ruby-throated Hummingbird; Orchard Oriole; and various thrushes, vireos, and warblers. *Fall and winter:* Black-crowned Night-Heron; Northern Pintail; Green-winged and Blue-winged Teal; Northern Shoveler; Gadwall; American Wigeon; Redhead; Ruddy and Ring-necked Duck; Lesser Scaup; Bufflehead; Black-bellied Plover; Western, Semipalmated, and Least Sandpiper; Dunlin; Long-billed Dowitcher; Wilson's Snipe; American Woodcock; Royal Tern; Brown Creeper; Winter Wren; Hermit Thrush; Cedar Waxwing; White-eyed and Blue-headed Vireo; Rusty Blackbird; and various gulls, kinglets, warblers, and sparrows. *Year-round:* Great Egret; American Bittern; American Black and Wood Duck; King and Virginia Rail; Greater and Lesser Yellowlegs; Forster's Tern; Tree Swallow; Marsh Wren; and various raptors, owls, and woodpeckers.

Nearby opportunities: Pocosin Lakes National Wildlife Refuge headquarters is located in Columbia. Information regarding hunting seasons, maps, and wildlife checklists are available from the headquarters office. For additional information call (252) 796-3004.

Directions: Mattamuskeet NWR is approximately 65 miles east of Washington, 30 miles south of Columbia, and 60 miles west of Manteo. From the north follow Highway 94 south to the entrance road, located 1.5 miles north of the Highway 94 and US 264 intersection. From the west follow US 264 east of Swan Quarter to Highway 94, and then go 1.5 miles north on Highway 94 to the entrance road.

From the west follow US 264 west from Engelhard to Highway 94, and then go 1.5 miles north on Highway 94 to the entrance road.

Unless otherwise posted, foot travel is permitted on the many miles of dikes and roads closed to vehicles, including the well-known Lake Landing area or East End. To reach the East End, follow US 264 for 6 miles east of refuge headquarters to the Lake Landing Canal. Turn north on the gravel road and park near the refuge gates. Walk under gates not marked with CLOSED AREA signs (dikes are occasionally closed due to maintenance and bird banding activities). The path beyond the northern gate leads to the Lake Mattamuskeet shoreline via a managed marsh impoundment; the unpaved farm road beyond the eastern gate runs along the refuge farm area and eventually along managed marsh impoundments. *Caution:* Use a refuge map to navigate the East End's 20 miles of looping dikes and roads.

A shorter dike that is open to hiking is near the south side of Highway 94. To bird this area, known as Sandy Dike and Marsh Impoundment 3 (MI-3), park near the gate on the west side of Highway 94 about 1.1 miles north of the US 264 intersection. Walk under the gate and along Sandy Dike Road, which runs adjacent to MI-3; the loop dike around MI-3 includes secluded views of the impoundment and Lake Mattamuskeet. *Caution:* Nutria holes in the dike create occasional walking hazards.

A third area for hiking is the refuge West End, located 5 miles northwest of the State Road 1304 and US 264 intersection. Turn east off SR 1304 onto the gravel road that runs along Rose Bay Canal and park near the gate. Follow the dike along Rose Bay Canal past a mixed pine and hardwood forest and eventually along managed marsh impoundments. On all refuge hikes, do not block gates, watch for venomous snakes, and be prepared for encounters with ticks and mosquitoes.

Due to its relatively remote and rural setting, Mattamuskeet NWR is not crowded anytime of the year. The refuge is open during daylight hours only. Much of the area described can be viewed from boats, including kayaks and canoes, from March 1 through November 1. Contact the refuge for a canoe trail map.

Access: Much of the refuge is accessible by car. Restrooms in the refuge headquarters are wheelchair-accessible.

Bathrooms: Available at the refuge headquarters, which is open weekdays from 7:30 A.M. to 4:00 P.M. Portable toilets are usually available at the refuge headquarters and the East End parking lot.

Hazards: Venomous snakes, ticks, and mosquitoes can be somewhat abundant during warmer months.

Nearest food, gas, and lodging: No food or drink is sold on-site, but there are small restaurants, service stations, and general stores in the villages of Swan Quarter, Engelhard, and Fairfield. One service station and general store is located near the south end of Highway 94.

Nearest camping: Privately owned campground in Swan Quarter.

DeLorme map grid: Page 68, A-B1–2.

North Carolina Travel Map grid: K2.

For more information: Mattamuskeet National Wildlife Refuge Headquarters, (252) 926–4021; http://mattamuskeet.fws.gov.

⑥ Alligator River National Wildlife Refuge

by Jeff Lewis

County: Dare.

Habitats: Swamp forests, pine forests, mixed pine-hardwood forests, pocosins, salt marshes, farm fields.

Key birds: *Summer:* Anhinga; Chuck-will's-widow; Whip-poor-will; Black-throated Green, Prothonotary, Worm-eating, Swainson's, and Hooded Warbler; Blue Grosbeak; Indigo Bunting. *Winter:* Tundra Swan; Golden and Bald Eagle; Rough-legged Hawk; Black Rail; Short-eared Owl; Sedge Wren; Horned Lark; American Pipit.

Best times to bird: Early breeding season and winter.

About this site:

Alligator River National Wildlife Refuge (NWR) is 152,000 acres managed by the U.S. Fish and Wildlife Service. The refuge consists primarily of wet swamp forest and pocosin with smaller areas of slightly drier habitat including pine forest and mixed pine-hardwood forest. It is virtually surrounded by water, with the Alligator River, Albemarle Sound, Croatan Sound, and Pamlico Sound bordering all but the southwest corner. In the center of the refuge is the 46,000-acre Dare County Bombing Range, which is partially off limits to the public. The refuge is open year-round during daylight hours only. Be aware that hunting is allowed on the refuge. Visitors should pick up a map and list of refuge restrictions at the kiosk at the Creef Cut parking area off U.S. Highway 64 at Milltail Road or at the U.S. Fish and Wildlife office in Manteo. On the refuge itself, access varies seasonally and is limited to some of more than 150 miles of mostly unimproved roads managed by the staff. Roads where access is not permitted are gated. Vehicles must remain on the roads or road shoulders at all times. Foot access is allowed into the wooded areas but not into the farm fields.

More than 250 species of birds have been seen on the Alligator River National Wildlife Refuge. In addition to birds, the refuge provides habitat for one of the largest concentrations of black bears on the East Coast and is also home to river otters, bobcats, and reintroduced red wolves.

During the breeding season Prothonotary and Prairie Warblers and Common Yellowthroats can be found over much of the refuge. Yellow-throated, Hooded, and Black-and-white Warblers and Northern Parulas are fairly easy to find in several areas throughout the refuge. The coastal race of Black-throated Green Warbler is common in the more coniferous areas of the refuge, especially in mature stands of Atlantic white cedar. A good example of this habitat can be found along the Sandy Ridge hiking trail at the end of Buffalo City Road. Also listen for Worm-eating Warblers in this area.

The Prairie Warbler is a breeder in old fields, second-growth clearings, and young pine-plantations of the Coastal Plain and Piedmont. PHOTO: JEREMY POIRIER

Ovenbirds are common in the mature deciduous woods of the refuge. Good locations for seeing all of these warblers are Buffalo City Road, Brier Hall Road, and Koehring Road. A particularly convenient spot for Yellow-throated Warblers is the Creef Cut parking lot on US 64. This is also a great spot for Pine Warblers and Brown-headed Nuthatches. The refuge hosts fairly good numbers of Swainson's Warblers during the breeding season. They are not that difficult to find beginning about the third week in April, provided you know their song. Some years they can be found on Brier Hall Road, on the north side of US 64. Set your odometer as you turn onto Brier Hall and listen for them beginning at 2.5 miles. Another good site is Milltail Road, a mile or so on either side of Milltail Creek. This is also a good area for Hooded, Prothonotary, and Black-and-white Warblers. If you spend a few early morning hours here, you will likely hear Barred Owls.

Watch farm field edges for Blue Grosbeaks and Indigo Buntings. Eastern Wood-Pewees and Acadian Flycatchers are common in several areas, including along Long-curve Road just north of Navy Shell Road. This is also a good spot for Yellow-billed Cuckoos and Black-throated Green Warblers. In some years Black-billed Cuckoos are present here in small numbers. When present, these cuckoos are often found near the intersection of Navy Shell and Long Curve Roads.

The most common breeding vireo on the refuge is the White-eyed, which can be found in low, dense cover. Chuck-will's-widows and Whip-poor-wills breed on the refuge primarily in the southern half. A couple of fairly reliable spots to listen for Whip-poor-wills are near the end of Lake Worth Road and along Navy Shell Road beginning about 1 mile from Highway 264.

Small numbers of Anhingas nest most years in the Great Blue Heron rookery on Whipping Creek Lake, which represents one of the northernmost breeding sites. Note that Whipping Creek Lake is accessible only by nonmotorized boats and then only when the roads are both open to the public and not too muddy to traverse.

Common year-round residents include Pine Warblers and Brown-headed Nuthatches. They are easily found in the areas dominated by pines. Red-shouldered Hawks are fairly common year-round over much of the refuge. Bald Eagles nest on the refuge. Northern Flickers and Red-bellied, Downy, Hairy, and Pileated Wood-peckers are fairly common in the wooded areas of the refuge. Red-cockaded Woodpeckers are uncommon on the central to southern end of the refuge and breed primarily in the inaccessible Air Force Bombing Range.

Wood Ducks, found throughout the year, are often seen in the roadside canals. The refuge boasts a large population of Northern Bobwhites, which are common in the farm field areas, as are Killdeer and Eastern Meadowlarks. Occasionally King and Virginia Rails are seen in the wetter sections of the fields. Wild Turkeys have been reintroduced to the refuge, and their population seems to be increasing. In the marshy areas along Croatan and Pamlico Sounds, Clapper Rails, Marsh Wrens, and Seaside Sparrows can be found. A good access point to this area is at the southern end of the refuge where Pamlico Road intersects with Highway 264. You may also get looks at fly by terns and gulls here.

Year-round owl residents on the Alligator Refuge include Great Horned, Barred, and Eastern Screech-Owls. Barred Owls can sometimes be seen during daylight hours. (Remember that access to the refuge is limited to daylight hours.) Great Horned Owls are sometimes seen at dusk along Milltail Road.

In the fall the refuge offers a good variety of migrating passerines, including warblers, flycatchers, swallows, and raptors. In September the farm fields attract flocks of Bobolinks. In mid-October American Pipits, Palm Warblers, and winter sparrows begin arriving.

In winter raptors take center stage. Farm fields attract Northern Harriers, Red-tailed Hawks, and Turkey and Black Vultures. Also look for Peregrine Falcons, Merlins, American Kestrels, Red-shouldered, Sharp-shinned, and Cooper's Hawks, and Bald Eagles. Much less common but sometimes seen are Rough-legged Hawks and Golden Eagles. At dusk Short-eared Owls might be seen in farm fields. Also during winter check flooded fields for waterfowl. The sites most accessible for viewing are from the end of Creef Cut Trail and a section of Milltail Road, although the high vegetation and distance on Milltail Road makes for less-than-desirable views. In these seasonal impoundments are found good numbers of Tundra Swans, Northern Pintails, and Green-winged Teal. Many other waterfowl species are often present. The flooded fields also provide habitat for a few species of shorebirds. Look for Greater and Lesser Yellowlegs, Long-billed Dowitchers, and Wilson's Snipes. Occasionally small sandpipers and Semipalmated Plovers can be seen. American Woodcocks can sometimes be seen in the roads or farm field edges very early in the morning or heard as they make their courtship flights in late winter.

In addition to raptors, waterfowl, and shorebirds, winter brings a good assortment of songbirds to the refuge. The farm fields host large numbers of Savannah Sparrows. Grasshopper Sparrows winter here at least some years. Swamp Sparrows are abundant along the farm field ditches, and often Lincoln's Sparrows can be seen with them. White-crowned Sparrows have been recorded here several times, and Vesper, Henslow's, and Le Conte's Sparrows are probably present in small numbers at least some winters. American Pipits are often found in the moist, bare fields. Lapland Longspurs and Horned Larks are occasionally present. Look in the wooded areas, particularly in the northern sections of the refuge, for Winter Wrens and White-throated and Fox Sparrows. In salt marsh areas look for Sedge Wrens, Sharp-tailed and Seaside Sparrows, and Virginia and Black Rails.

Other key birds: *Summer:* Yellow-billed Cuckoo; Eastern Wood-Pewee; Acadian Flycatcher; White-eyed Vireo; Northern Parula; Yellow-throated, Prairie, and Black-and-white Warbler; Ovenbird. *Winter:* American Wigeon; Northern Pintail; Green-winged Teal; Northern Harrier; Cooper's Hawk; American Kestrel; Yellow-bellied Sapsucker; Eastern Phoebe; Blue-headed Vireo; Tree Swallow; House and Winter Wren; Golden and Ruby-crowned Kinglet; Hermit Thrush; Orange-crowned Warbler; Savannah, Fox, Lincoln's, and Swamp Sparrow. *Year-round:* Wood Duck; Red-shouldered Hawk; Northern Bobwhite; Eastern Screech-Owl; Great Horned and Barred Owl; Hairy and Pileated Woodpecker; Brown-headed Nuthatch; Eastern Meadowlark; Red-winged Blackbird.

Nearby opportunities: Palmetto Peartree Preserve consists of 9,732 acres primarily of pine forest, transected by both paved and unimproved roads. This newly formed preserve is excellent for finding the endangered Red-cockaded Woodpecker. There are well over one hundred cavity trees with an estimated one hundred birds in more than twenty active clusters. Additional details for this site are available online at the Carolina Bird Club Web site, www.carolinabirdclub.org.

Directions: The Alligator River National Wildlife Refuge is located between the Alligator River and the Croatan Sound, encompassing most of the Dare County mainland. The main entrance is at Milltail Road, off U.S. Highway 64. The entrance is marked with a kiosk, and there is a paved parking lot. Maps of the refuge are available here. This entrance also marks the beginning of the Creef Cut Trail. Driving from the west, Creef Cut is approximately 24 miles from Columbia. From Manteo the distance is about 11 miles.

Access: This site has some habitats that may be birded from the road by car. Other habitats are reachable only on foot.

Bathrooms: Facilities are limited to portable restrooms at Creef Cut and at the end of Buffalo City Road.

Hazards: Poison ivy, insect pests, ticks, and venomous snakes.

Nearest food, gas, and lodging: Manteo.

Nearest camping: Privately owned campground in Manteo.

DeLorme map grid: Page 48, C3.

North Carolina Travel Map grid: L3.

For more information: U.S. Fish and Wildlife Service, Manteo, (252) 473-1131; http://alligatorriver.fws.gov.

Pea Island National Wildlife Refuge

by Jeff Lewis

County: Dare.

Habitats: Tidal creeks, freshwater and brackish ponds and impoundments, marshes, ocean beaches, barrier dunes, adjacent ocean and sound shoreline and waters.

Key birds: *Spring and summer:* Glossy Ibis; Black Skimmer; Black-necked Stilt; Roseate Tern. *Fall:* Peregrine Falcon; Marbled Godwit; Black-billed Cuckoo; Dickcissel. *Winter:* Red-throated Loon; Horned and Red-necked Grebe; Great Cormorant; Snow Goose; Ross's Goose; Tundra Swan; Eurasian Wigeon; Harlequin Duck; Red-breasted Merganser; Peregrine Falcon; Yellow Rail; American Avocet; Marbled Godwit; Purple Sandpiper; Short-eared Owl; Sedge Wren; American Pipit; Nelson's Sharp-tailed and Saltmarsh Sharp-tailed Sparrow. *Year-round:* Brown Pelican; Little Blue Heron; Snowy Egret; White Ibis; Piping Plover; American Oystercatcher; Short-billed Dowitcher; Seaside Sparrow.

Best times to bird: Good to excellent opportunities year-round, especially spring and fall migrations and during winter for waterfowl.

About this site:

Located midway on the Atlantic Flyway, Pea Island National Wildlife Refuge is one of the premier birding areas of the Atlantic Coast, with over 350 bird species documented. The refuge includes 5,834 acres located on a barrier island, bordered on the east by the Atlantic Ocean and on the west by Pamlico Sound. The habitat on the west side of Pea Island consists primarily of salt marshes, with numerous small creeks and bays. The east side is ocean beach, subject to the severe pounding and tidal influence of the Atlantic Ocean. In between the salt marshes and the beaches lie dunes, salt flats, stunted shrub and tree thickets, and freshwater and brackish ponds and impoundments.

The impoundments, salt flats, and ocean beaches are a great place to look for shorebirds during spring and fall migration. In addition to thirty or so more common species, such as the Black-bellied Plover, Black-necked Stilt, and American Avocet, that visit Pea Island regularly, rarities such as the Long-billed Curlew, Bar-tailed Godwit, Curlew Sandpiper, or Ruff turn up from time to time. In fall and winter the impoundments hold Tundra Swans, Snow Geese, and up to twenty-five other species of waterfowl. Reliable during this season are Gadwalls, American Wigeons, American Black Ducks, Northern Shovelers, Northern Pintails, and Green-winged Teal. This is a great time to look for rare species such as Ross's Goose, Greater White-fronted Goose, and Eurasian Wigeon. While at Pea Island during this period, you are likely to find Peregrine Falcons. Bald Eagles are increasing on the refuge.

Wading birds are numerous in the impoundments and marshes. Some species, such as Great Egret, Black-crowned Night-Heron, and White Ibis, are present year-round, while others, such as Green Heron, Yellow-crowned Night-Heron, and Glossy Ibis, are more likely during warmer months. American Bitterns are routine here in fall and winter.

The marshes just west of the impoundments and along Pamlico Sound provide great rail habitat. Clapper and Virginia Rail are present year-round, while other species, such as Sora, Black Rail, and Yellow Rails, are most often found during migration or in winter. These marshes are also home to Seaside Sparrows and Marsh Wrens year-round and Sedge Wrens during the fall-to-spring period. The salt flats area just north of North Pond is a good spot to find Seaside Sparrows during the breeding season. The two types of Sharp-tailed Sparrows, Nelson's and Saltmarsh, are easier to find in the more tidal areas of the marsh, closer to the sound or the inlet.

The refuge is a great place for terns and gulls. Summer terns easily seen include Royal, Sandwich, Common, Forster's, and Least. Gull-billed Terns are fairly common some years, especially in the salt flats area, north of North Pond. Black Terns can be numerous in late summer, in a myriad of plumages. Caspian Terns are common during fall migration in September and October, and Roseate Terns are

A view of North Pond at Pea Island National Wildlife Refuge. PHOTO: KAREN BEARDEN

sometimes seen in summer or fall. Even Sooty and Bridled Terns show up infrequently, especially during or after tropical storms. Winter is a good time for gulls, particularly the Great Black-backed Gull. Little Gulls, Black-headed Gulls, California Gulls, Iceland Gulls, and Glaucous Gulls are among the rare gulls that have been seen here.

Ocean watching in late fall and winter can be productive at Pea Island. In October and November, long strings of Surf, Black, and White-winged Scoters can often be seen migrating south. Also seen are Red-breasted Mergansers and flocks of Double-crested Cormorants. Common and Red-throated Loons are common all winter. Horned Grebes are fairly common, and sometimes Eared and Red-necked Grebes are found. Common Eider, King Eider, and Harlequin Duck are seen on rare occasions, especially in the vicinity of the Oregon Inlet Bridge and rock groin.

The north end of the island at the shrubby area near the old Coast Guard Station is this area's best migrant trap. On mornings after nights with clear skies and northwest winds, many birds fly back to the northwest in an effort to reorient themselves. North Pond can also be rewarding during these weather conditions, offering many of these same species. One approach to look for migrants is to begin early at the Coast Guard Station, bird a few hours or until the action slows, and then drive to North Pond to check out the shrubs along the impoundment dikes.

Later in October and into November, when Bobolinks, orioles, and most species of warblers have migrated through, there are still birds present. Several species of sparrows come through now, and most of the winter birds are showing up as well. Sparrows seen may include White-crowned, Grasshopper, Vesper, Savannah, and Fox. Lapland Longspurs and Snow Buntings are possible. This is a good time for songbird rarities. Western Kingbirds are almost regular at Pea Island.

Other key birds: *Spring and summer:* Yellow-crowned Night-Heron; Gadwall; American Black Duck; Osprey; Prairie Warbler; over thirty species of shorebirds. *Fall:* American Bittern; Sora; Common Moorhen; Baird's Sandpiper; Hudsonian Godwit; Western Kingbird; over fifteen species of sparrows. *Winter:* Common Loon; American Bittern; over twenty-five species of ducks; Northern Harrier; Wilson's Snipe; Tree Swallow; Marsh Wren; Orange-crowned Warbler; over twenty species of shorebirds. *Year-round:* Great Egret; Tricolored Heron; Black-crowned Night-Heron; Gadwall; American Black Duck; Clapper and Virginia Rail; Black-bellied Plover; Sanderling; Great Black-backed Gull; Royal and Forster's Tern.

Nearby opportunities: Fort Raleigh National Historic Site and the Elizabethan Gardens are located at the north end of Roanoke Island approximately 3 miles from Manteo. Fort Raleigh National Historic Site is a 450-acre park managed by the National Park Service. It is located on the site of the first English colony in the New World, established over 400 years ago. Jockeys Ridge State Park and Nags Head Woods Ecological Preserve are also located nearby in the Nags Head area. Additional details for these sites are available online at the Carolina Bird Club Web site, www.carolinabirdclub.org.

Directions: Pea Island National Wildlife Refuge is located on Highway 12 in Dare County south of Nags Head. To get there from the west, drive east on U.S. Highway 64 or 264 until you come off the Manteo/Nags Head Causeway at Whalebone Junction. At the first light, turn right onto Highway 12 and head south. Coming from the north, drive south on Highway 158 until you reach this same intersection, with signs directing you toward Hatteras. At 8.4 miles you will reach the Bonner Bridge, a 2.3-mile-long bridge which spans Oregon Inlet. As you leave the bridge at the south end, you are entering Pea Island Refuge. To reach the visitor center, continue for another 4.2 miles, or 14.9 miles total. The center will be on your right.

Access: Pea Island Visitor Center is wheelchair-accessible.

Bathrooms: At Pea Island Visitor Center.

Hazards: In the warmer months biting insects and high daytime temperatures.

Nearest food, gas, and lodging: There are numerous stores, restaurants, and accommodations, including motels and rental cottages within twenty to thirty minutes' drive of the refuge.

Nearest camping: Oregon Inlet Campground has 120 campsites.

DeLorme map grid: Page 49, C and D7, and page 69, A7.

North Carolina Travel Map grid: L2.

For more information: Pea Island National Wildlife Refuge, U.S. Fish and Wildlife Service, (252) 473-1131; http://peaisland.fws.gov.

8 Cape Hatteras National Seashore

by Sidney Maddock and Patricia Moore

County: Dare.

Habitats: Ocean beach, dunes, saltwater and freshwater marshes, maritime forest, shrub swamps, thickets.

Key birds: *Summer:* Little Blue Heron; Snowy Egret; White Ibis; Swallow-tailed Kite; Wilson's Plover; Piping Plover; American Oystercatcher; Least and Gull-billed Tern; Black Skimmer; Seaside Sparrow. *Winter:* Red-throated Loon; Hooded Merganser; Horned Grebe; Long-tailed Duck; Brown Pelican; Snow Goose; Brant; Lesser Black-backed Gull; Peregrine Falcon; American Pipit; Saltmarsh Sharp-tailed Sparrow.

Best times to bird: Good opportunities year-round, with summer being an excellent time for observing breeding solitary and colonial waterbirds.

About this site:

More than 300 species of birds have been documented at Cape Hatteras National Seashore. Hurricane Isabel dramatically changed the topography and plant cover in 2003, removing the artificially constructed dunes and causing a shift from dense scrub and grass habitats in the middle and soundside areas of the island toward open sand and overwash fan areas. Future habitat conditions and the resulting birds that use this narrow barrier island area will depend on storm intensity and frequency.

Hatteras Inlet spit is an excellent site to observe breeding waterbirds. The spit is one of the best Piping Plover nesting habitats in this area, and American Oyster-catchers, Willets, Common and Least Terns, and Black Skimmers also nest here. Wilson's Plovers historically nested here, and Hurricane Isabel's restoration of shorebird feeding and nesting habitats may allow their return. This section of Hatteras Island runs roughly in an east-to-west direction, with the beach facing south. From the end of the paved road, Hatteras Inlet is about 2.9 miles to the west, although that distance varies as the inlet moves.

As you start your walk from the parking lot at the ferry dock, if it is winter, look toward the sound for Brant. Then walk west, and turn toward the ocean to walk over Ramp 55 and scan the ocean for Northern Gannets and scoter species. As you proceed west toward the inlet, at about 0.7 mile below the ramp, the first of the overwash fans created by Hurricane Isabel can be found. This area should be scanned for species that like to use sand and mudflats for feeding, such as Piping and Semipalmated Plovers. On the sound side of the island, above and below the overwash fans can be found patches of high and low salt marsh areas that attract Great Blue and Tricolored Herons. In the summer Seaside Sparrows may be observed in the early morning, and White Ibises and Black-crowned and Yellow-crowned Night-Herons are possible. In the winter Saltmarsh Sharp-tailed Sparrows are present in the same habitat.

The largest numbers of waterbirds have been found in the sandy, open beach areas within half a mile above the inlet, but Hurricane Isabel created extensive areas of additional shorebird habitat farther east. The long-term maintenance of these large sand flats and their associated feeding areas will influence species composition and numbers; a period without strong storms would allow these areas to return to thick dune grasses and shrub thicket, which favors Palm Warblers and Mourning Doves. More frequent storms would maintain the area in the open sand and minimal vegetation favored by Least and Common Terns and Black Skimmers.

The dry sand flats near the inlet are often a roosting area for hundreds of gulls during the winter, and the Lesser Black-backed Gull or even rarer gull species may be seen. Look for Red Knots and Piping Plovers feeding in the wet intertidal areas. Other rarities may be found during fall migration.

Cape Point is accessed from Highway 12 in Buxton. Begin your tour alongside this road. Between the intersection and the lighthouse, you will find 1.4 miles of freshwater marshes, swamps, and wooded areas. In any season look for songbirds and waders. At mile 0.5 linger at the first pond on the left. In spring look for Prothonotary Warblers, Marsh Wrens, and Common Yellowthroats in the marsh across the road. In winter look for waterfowl.

Wilson's Plovers tend to feed on the higher parts of the beach. PHOTO: HARRY SELL

From here the next left turn leads to the Old Lighthouse site. A short walk toward the beach will take you to the old site, marked by a circle of granite stones inscribed with the names of lighthouse keepers. This is a good spot for ocean watching. In winter watch for Northern Gannets, Red-breasted Mergansers, scoters, Brown Pelicans, and Bonaparte's Gulls. Purple Sandpipers often feed on the groins and rocks. In the winter look for American Bitterns and Wilson's Snipes around the edges of the small pond adjacent to the parking lot.

From the parking area drive 0.2 mile to the Buxton Woods Nature Trail. This wooded area can be very productive during spring and fall migration for migrant warblers. From here continue to the ranger station. The lawn between the building and the road merits a quick look for foraging shorebirds. In spring watch overhead for Swallow-tailed Kites. Continue from the ranger station toward Cape Point Campground, watching the marshy thickets, stunted vegetation, and tree snags along the road for Blue Grosbeaks, Prairie Warblers, American Woodcocks, and Green Herons.

In the summer ask permission to drive around the campground. In the winter, when the campground is closed, park outside the gate and walk through the campground, watching for herons, egrets, American Kestrels, Merlins, Northern Harriers, Wilson's Snipes, and American Pipits.

From the campground continue to the first parking area on the left. The pond to the north will have herons, egrets, and gulls in summer and diving ducks in winter. In summer expect Common Nighthawks over the dunes south toward the ocean. In winter a Short-eared Owl might appear. Take note of the beach regulations that are posted on the brown sign that is directly across from the parking area. The sand road beside the sign leads to Ramp 44; the paved road to the left goes to Ramp 43. Note that a four-wheel-drive vehicle is needed to access either Ramp 43 or 44. Either ramp will give you access to the Salt Pond. The advantage of going over Ramp 43 is that it gives access to the north end of the adjacent pond and toward the ocean edge for a good look at gulls and terns. In winter look for Lesser Black-backed Gulls in this area. To reach the Salt Pond, follow the shoreline until you are well past the nearest dune, then swing right and slightly uphill toward the west. To get to the Salt Pond from Ramp 44, go over the ramp and follow the left fork.

Watch for White and Glossy Ibises, which sometimes feed in the surrounding marshy areas. As soon as you clear the dunes that mark this road, turn right and stop at the large area of water, the Salt Pond. Look for a variety of waterfowl in winter including Tundra Swans, White-winged Scoters, and Lesser Scaup. During the breeding season several tern species, including Royal, Gull-billed, Common, and Least, are often present.

From the Salt Pond cross to the ocean for shorebirds as you continue toward the point. In past years the posted areas between the wet beach and the dunes have been home to Least and Common Terns, American Oystercatchers, and Black

Skimmers. The nesting area has been home to a few pair of Piping Plovers, but the combination of predation, storm overwash, and human interference has decreased nesting pairs dramatically.

Season and weather determine the best birding at the point. If the winds are right in late May, a number of pelagic species might fly by, including Wilson's Storm-Petrel, various shearwaters, and jaegers. In winter thousands of assorted gulls rest on the beach all the way from Ramp 43, around the point and to the drain. To approach these flocks closely enough for firsthand study, a four-wheel-drive vehicle is recommended, since a person on foot will put the birds to flight. Look for Snow Buntings hiding in beach debris or Lapland Longspurs out on the flats. In winter loons, grebes, and Bonaparte's Gulls are common, both in and over the water. Farther out, thousands of gannets will be gliding along and diving for fish.

From the point the shoreline curve leads toward the drain for about 1.3 miles. On the west side of a line of low dunes that separates the point from the bight, there are seasonal watery flats where ducks, gulls, and terns can be found. Look closely for a possible Peregrine Falcon perched on a dune, or a wintering flock of Snow Geese. On the way to the drain, look along the shoreline for Sanderlings, Ruddy Turnstones, and American Oystercatchers on the higher beach. In winter Black-bellied Plovers favor this area, as do gull flocks.

To return from the drain to Ramp 44, go back half a mile toward the point and turn left to the west end of the Salt Pond to search for American Bitterns, Black-crowned Night-Herons, and Marsh Wrens along a ditch that flows from the pond. Just before the ditch, pull your car to one side and walk up the easy slope to view the west end of the pond. The shallows there can be very productive for ducks in winter and shorebirds during fall migration. Continue another tenth of a mile to the interdunal road and head east about 0.8 mile to the intersection with the Ramp 44 road. Turn left; go over the ramp and back to the paved road.

Other key birds: *Summer:* Common, Royal and Black Tern, Clapper Rail. *Winter:* Common Loon; Northern Gannet; White-winged, Surf, and Black Scoter; Bufflehead; Red-breasted Merganser; Ring-necked Duck; Dunlin. *Year-round:* Gadwall; American Black Duck; American Wigeon; Black-bellied Plover; Red Knot; Royal and Forster's Tern; Merlin; American Bittern.

Nearby opportunities: For additional birding opportunities, see the site descriptions for Ocracoke Island (site 10) and Pea Island National Wildlife Refuge (site 7).

Directions: Hatteras Island Spit is located at the western end of Hatteras Island, below Hat- teras Village and above Hatteras Inlet. To reach the spit from Whalebone Junction in Nags Head, take Highway 12 south toward Hatteras Inlet. Upon approaching the Hatteras ferry landing location, remain in the left lane and go through the light; there is parking adjacent to the ferry visitor center, and just farther west, there is a lot on Seashore property with very limited parking. If you are coming from Ocracoke, take the Ocracoke-Hatteras ferry to Hatteras, and after exiting the ferry, turn right at the light and right again into the parking area. To reach the Cape Point near Buxton, turn into the park at the CAPE HATTERAS NATIONAL SEASHORE sign just before milepost 61 (if coming from Hatteras Spit).

Access: Cape Hatteras Visitor Center restrooms are accessible. Campground restrooms also have accessible facilities. Beach wheelchairs are available for rental from the visitor center.

Bathrooms: At Ferry Visitor Center and Cape Hatteras Visitor Center. Portable toilets can be found at the Buxton Woods Nature Trail and near the Old Lighthouse site.

Hazards: Deep sand not suitable for two-wheel-drive vehicles and the possibility of venomous snakes along Buxton Woods Nature Trail.

Nearest food, gas, and lodging: Hatteras Village and Buxton.

Nearest camping: Cape Point Campground has setups for tent and RV camping, with a total of 202 sites.

DeLorme map grid: Page 69, D6.

North Carolina Travel Map grid: L3.

For more information: Cape Hatteras National Seashore National Park Service, (252) 995–4474; www.nps.gov/caha.

9 Gulf Stream Pelagic Birding

by Brian Patteson

County: Dare.

Habitats: Open ocean over continental shelf and slope, Gulf Stream, Labrador Current.

Key birds: *Summer:* Audubon's Shearwater; Band-rumped Storm-Petrel; Bridled and Sooty Tern; Black-capped, Herald, Fea's, and Bermuda Petrel; White-tailed Tropicbird; Masked Booby; South Polar Skua. *Migration:* Sooty and Manx Shearwater; Leach's Storm-Petrel; Long-tailed Jaeger. *Winter:* Manx Shearwater.

Best times to bird: May through September and January through March.

About this site:

The close proximity of the warm Gulf Stream current, the cooler Labrador Current, and the edge of the continental shelf make the waters offshore of Cape Hatteras some of the best for seabirds in the western North Atlantic. Consequently, just 20 to 40 miles offshore, there is a crossroads in the ocean for birds that breed in the Arctic, the Antarctic, the tropics, and the eastern Atlantic. Such close proximity makes it possible for boat trips departing from Oregon Inlet or Hatteras Inlet to see both large numbers and a good diversity of pelagic bird species over the course of a ten- to twelve-hour trip.

Several trips are organized each year aboard local fishing boats with the express purpose of searching for birds. Because the pelagic seabirds that occur off Cape Hatteras come from all over the Atlantic Ocean and breed at different seasons, a trip on any day of the year could conceivably yield interesting sightings and a diverse list of species. Nevertheless, certain times of year have proven to be more consistently productive than others. For a chance to see most of the summer visitors, the period from late May through September is usually the best time, and most trips during this time frame average seeing eight to twelve pelagic species. Most trips encounter Black-capped Petrels; Cory's, Greater, and Audubon's Shearwaters; Band-rumped and Wilson's Storm-Petrels; and Bridled and Sooty Terns. Trips in late May or September tend to offer the best chance for a really long list, with the addition of migrating jaegers, phalaropes, and terns, though overall numbers of birds might be somewhat lower than those encountered between June and August.

Cold water temperatures between January and March bring another mix of pelagic birds to the continental shelf off Cape Hatteras, and these visitors frequently include Northern Fulmars, Manx Shearwaters, Great Skuas, Black-legged Kittiwakes, and a variety of alcids. The continuing presence of warm water in the Gulf Stream (usually in excess of seventy degrees) can be good for large numbers of Red Phalaropes and even small numbers of Black–capped Petrels and Audubon's Shearwaters, the former of which are breeding at this time. Most winter trips all but ignore the Gulf Stream and focus on the colder Labrador Current.

Other key birds: *Summer:* Cory's and Greater Shearwater; Wilson's Storm-Petrel; Red-billed Tropicbird. *Migration*: Sooty Shearwater; Red-necked Phalarope; Pomarine and Parasitic Jaeger; Arctic Tern. *Winter:* Northern Fulmar; Red Phalarope; Great Skua; Black-legged Kittiwake; Little Gull; Razorbill; Dovekie; Atlantic Puffin.

Nearby opportunities: If you wish to plan your own trip for offshore birding, many other boats are available for charter at these points, as well as at the Oregon Inlet Fishing Center, the village of Wanchese, and other marinas within Hatteras Village. Such a trip, however, should be undertaken only by a highly experienced crew, and even then with a careful eye on the weather. Conditions at both Oregon Inlet and Hatteras Inlet can be very treacherous at times and can change quickly.

Directions: Reservations for pelagic trips are required. Boats leave from Oden's Dock in Hatteras Village and Pirate's Cove Marina in Manteo. Oden's Dock is the first of three major marinas on the right on the Pamlico Sound side of Highway 12, just past "Nedo's" True Value Hardware store and the Hatteras Harbor Motel. Pirate's Cove Marina is located at the east end of Roanoke Island.

Access: Facilities and boats are not accessible for persons with disabilities.

Bathrooms: At docks and aboard boats.

Hazards: Seasickness, unpredictable weather.

Nearest food, gas, and lodging: Village of Hatteras, Nags Head, and Manteo.

Nearest camping: Cape Point Campground has setups for tent and RV camping, with a total of 202 sites.

DeLorme map grid: Page 46, B6, and page 69, D5.

North Carolina Travel Map grid: L2, L3.

For more information: Brian Patteson, Inc., (252) 986–1363, or Seabirding Pelagic Trips, www.seabirding.com.

10 Ocracoke Island

by Elizabeth Hanrahan

County: Hyde.

Habitats: Ocean beach, natural and artificial dunes, shrub thickets, brackish and freshwater ponds, dune fields, maritime forests, young pine forests, forested hammocks, salt marsh, near shore shallows.

Key birds: *Summer:* Little Blue Heron; Snowy Egret; Glossy Ibis; Black-necked Stilt; Wilson's Plover; Least Tern; Marbled Godwit; Gull-billed Tern; Sandwich Tern; Black Skimmer; Chuck-will's-widow; Great Crested Flycatcher; Eastern Kingbird. *Winter:* Red-throated Loon; Brant; Peregrine Falcon; Brown-headed Nuthatch; Sedge Wren. *Year-round:* Brown Pelican; White Ibis; Piping Plover; American Oystercatcher; Seaside Sparrow.

Best times to bird: Year-round and during spring and fall migrations and after strong cold fronts or storms.

About this site:

Ocracoke Island is located approximately 25 miles off the mainland across the Pamlico Sound. The island extends approximately 18 miles from Hatteras Inlet to Ocracoke Inlet. It is accessible by ferries operated by the North Carolina Department of Transportation, by private boat, or by private plane. The entire island, except the village, is part of the Cape Hatteras National Seashore Park.

More than 300 species of birds have been documented on Ocracoke Island. Land birds can be found at various locations, including the village by the Park Service Visitor Center and Howard Street, Hammock Hills Nature Trail, the Woods (a maritime forest on Highway 12), Pony Pasture, South Point Road, and the beach.

Wading birds can be found throughout the year on South Point Road, at the Hammock Hills Nature Trail overlook, and at Bird Pond near the Hatteras ferry docks. Check for waterfowl in winter at the following sites: Silver Lake, Pamlico Sound, the public boat ramp, Bird Pond, and South Point or anywhere on the beach. Numerous gulls and terns can be seen from the beach throughout the year. During migration, however, South Point is the preferred place to view impressive numbers and species. During winter loons, gannets, cormorants, and scoters are easily seen from the beaches. In late fall and winter, raptors are frequently found over the grassy areas on South Point Road. Peregrine Falcons frequent the South Point beach. Merlins and American Kestrels are seen in the village as well as on the power lines along Highway 12. Most people arrive on Ocracoke Island via the Hatteras Inlet Ferry from Hatteras Village. Therefore, the distances to points for specific sites are measured from the comfort station and parking lot at the Hatteras ferry.

Bird Pond, a small freshwater pond, 0.2 mile from the ferry, is on the left side of the road. Pull over by the FERRY 20 MPH sign. Early morning or just before sunset are the best times to bird this pond. You may see Laughing Gulls in the summer and Ring-billed, Herring, and Great Black-backed Gulls at any time. In the summer Black-necked Stilts are possible, and Forster's, Least, and Royal Terns and Glossy Ibises are present. White Ibises are found throughout the year, and Common Moorhens are seen here occasionally. During winter you may see American Coots and Clapper and Virginia Rails, as well as an occasional American Bittern and small rafts of waterfowl. In the summer, large mixed flocks of wading birds are often found across Highway 12 toward Pamlico Sound. Seaside Sparrows breed in this marsh.

Continue your drive down the island. At 9.4 miles from the ferry you will cross a small bridge over Island Creek. To the right, just beyond the bridge and across from the Park Service Campground, is Hammock Hills Nature Trail. The nature trail is mixed pine and shrub thicket. Throughout the year you should see Common Yellowthroats, Gray Catbirds, Brown Thrashers, and Eastern Towhees at the trail entrance. The trail boardwalk begins at and overlooks Island Creek. Wading birds often forage on the edges of the freshwater pond. In the winter look for Brown-headed Nuthatches in the pines and Northern Harriers over the marsh.

A view of marsh and the sound along Ocracoke Island. PHOTO: KAREN BEARDEN

On the left at the 12.4-mile point is South Point Road, a sand track road. The very best time to bird this area is after a storm when the road has been closed to traffic because of flooding. The 2-mile walk will provide you with vast numbers of wading birds, shorebirds, sandpipers, plovers, and passerines. South Point Road can be driven in a regular vehicle. Look for American Bitterns in the ditches with tall grasses. At dawn and dusk you may hear or see Chuck-will's-widows or American Woodcocks flying over the flats. Seaside Sparrows and Eastern Kingbirds are regularly found in the area during summer. In the winter look for Savannah and Sharp-tailed Sparrows and Sedge and Marsh Wrens.

Return to the main part of South Point Road and drive to the end. If you have a four-wheel-drive vehicle, you can continue to drive down to South Point. You may also walk to and around South Point. Be sure to obey posted signs, because areas of the beach are frequently closed during nesting season. A walk or ride to and around the point from Ramp 72 is productive. Note that driving on the beach or loose sand requires four-wheel drive. Walk along the shoreline to observe gulls, terns, and other shorebirds. Look along the shoreline and walk to the overwash area around the point to seek Solitary Sandpipers, Ruddy Turnstones, Marbled Godwits, Wilson's Plovers, and Black, Least, Sandwich, and Common Terns. American Golden-Plovers and Sooty Terns are two of the rarities found here.

Continue to Ocracoke Village via Highway 12. A walking map of the village is available at most stores, the Park Visitor Center, or the Preservation Society. It is easiest to walk or bike through the village. Park your car at the Park Service public parking area. In winter you will often find Buffleheads, rafts of various ducks, Brant, and the occasional unusual sandpiper. During winter check the water tower for falcons.

The Hatteras Inlet Ferry is a forty-minute, free ferry from Hatteras Village to Ocracoke Island which can usually provide some interesting birding. In the summer you can expect to see the usual gulls and terns as well as wading birds, Brown Pelicans, and an occasional nonbreeding Common Loon on both the Hatteras and Ocracoke side. November through March is the best time to look for ducks and Brant that frequent the area along with Buffleheads, Common Goldeneyes, and an occasional Common Eider.

Reservations are required for Cedar Island and Swan Quarter toll ferries from Ocracoke. The best time for birding is during the winter from late October through March. Expect to see a variety of waterfowl during the winter. About twenty minutes out of Ocracoke, you will see a large dredge spoil known locally as Bird Island or Dredge Island. In the summer you will see thousands of nesting Brown Pelicans, gulls, and terns. As you enter Swan Quarter, you can expect to see many wading birds. If you are on the Cedar Island Ferry, check the pilings on the left side of the boat for Osprey nests.

Other key birds: *Summer:* Yellow-crowned Night-Heron; Clapper Rail; Whimbrel; Ruddy Turnstone; Semipalmated Plover; Sandwich Tern; Great Crested Flycatcher; Barn Swallow; Prairie Warbler. *Winter:* Common Loon; Northern Gannet; American Bittern; Red Knot; Northern Pintail; Bufflehead; Surf Scoter; Northern Harrier; Merlin; Virginia Rail; Dunlin; Razorbill; Swamp Sparrow. *Year-round:* Great Egret; Tricolored Heron; Black-crowned Night-Heron; Black-bellied Plover; Forster's Tern.

Nearby opportunities: For additional birding opportunities, see the site descriptions for Mattamuskeet National Wildlife Refuge (site 5) and Cape Hatteras National Seashore (site 8).

Directions: Ocracoke Island is accessible from the north by the Hatteras-Ocracoke ferry across Hatteras Inlet. The drive from the ferry to Ocracoke Village provides views of the undeveloped beach and Pamlico Sound. From the south end of the island, Ocracoke is accessible by toll ferries from the mainland at Cedar Island and Swan Quarter. Reservations are required for these ferries.

Access: The National Park Service Visitor Center, the ferry docks, and several National Park Service Beach Access locations are wheelchair-accessible.

Bathrooms: National Park Service Visitor Center, the ferry docks, and some NPS Beach Access locations; also some in Ocracoke Village.

Hazards: High daytime temperatures during the summer.

Nearest food, gas, and lodging: Ocracoke Village.

Nearest camping: Ocracoke Campground.

DeLorme map grid: Page 68, C3.

North Carolina Travel Map grid: L3.

For more information: Cape Hatteras National Seashore National Park Service, (252) 995–4474; www.nps.gov/caha. North Carolina Ferry System, (800) 293–3779; www.icw-net.com/nc/ncferry.

11 Merchants Millpond State Park

by Linda J. Ward

County: Gates.

Habitats: Black-water coastal millpond, swamp forest, mixed pine-hardwood forest.

Key birds: *Summer:* Eastern Kingbird; Great Crested Flycatcher; Prothonotary Warbler; Blue Grosbeak; Summer Tanager. *Winter:* Hooded Merganser. *Year-round:* Brown-headed Nuthatch.

Best times to bird: Spring into early summer.

About this site:

The highlight of Merchants Millpond State Park is the 760-acre shallow millpond, which has large bald cypress and tupelo gum trees draped with Spanish moss. Beyond the main millpond, Lassiter Swamp is the home of old-growth cypress. The trails wind through mixed pine and hardwood forests surrounding the pond. At least 210 bird species have been identified in Merchants Millpond State Park. Bird the roads and parking areas nearby for forest species such as Summer Tanager, Carolina Chickadee, and Red-bellied and Downy Woodpeckers. Scarlet Tanagers are uncommon during spring and occasionally may be seen in summer and fall along the wooded roads to the family campground.

Turn left out of the park entrance, and then take another left onto Millpond Road (State Road 1403), which will take you to the entrance to the canoe rental area on your left after crossing a small bridge. In spring scan the trees around the launch site for White-eyed and Yellow-throated Vireos, and watch and listen for Prothonotary Warblers.

To bird from the water, put in at the canoe rental area. Once on the water, look for Northern Parula and Blue-gray Gnatcatcher. Follow first the orange canoe trail markers and then the yellow, which bring you near the family and group camping areas. In this section of the pond, Yellow-throated Warblers, Orchard Orioles, Eastern Kingbirds, and Yellow-billed Cuckoos are often seen in spring and early summer. Scan the shoreline for Great Blue and Green Herons, and check decaying trees and snags on the millpond for Downy, Hairy, Red-bellied, and Pileated Woodpeckers. Red-shouldered Hawks nest on and around the millpond. Wood Ducks, Mallards, and Canada Geese can be glimpsed among the cypress knees and stumps all year. The paddling in Lassiter Swamp can become difficult in summer with drier conditions and heavy mats of duckweed, but in fall and winter the water is more open, and waterfowl such as Ring-necked and American Black Ducks and American Wigeons can be found.

After returning to the canoe launch area, walk along Cypress Point Trail where Northern Cardinals, Tufted Titmice, Carolina Chickadees, and White-breasted Nuthatches are easily spotted all year. During the late fall and winter, look for

Winter Wrens, Hermit Thrushes, Brown Creepers, Swamp Sparrows, and Golden and Ruby-crowned Kinglets along the edges of Cypress Point Trail. Cypress Point Trail is wheelchair-accessible, with benches and decks overlooking the millpond.

The entrance to Coleman Trail is just off the parking lot of the canoe rental area. This hilly 2-mile walk leads through mixed woods and borders the millpond. Wild Turkeys, though rarely seen, are possible all seasons, and Yellow-bellied Sapsuckers can be found in late fall and winter.

Lassiter Trail can be accessed from Millpond Road or the picnic area off of Millpond Road. For those wishing a wilderness experience, follow this winding trail to the backpack camping area. For a shorter hike take a leisurely walk along the Fire Trail that interconnects the north and south sections of Lassiter Trail. Along the Fire Trail look for Blue Grosbeaks, Prairie and Pine Warblers, Common Yellowthroats, Indigo Buntings, Orchard Orioles, Northern Bobwhites, and Summer Tanagers in spring and summer.

Merchants Millpond State Park. PHOTO: KAREN BEARDEN

Other key birds: *Summer:* Osprey; Yellow-billed Cuckoo; Acadian Flycatcher; Eastern Wood-Pewee; Purple Martin; Wood Thrush; Yellow-throated, Black-and-white, and Prairie Warbler; Northern Parula; White-eyed Vireo; Ovenbird; Indigo Bunting; Field Sparrow; Orchard Oriole; American Goldfinch. *Winter:* American Wigeon; Northern Pintail; Wilson's Snipe; American Bittern; American Woodcock; Yellow-bellied Sapsucker; Brown Creeper; Winter Wren; Cedar Waxwing. *Year-round:* Wood Duck; Great Horned, Barred, and Eastern Screech-Owl; Northern Flicker.

Nearby opportunities: Great Dismal Swamp National Wildlife Refuge is located in southeastern Virginia and northeastern North Carolina. The refuge consists of over 109,000 acres of forested wetlands that have been greatly altered by drainage and repeated logging operations. Lake Drummond, a 3,100-acre natural lake, is located in the heart of the swamp. More than 200 bird species have been identified since the refuge's establishment, 96 of which have been reported as nesting on or near the refuge. Birding is best during spring migration from April to June when the greatest diversity of species, particularly warblers, occurs. Winter brings massive movements of blackbirds and robins to the swamp. Thousands of ducks, geese, and swans can be seen on Lake Drummond during the winter months. For additional information call the refuge office at (757) 986–3705 or visit http://greatdismalswamp.fws.gov.

Directions: Merchants Millpond State Park is approximately 140 miles northeast of Raleigh and 30 miles north of Edenton. The park office and family campground are half a mile east of the U.S. Highway 158 and SR 1403 (Millpond Road) crossroads, 4 miles west of Sunbury. The picnic area has a separate entrance located 1 mile south of US 158 on Millpond Road. The millpond and canoe rental area are half a mile farther south on Millpond Road. Each entrance is well marked.

Access: Cypress Point Trail and restrooms at the park office are wheelchair-accessible.

Bathrooms: At park office, canoe rental area, and picnic grounds and off the Fire Trail near the group campground.

Hazards: Ticks, poison ivy, and venomous snakes along trails during late spring and summer. At times the creek may be dangerous for canoeing. Check with park staff for the water level before embarking on a canoe trip.

Nearest food, gas, and lodging: A country store with gas pumps can be found at the intersection of US 158 and Millpond Road.

Nearest camping: Facilities include twenty sites for tents and trailers in the family campground. Primitive campsites are accessible by trail and canoe.

DeLorme map grid: Page 24, B4.

North Carolina Travel Map grid: K1.

For more information: Merchants Millpond State Park, (252) 357–1191; www.ils.unc.edu/parkproject/visit/memi/home.html.

12 Roanoke River

by Jean Richter

Counties: Halifax, Northampton, Martin, Bertie, and Washington.

Habitats: Bottomland hardwoods, cypress and tupelo swamps, mixed hardwood and levee forests.

Key birds: *Summer:* Bald Eagle; Mississippi Kite; American Redstart; Kentucky, Swainson's, and Cerulean Warbler; Summer and Scarlet Tanager. *Winter:* Red-headed Woodpecker.

Best times to bird: Spring and early summer for neotropical migrants. Fall birding can be quite rewarding.

About this site:

The Roanoke River flows through northeastern North Carolina, supporting a floodplain that covers more than 150,000 acres. Over 219 bird species have been recorded on the floodplain. Between the Nature Conservancy, the North Carolina Wildlife Resources Commission, and the U.S. Fish and Wildlife Service, which administers the Roanoke River National Wildlife Refuge, more than 70,000 acres of floodplain forestlands are protected or managed, with additional protection efforts still in progress. Over hundreds of years, floods of varying magnitudes have sculpted the various geomorphological features (ridges, swales, flats, and natural levees) found on the floodplain, creating a rich mosaic of plant and animal communities that provide great birding opportunities. Although much of the floodplain is under private ownership, birding opportunities are available on the public lands and by floating the river.

For the sake of simplicity, the river has been divided into three sections: the Upper Reach, starting at the base of the dam in Roanoke Rapids to Scotland Neck (U.S. Highway 258); the Middle Reach, from Scotland Neck to Devil's Gut, which is located approximately 5 miles downstream from Williamston (U.S. Highway 13/17); and the Lower Reach, from Devil's Gut to the mouth of the river.

The Upper Reach river channel from the base of the dam to just above Weldon is braided with channel islands supporting mixed hardwood forests. From Weldon to the US 258 bridge, the river is a single channel consisting of a well-developed levee that is distinctly higher than the floodplain. Most of the floodplain on this stretch of the river is owned by private individuals and is being farmed or managed for hardwoods or hunt clubs. Mississippi Kite, Bald Eagle, and Cerulean Warbler are the highlight species for this reach.

The Middle Reach section contains the highest overall bird diversity due to expansive forests behind the levees. A well-defined river levee is still apparent but decreases in elevation as you proceed downstream and the floodplain begins to

Mississippi Kites commonly eat large flying insects like dragonflies. PHOTO: HARRY SELL

widen. River levees that can be up to a quarter of a mile wide merge with expansive bottomland flats that either transition into large cypress and water tupelo swamps or narrow sloughs defined by low and high hardwood ridges. Stands of river cane are common along the levee, providing habitat for Swainson's and Kentucky Warblers. Numerous heron rookeries and many neotropical migrants such as the Prothonotary Warblers and Yellow throated Vireos are common in the large swamps found in this reach. Also watch for Cerulean Warblers, Louisiana Waterthrushes, American Redstarts, Summer and Scarlet Tanagers, Mississippi Kites, and Bald Eagles.

The Lower Reach section begins near the mouth of the river as the levee forest becomes less well defined. In the upper part of the Lower Reach is Devil's Gut Island, a preserve managed by the Nature Conservancy. This almost 10,000-acre island contains a diverse forest community with old-growth swamp forests interrupted by narrow ridges that support everything from beech forests on the higher ridges to floodplain oak communities on the lower ridges. As you move downriver these communities disappear due to the lower elevation. Major creeks and smaller rivers (such as the Eastmost, Middle, and Cashie Rivers) join the Roanoke River, giving this reach near the mouth a braided configuration. Just upstream of Plymouth is a thoroughfare that joins the Cashie River to the Roanoke River. Both the Cashie River and the thoroughfare are worth checking out by boat. The Cashie River is a slow-moving, meandering black-water river whose banks are dominated by bald cypress and other trees.

The floodplain in this reach is at its widest—more than 5 miles across in some areas. Most of the habitat is dominated by cypress and tupelo swamps. Here the canopy is dominated by bald cypress and other trees with thick layers of shrubs and small trees. Wood Ducks, Northern Parulas, Bald Eagles, Yellow-throated Warblers, Summer Tanagers, Indigo Buntings, Great Crested Flycatchers, and Ospreys are typical along this reach.

Other key birds: *Summer:* Acadian Flycatcher; Wood Thrush; Louisiana Waterthrush; Northern Parula; Yellow-throated Warbler. *Winter:* American Black Duck, Blue-winged Teal. *Year-round:* Wood Duck; Red-shouldered Hawk; Barred Owl; woodpeckers; White-eyed Vireo.

Nearby opportunities: The Roanoke Canal Trail is a walking trail located between Roanoke Rapids and Weldon. This historic area offers some good birding opportunities. There are five access locations to the canal trail, allowing for enjoyment in short lengths. The trail starts at the Roanoke Rapids Dam Access Point. For more information visit www.visithalifax.com.

Directions: The Roanoke River traverses several rapids, the most significant being just below U.S. Highway 301 at Weldon. As the river passes the fall line and makes its way to the coast, it begins to widen and become better for birding from the river. The boat access points listed here are those maintained by the North Carolina Wildlife Commission. There are, however, numerous access points from land. If you are interested in more specific information than provided here, then use the contact information provided at the end of this entry to help in planning your birding trip.

The first two boat access points for the Upper Reach can be accessed from Highway 48 north of Roanoke Rapids and US 301/158 northeast of Weldon. Note, however, that rapids are located in this portion of the Upper Reach. The more easterly portion, below the fall line, can be accessed approximately 7 miles north of Scotland Neck where US 258 crosses the Roanoke River.

The Roanoke River National Wildlife Refuge

begins in the vicinity of the Middle Reach with the Broadneck Swamp tract. Heading downstream from there is Company Swamp, the Askew tract, and in the vicinity of Williamston is Conine Island. On portions of Broadneck Swamp located upstream of Hamilton and along Company Swamp are trails that run for the most part adjacent to the river, making walking in this habitat easier. All these tracts, except Conine Island, are accessible by boat only. US 13/17 runs through the Conine Island and Askew tracts, allowing visitors to stop and walk on the old logging trails, which are distinguished by the gates that prevent vehicular access. There are two small parking lots located on the northbound lane of US 13/17 on Conine Island. Of special note is the Charles Kuralt birding and self-guided interpretive trail located approximately 1 mile north of the Roanoke River, off of US 13/17 north.

The North Carolina Wildlife Resources Commission also has several tracts of land in the Middle Reach section. They include the Boone Tract (Northampton County), Urquhart (Halifax County), and Beech House Swamp, Deveraux Swamp, and Conoho Farms, all located in Martin County. All these tracts, except Conoho Farms, are accessible only by boat. There is a public boat ramp located off Highway 125 in Hamilton. Turn east onto East Main Street and continue to the boat access point. Another public ramp is located at the river crossing on US 17 just north of Williamston. In addition, access to Conoho Farms from land can be from Moratoc Park in Williamston. On the entrance road to the park there is a gravel road that veers off to the left. Follow this road, and follow the signs to the Game Lands. You will see a sign that says NO ENTRY WITHOUT A PERMIT; this restriction applies only during the permitted hunts, otherwise travel by foot beyond the gate is allowed. A second access point is from Poplar Point Road off of Highway 125, which heads west out of Williamston. This road will also take you to the back side of Deveraux Swamp.

Movement on foot in the habitat in the Lower Reach of the river is difficult and oftentimes wet. The Roanoke River Partners organization has developed a paddle trail here, with future plans of extending it to the Middle and Upper Reaches. This trail is the best and most enjoyable way to visit the Lower Reach.

Access: Very limited.

Bathrooms: No public services.

Hazards: High water, venomous snakes, biting insects, and ticks.

Nearest food, gas, and lodging: Roanoke Rapids/Weldon, Williamston, Plymouth.

Nearest camping: Privately owned campground in Williamston.

DeLorme map grid: Pages 22–23, B3–D6; page 43, A6–B7; page 46, B1–4.

North Carolina Travel Map grid: J1/2.

For more information: Roanoke River National Wildlife Refuge, (252) 794–3808; http://roanokeriver.fws.gov. The Nature Conservancy, (252) 794–1818; http://nature .org/wherewework/northamerica/states/north carolina/. NC Wildlife Resources Commission, (252) 792–3868; www.ncwildlife.org. Roanoke River Partners, (252) 798–3920; www.roanokeriverpartners.org.

⑬ Greenville Area

by Howard Vainright and Ernie Marshall

Counties: Pitt and Beaufort.

Habitats: Freshwater ponds, grass and shrub areas, mixed pine-hardwood forest, floodplain hardwood forest.

Key birds: *Summer:* Eastern Kingbird; Great Crested Flycatcher; Loggerhead Shrike; Pro-thonotary Warbler; Henslow's and Grasshopper Sparrow; Summer Tanager. *Winter:* Short-eared Owl. *Year-round:* Bald Eagle.

Best times to bird: Birding is typically good during all seasons. Spring and fall are the best periods for migrants.

About this site:

River Park North is 324 acres of varied habitats. These include 250 acres of bottomland forest, over 20 acres of open grassland, and 45 acres of small lakes. The park is managed by the Greenville Recreation and Parks Department. An unpaved road with connecting trails makes many of the habitats easily accessible to birding. The park is open from sunrise to sunset. River Park North is one of the best places in the Greenville area for both spring and fall warbler migration. Northern Parulas, Magnolia Warblers, and American Redstarts are common, and Black-throated Blue and other warbler species are likely. Prothonotary Warblers nest in the park in good numbers. The ponds attract waterfowl in winter. American Wigeons and Ring-necked Ducks are usually present in small flocks, along with a few representatives of several other duck species.

Voice of America (VOA) sites A and B constitute the largest open grassy area in the region, created as a setting for the high-powered transmission towers and thus a unique even if somewhat limited environment. The VOA sites have some of the only nesting populations of Henslow's Sparrows in the state. This concentration of Henslow's Sparrows is the largest population east of the Mississippi in the Southeast. The birds can sometimes be seen and heard singing from the road. Access to the sites is restricted so that birding has to be done from the perimeter outside the fences. Key birds to look for in summer are Henslow's and Grasshopper Sparrows and Loggerhead Shrikes. Birds to watch for during the winter include Yellow-rumped and Palm Warblers, Short-eared and Great Horned Owls, Northern Harriers, and Sharp-shinned Hawks.

The Ayden and Pactolus Catfish Ponds sites are commercial catfish operations, with large ponds visible from the main road. They are probably the best locations in the area for Bald Eagles. At the Ayden site the ponds are on the north side of the road, and at the Pactolus site they are on both sides of the road. The ponds and the trees beyond can be scoped from the side of the road for waterfowl, eagles, and shorebirds.

The Grimesland Sand Pits have been a popular local fishing spot for many years. Recently the North Carolina Department of Transportation (NCDOT) has worked to restore portions of the property to a more natural wetland habitat. Native trees and plants have been planted for wetland mitigation. Plans are to continue to improve the site for visitation and use by nature enthusiasts. The Grimesland Sand Pits offer good chances for observing waterfowl in fall and winter, shorebirds in spring and late summer, and year-round viewing of Bald Eagles, Ospreys, various hawks, Turkey and Black Vultures, and Double-crested Cormorants. The site is also a regular feeding area for gulls, terns, and an occasional Brown Pelican.

Other key birds: *Summer:* Green Heron; Osprey; Solitary, Least, Western, and Spotted Sandpiper; Yellow-billed Cuckoo; Acadian Flycatcher; Eastern Wood-Pewee; Blue-gray Gnatcatcher; Wood Thrush; Gray Catbird; Northern Parula; Common Yellowthroat; Yellow-breasted Chat. *Winter:* Ring-necked Duck; American Wigeon; Northern Harrier; Sharp-shinned Hawk; Tree Swallow; Winter and House Wren; Blue-headed Vireo; Palm Warbler. *Year-round:* Great Egret; Double-crested Cormorant

Nearby opportunities: At Goose Creek State Park, the brackish marshes are home to Marsh Wrens, rails, and several species of herons and egrets. Barred Owls and Red-shouldered Hawks reside in the wooded swamps. Birdlife at Goose Creek varies dramatically with the seasons, with breeding populations of Bald Eagles and Ospreys as well as a variety of waterfowl present during winter. For more details visit www.ils.unc.edu/parkproject/visit/gocr/home.html.

Directions: River Park North is located on the north side of the Tar River, on Mumford Road, which is a main road connecting Greene Street and Highway 33. Coming into Greenville on U.S. Highway 264, signs direct visitors to the park from the intersection of that major highway and Highway 33. From downtown Greenville, turn right onto Mumford Road at the first traffic light after crossing the Greene Street Tar River Bridge.

VOA site A is located northeast of Greenville, and site B is southeast of Greenville. For VOA site A, from the intersection of US 264 East and Highway 33 East, proceed east 8.5 miles to Sheppard Mill Road, turn left (north), and continue 3 miles to Ward's Bridge Road, and then turn right and go 2 more miles to the site. For VOA site B Road, take Highway 43 south of Greenville to Hollywood Crossroads, and then turn left onto Mills Road and continue 5 miles to Black Jack. From Black Jack jog left, then right, onto VOA site B Road and continue 3.5 miles to the site.

To reach the Pactolus catfish ponds, follow the directions for VOA site A to Ward's Bridge. At this point continue straight ahead for another 0.7 mile to the ponds. For the Ayden catfish ponds, take Highway 11 south from Greenville to Ayden and the intersection with Highway 102. Go east on Highway 102 for 5.0 miles to the intersection with Emma Cannon Road. Turn right and continue 5.0 miles on Emma Cannon Road to the ponds (2.2 miles beyond Helen's Crossroads).

The Grimesland Sand Pits are located north of the Tar River on the Grimesland Bridge Road. Grimesland Bridge Road is accessible from Highway 33 in Grimesland or by US 264 between Greenville and Washington.

Access: In the park an unpaved road with connecting trails provides limited access to birding for people who have difficulty walking. The park is closed Monday. Other sites can be birded from the car.

Bathrooms: Available at the River Park North near the park entrance in the Visitor Reception Building. The Science and Nature Center—with nature exhibits, an assembly room, and a gift shop—was destroyed in 1999 by Hurricane Floyd and is being upgraded.

Hazards: None.

Nearest food, gas, and lodging: Greenville area.

Nearest camping: Goose Creek State Park has twelve sites for primitive camping.

DeLorme map grid: Page 65, A7–8, B6.

North Carolina Travel Map grid: J2.

For more information: Greenville Recreation and Parks Department, (252) 329–4562.

Howell Woods Environmental Learning Center

by Jamie Sasser

County: Johnston.

Habitats: Bottomland hardwood, mixed pine-hardwood, loblolly pine, longleaf pine, and pine and scrub oak sandhill forests; cypress-gum swamp; managed fallow fields.

Key birds: *Summer:* Mississippi Kite; American Redstart; Hooded, Prothonotary, Kentucky, and Swainson's Warbler; Summer Tanager;

Indigo Bunting. *Winter:* Baltimore Oriole. *Year-round:* Red-headed Woodpecker; Loggerhead Shrike; Brown-headed Nuthatch.

Best times to bird: Most anytime will yield excellent daily counts, especially during spring and fall migration, when counts of sixty-five to eighty species a day are common.

About this site:

Howell Woods Environmental Learning Center is owned and operated by Johnston Community College. The 2,856-acre property is actively managed for the benefit of wildlife, educational opportunities, and low-impact outdoor recreation. The Howell Woods property contains a great diversity of habitats and wildlife within the 2,800 acres situated between the Neuse River and Hannah and Mill Creeks. The dominant community is over 1,600 acres of bottomland hardwood forest. There are more than 25 miles of unpaved roads and trails on the property.

More than 160 bird species have been documented on the property. A bird feeding station is located near the entrance of the Learning Center building, where Brown-headed and White-breasted Nuthatches, woodpeckers, and other common feeder birds can be easily watched year-round. Ruby-throated Hummingbirds are numerous during the summer.

The Learning Center Habitat Diversity Hiking Trail system contains more than fifteen short (0.10- to 0.75-mile) connected trails that pass through bottomland hardwood forest; open fallow fields; mixed pine-hardwood, longleaf, and loblolly forests; and creek-side habitat. Other areas on the property with great birding opportunities require staff guidance or granted access. These areas include the River Loop Bottomland Hardwood Trail system, Monkey Ridge Road (bottomland hardwood and cypress-gum slough habitat), and the wetland restoration area. It is easily possible to pick up thirty-five to fifty species of birds on any given day by walking any number of the trail systems mentioned.

Swainson's, Kentucky, Hooded, and Prothonotary Warblers; American Redstarts; Acadian Flycatchers; Indigo Buntings; Yellow-throated and White-eyed Vireos; Summer Tanagers; Yellow-billed Cuckoos; Mississippi Kites; and Wood Thrushes are common throughout the property in the spring and summer. During the winter

Cypress slough near Howell Woods Environmental Learning Center. PHOTO: JAMIE SASSER

Song, Fox, and White-throated Sparrows; Dark-eyed Juncos; Pine and Yellow-rumped Warblers; Hermit Thrushes; Red-headed Woodpeckers (along with six other woodpecker species); and Ruby-crowned Kinglets can be found. The wetland restoration project has resulted in the development of an area that attracts a variety of migrating shorebirds and waterfowl.

Other key birds: *Summer:* Yellow-billed Cuckoo; Yellow-throated Vireo; Wood Thrush. *Winter:* Hermit Thrush; waterfowl.

Nearby opportunities: The Middle Creek Bottomlands II was donated to the Triangle Land Conservancy and comprises 160 acres. Much of the tract is covered by buttonbush, alder, and black willow. Additional details for this site are available online at the Carolina Bird Club Web site, www.carolinabirdclub.org.

Directions: Howell Woods Environmental Learning Center is located on Devil's Racetrack Road approximately 9 miles from the town of Four Oaks. Devil's Racetrack Road

(State Road 1009) is easily accessed from Interstate 95 at exit 90 at the U.S. Highway 701 and Highway 96 intersection at the Citgo and BP gas stations. Devil's Racetrack Road is the access road to get back onto I-95 North. Once on Devil's Racetrack travel about 8.2 miles, and the Learning Center will be located on the left down a gravel drive lined with young longleaf pine trees.

Access: The Learning Center building is accessible for persons with disabilities.

Bathrooms: At the Learning Center.

Hazards: Biting insects, ticks, and venomous snakes.

Nearest food, gas, and lodging: Four Oaks, about 8 miles from the site.

Nearest camping: On-site. Reservations required.

DeLorme map grid: Page 63, B5.

North Carolina Travel Map grid: I3.

For more information: Howell Woods Environmental Learning Center, (919) 938–0115; www.johnstoncc.edu/information/howell woods/howellwoods.htm. Normal business hours for the Learning Center are Monday through Friday from 8:00 A.M. to 5:00 P.M. Hiking trails are generally open seven days a week during daylight hours but may be temporarily closed for special training or hunting events, so please call if you are traveling a long distance to ensure desired access. Trail maps and information brochures are available in the Learning Center building.

⑮ Weymouth Woods Sandhills Nature Preserve
by Scott Hartley

County: Moore.

Habitats: Longleaf pine and scrub oak, mixed pine-hardwood, small stream and bottomland hardwoods, stream-head pocosins.

Key birds: *Summer:* Chuck-will's-widow; Great Crested Flycatcher; Kentucky and Hooded Warbler; Bachman's Sparrow; Summer Tanager; Blue Grosbeak. *Winter:* Pine Siskin. *Year-round:* Red-headed and Red-cockaded Woodpecker; Brown-headed Nuthatch.

Best times to bird: Anytime of the year.

About this site:

Weymouth Woods Sandhills Nature Preserve is a State Nature Preserve operated by the North Carolina Division of Parks and Recreation. The preserve consists of 900 acres on three separate tracts of land. The Weymouth Tract is 515 acres with 4.5 miles of trails that give access to all habitat types. It is important to remain on the trails at all times.

More than 135 species of birds have been documented at Weymouth Woods. It is considered the best place in North Carolina to see Red-cockaded Woodpeckers. Two groups of birds live within 100 to 200 yards of the parking area. The best time for viewing is between the first of April and the end of June. Bachman's Sparrows are also present in this area. The Bower's Bog Trail and Pine Barrens Trail are the best spots for locating them. The upland longleaf area around the office is good for Pine Warblers, Brown-headed and White-breasted Nuthatches, Eastern Bluebirds, and Red-cockaded Woodpeckers year-round. In the spring listen for Northern Bobwhites in the area behind the office. Great Horned Owls are vocal during October and early November in late afternoon and can be seen and heard behind the park office. During summer the area around the park office and on the short Bower's Bog Trail will yield Summer Tanagers, Great Crested Flycatchers, Eastern Wood-Pewees, Hairy Woodpeckers, and Blue-gray Gnatcatchers. Chimney Swifts and Common Nighthawks are often seen overhead.

For a good variety of birds year-round take the Lighter Stump Trail to the Pine Island Trail. A trail map is available at the park office. The Lighter Stump Trail descends from the park office half a mile between a frequently burned upland area and an unburned stream-head pocosin and mixed hardwood forest. During the summer Prairie Warblers, Summer Tanagers, Great Crested Flycatchers, Eastern Wood-Pewees, Indigo Buntings, and Blue Grosbeaks are found on the west side of the trail. The east side, with its thick evergreen vegetation and mixed hardwoods, is good for Blue-gray Gnatcatchers, Red-eyed and White-eyed Vireos, Gray Catbirds, and Brown Thrashers. Near the lower end of the Lighter Stump Trail are a set of wooden steps. Look for Kentucky and Hooded Warblers along the small stream. After crossing the small bridge listen for Black-and-white Warblers.

Beyond the bridge bear to the right onto the Pine Island Trail, a half-mile loop. To the left is James Creek. On a good migration day you can get all the eastern thrushes, as well as tanagers, several woodpecker species, and a number of warblers. Take some time to scan this area. Barred Owls are often seen and heard in this area year-round. Red-shouldered Hawks, Wood Ducks, and Green and Great Blue Herons may be seen downstream from the bridge. During the summer stop at each bridge crossing and listen for Acadian Flycatchers, Louisiana Waterthrushes, Yellow-throated Warblers, and Yellow-throated Vireos. In the winter, Fox Sparrows, Winter Wrens, Brown Creepers, Blue-headed Vireos, Yellow-bellied Sapsuckers, Hermit Thrushes, and both Ruby and Golden-crowned Kinglets are present. Check the trees for Pine Siskins, Purple Finches, and grosbeaks. The Pine Island Trail will bring you back to the Lighter Stump Trail, or you may choose to take the Holly Road Trail for a different route back to the visitor center.

The endangered Red-cockaded Woodpecker is dependent on mature pine forests of the southeast United States. PHOTO: HARRY SELL

Other key birds: *Summer:* Acadian Fly-catcher; Eastern Wood-Pewee; Wood Thrush; Blue-gray Gnatcatcher; Red-eyed, Yellow-throated, and Blue-headed Vireo; Common Nighthawk; Black-and-white and Prairie Warbler; Louisiana Waterthrush; Ovenbird; Indigo Bunting. *Winter:* Yellow-bellied Sapsucker; Brown Creeper; White-throated, Chipping, and Fox Sparrow; Winter Wren; Hermit Thrush; Golden and Ruby-crowned Kinglet; Yellow-rumped Warbler; Cedar Waxwing. *Year-round:* Great Horned Owl; Northern Bobwhite; wood-peckers; Blue-headed Vireo.

Nearby opportunities: Sandhills Game Land comprises approximately 58,000 acres and provides an excellent example of a longleaf pine ecosystem. Bachman's Sparrows are abundant in areas of open pine forest with a grass understory. Red-cockaded Woodpeckers are common. Additional details are available online at the Carolina Bird Club Web site, www.carolinabirdclub.org.

Directions: Weymouth Woods is located at 1024 Fort Bragg Road just outside of Southern Pines, North Carolina. If coming from Southern Pines, take U.S. Highway 1 to the intersection with Saunders Boulevard. There is a brown WEYMOUTH WOODS SANDHILLS NATURE PRESERVE sign at the intersection. Turn onto Saunders Boulevard and proceed to a stop sign at the intersection of Saunders Boulevard and Bethesda Road. Turn left at this stop sign. Continue to a four-way stop at the intersection of Fort Bragg Road and Indiana Avenue. Go straight at this intersection. The preserve entrance is half a mile on your left, marked by a large brown WEYMOUTH WOODS sign.

Access: The visitor center is wheelchair-accessible.

Bathrooms: At the park visitor center.

Hazards: Ticks are a year-round concern and can be excessively abundant during the warmer months. Poison oak, poison ivy, and poison sumac are present. Watch for cotton-mouths, particularly along James Creek. Stay on trails to minimize these hazards.

Nearest food, gas, and lodging: Pines and Aberdeen, which are within a five-minute drive.

Nearest camping: None.

DeLorme map grid: Page 60, D4.

North Carolina Travel Map grid: G3.

For more information: Weymouth Woods Sandhills Nature Preserve, (910) 692–2167; www.ils.unc.edu/parkproject/visit/wewo/home.html. The preserve gates open daily at 9:00 A.M. and remain open until 6:00 P.M. from November through March and 7:00 P.M. from April through October.

Piedmont

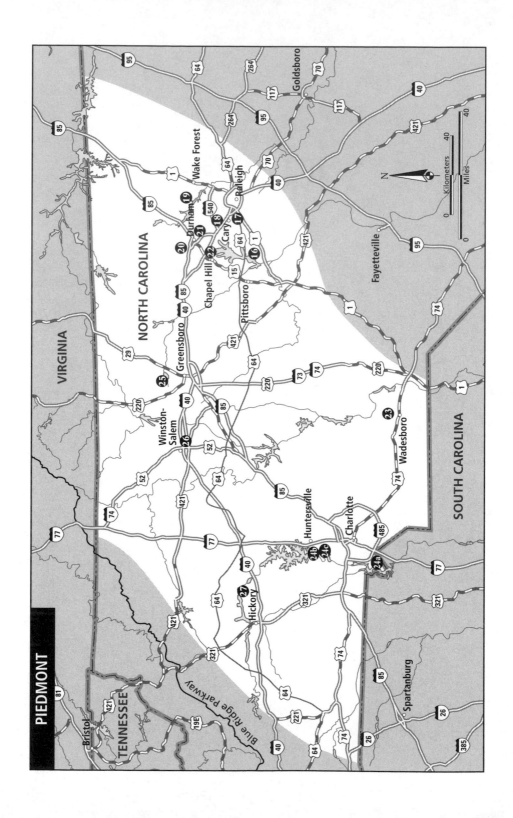

PIEDMONT

16 Jordan Lake State Recreation Area

by Will Cook

County: Chatham, with outlying areas in Wake and Durham.

Habitats: Lake, pine forest, mixed pine-hardwood forest, mature oak-hickory forest, fields, mudflats, streams, waterfowl impoundments, beaver impoundments.

Key birds: *Spring and summer:* Whip-poor-will; Eastern Kingbird; Great Crested Flycatcher; Cliff Swallow; Kentucky, Hooded, and Prothonotary Warbler; Summer and Scarlet Tanager; Indigo Bunting; Blue Grosbeak. *Winter:* Hooded and Common Merganser; Horned Grebe. *Year-round:* Bald Eagle; Red-headed Woodpecker; Brown-headed Nuthatch.

Best times to bird: Year-round, especially fall through spring.

About this site:

Jordan Lake is an outstanding birding location year-round, with more Bald Eagles than any other site in the state. The site also attracts more stellar rarities than just about any other spot in the Piedmont. Jordan Lake has 13,900 acres of water and is surrounded by 32,868 acres of game land and state recreation areas.

Jordan Lake is dependable all year for seeing the Bald Eagle, with highest numbers in summer and a few nesting pairs. Bald Eagles may be seen from any of the lake accesses mentioned subsequently. Cliff Swallow colonies are found under most of the large bridges over the lake. Tree Swallows, near their southeastern breeding limit here, nest in the dead trees in the middle of the lake, along with Ospreys and Double-crested Cormorants. Gulls are abundant in winter. Waterfowl can be scarce at times, but in late winter rarities such as Long-tailed Ducks, Common Mergansers, and Common Goldeneyes are almost expected. Hurricanes have brought outstanding pelagic rarities. Brown-headed Nuthatches and Pine Warblers are common in the pines surrounding the lake.

Begin your tour of the lake by visiting the dam area. The high dam that creates Jordan Lake has excellent vistas of the south end of the lake and the Haw River downstream, plus some nice field and woodland birding. From U.S. Highway 64 at Wilsonville, take Beaver Creek Road south 1.0 mile past Ebenezer Church State Recreation Area, turn right on Pea Ridge Road (State Road 1972), and reset the odometer. After 3.0 miles on Pea Ridge, bear right to stay on Pea Ridge. At 3.6 miles, stop at the gated road on the right. This long, straight road is excellent for both Chuck-will's-widows and Whip-poor-wills in spring and summer and Blue-headed Vireos, Brown Creepers, and kinglets in winter. Continuing driving south, at 5.1 miles turn right onto U.S. Highway 1 south. Take exit 79, 1.5 miles west of the Haw River. Turn right at the stop sign onto Moncure-Pittsboro Road (State

The Great Crested Flycatcher is a common summer resident in most areas of the state.
PHOTO: HARRY SELL

Road 1012). In 0.2 mile, turn right onto Jordan Dam Road (State Road 1970) and follow it to the end, bearing right at a fork, and park in the parking lot near the dam. Scope the south end of the lake for ducks and gulls. Downstream is good for herons, Hooded Mergansers, and woodland birds. Cliff Swallows nest under the dam control tower.

The epicenter of Jordan Lake birding is Ebenezer Point, which is officially called Ebenezer Church State Recreation Area. This is the best spot to look for rare waterbirds, with a commanding view of the heart of Jordan Lake. It can be a migrant trap in fall. Ebenezer is 2.3 miles south of US 64 on Beaver Creek Road on the east side of the lake. There is a well-marked entrance on the right. Drive to the end of the main road and park. Walk to the point for the best vantage. Diving ducks, loons, grebes, and gulls are common during the winter, though usually not close to shore. Bonaparte's Gulls are particularly abundant.

The Seaforth area offers a good view of the center of Jordan Lake, but not as commanding as Ebenezer Point. It is also great for land birds. The well-marked entrance is on the south side of US 64 between two arms of the lake. Drive to the end of the main road and park. The loop nature trail is good for woodland birds. The sandy beach has the best vantage point for scoping. Diving ducks, loons, grebes, and gulls are common during the winter. Continue south through the woods, following an old road and cutting through the woods to get to the point.

Opposite Ebenezer, with similar birding possibilities, is Vista Point. From US 64 just west of the lake, take Seaforth Road south 2.0 miles to North Pea Ridge Road. Turn left onto North Pea Ridge Road, and go 0.7 mile to the entrance.

Drive to the end of the main road and park. Walk to the point for the best vantage point to use a scope. Diving ducks, loons, grebes, and gulls are common during the winter. The loop nature trail is good for Brown-headed Nuthatches and migrants, the open areas for Blue Grosbeaks, and the woods for Blue-headed Vireos.

Big Woods Road is the main road that runs north-south on the western side of Jordan Lake north of US 64. There are a few places to stop to scan the lake, great land birding, and a nice beaver swamp at the north end. Traveling west on US 64, Big Woods Road is the first road to the right after crossing the lake and pass Parker's Creek Recreation Area. It is 3.2 miles west of the intersection of US 64 and Farrington Road. The best stops are at 1.6 miles north of US 64 at a small gravel pull-off and gated road on the right; 2.8 miles at Jordan Lake Educational State Forest; 3.5 miles at the NC Forest Resources Center; 4.9 miles at an old orchard and fishing access; and 6.2 miles at a beaver impoundment.

A good place to spend a few minutes checking in winter and during migration, when gulls and other assorted birds are resting on a breakwater, is at Crosswinds Marina. This is one of the best spots at Jordan to scan for rare gulls and terns, since they are concentrated and relatively close. The marina is a short distance north of US 64 on Farrington Road (1008). It is well marked on the left, just before the first bridge over the lake.

Farrington Point offers one of the best vantage points of the lake. From US 64 take Farrington Road north 4.4 miles to the bridge over Jordan Lake. Stop and scan at several spots along the long causeway. Cliff Swallows nest underneath the bridge. Continue north and turn left into the Farrington Point Boat Ramps area (5.0 miles north of US 64). Also, explore the ramp area, several short trails, and causeway. Ospreys and Bald Eagles are common in summer.

Indian Creek Wildlife Observation Site is located on Highway 751 about 5 miles north of US 64 and a mile south of the Highway 751 causeway. The entrance is a small gravel driveway opposite a convenience store, marked by a small brown park sign. The driveway leads a short distance to the parking lot. A nice woodland trail leads to a small platform with a good view of north-central Jordan Lake, also known as the Eagle Platform, since Bald Eagles are often seen here.

The Highway 751 bridge is one of the most frequently birded spots at Jordan Lake. From this bridge one has an expansive view of the lake to the west of the bridge and the Northeast Creek arm of the lake to the east. To reach the bridge from US 64 take Highway 751 north about 6 miles. Park along the causeway where permitted. In the fall when the water level is low, the area east of the bridge is great for wading birds and shorebirds. A short distance north of the bridge on the west side of the road, there is a small gravel parking lot. The trail beyond the gate here is good for woodland and field birds.

One of the best spots for migrant warblers, ducks, and Whip-poor-wills is Old Hope Valley Farm Road. When the water level is low, it is excellent for seeing shorebirds. If coming from US 64, take Farrington Road north 3.8 miles, and then turn right on Old Farrington Road. After 2.1 miles on Old Farrington, turn right onto Old Hope Valley Farm Road. This is the first right after the Orange County line. Park at the end of the road. Be careful not to block the gate. Walk past the gate and explore the main road and site trails. Turn left at the large power line and follow the trail to the lake.

Almost every species of shorebird that has been seen in the Triangle has been seen at New Hope Creek Mudflats. The mudflat area can also be great for egrets, dabbling ducks, migrant passerines, and raptors. The mudflats begin to appear when the lake level is less than 214 feet above sea level. Access is not easy, but it's often worth the long trek. In the morning walk in to the east side of the mudflats from the Highway 751 bridge. Park at the small gravel lot on the west side of Highway 751 just north of the bridge, walk into the woods on the game land trail, and take the second fork to the left. At the lake, follow the shore to the north to the mudflats. Total distance is about 2 miles one way. In the afternoon walk in to the west side from Old Hope Valley Farm Road. Park at the end of the road, walk past the gate, turn left at the power line, and follow the trail along the power line to the railroad peninsula jutting out into the mudflats. Depending on where the mudflats are, walking distance is 1 to 2 miles one way.

The Army Corps of Engineers created several impoundments to mitigate some of the loss of wetlands caused by the creation of the lake. All are of a similar design, with a small gravel parking space and gate leading to a long straight cause-way, which leads to a concrete dam and water gate at a stream crossing. They have similar suites of birds, such as Great Blue Herons, Wood Ducks, Red-headed Woodpeckers, Yellow-throated and Prothonotary Warblers, and Rusty Blackbirds (winter). The most popular impoundments for birding are Little Creek, from Interstate 40 at Highway 54, take Highway 54 west and pull off to the right in about a mile to the brown sign; New Hope Creek, from I–40 at Highway 54, take Highway 54 east and pull off to the left in about a mile to the brown sign marked (in apparent error) NEW HOPE RIVER WATERFOWL IMPOUNDMENT; Stagecoach Road, take Highway 751 south from Highway 54 and turn right on Stagecoach Road to find the impoundment access on the right just across New Hope Creek; Northeast Creek, take Highway 751 south from Highway 54, cross into Chatham County, and turn left on O'Kelly Chapel Road to find the impoundment on the left in about a mile; and Beaver Creek, from the intersection of Highway 751 and US 64, take New Hill Road south to find the impoundment on the left in about 1.5 miles.

Other key birds: *Spring and summer:* Tree Swallow. *Fall:* Herons and shorebirds. *Winter:* Common Loon; Bonaparte's Gull; Fox Sparrow. *Year-round:* Blue-headed Vireo.

Nearby opportunities: Raven Rock State Park is located in the fall zone of the eastern Piedmont along the Cape Fear River. Within 3,953 acres of land, visitors can find a rich diversity of bird and plant life. The park can be a very pleasant experience, with approximately 11 miles of foot trails.

White Pines Nature Preserve, acquired by the Triangle Land Conservancy (TLC) in 1986, is located at the confluence of the Deep and Rocky Rivers and covers 258 acres. The preserve is home to several stands of white pine, with some trees over 150 years old and 30 inches in diameter.

Additional details for these sites are available online at the Carolina Bird Club Web site, www.carolinabirdclub.org.

Directions: The Jordan Lake area is about 25 miles west of Raleigh and 15 miles south of Durham. The center of Jordan Lake activity is at Wilsonville, the intersection of US 64 and Farrington Road, which is the first stoplight east of the lake on US 64. From Raleigh, take U.S. Highway 1 south, then US 64 west to the lake area. If coming from Durham, take Highway 751 south to US 64, then US 64 west.

Access: Wheelchair-accessible sites include all sections of the Jordan Lake State Recreation Area, the dam area, and Crosswinds Marina.

Bathrooms: Available in most sections of the recreation area.

Hazards: Areas in the New Hope Game Land should be avoided during deer gun season.

Nearest food, gas, and lodging: Snacks and gas are available on US 64 east of the causeway. Lodging is available in the Raleigh-Durham area.

Nearest camping: More than a thousand campsites for tents and RVs are available in the state park at Crosswinds Campground, Parkers Creek, and Poplar Point.

DeLorme map grid: Page 39, D6–C7.

North Carolina Travel Map grid: H2.

For more information: Jordan Lake State Recreation Area, (919) 362-0586; www.ils.unc.edu/parkproject/visit/jord/home.html.

Hemlock Bluffs Nature Preserve, Ritter Park, and Swift Creek Bluffs

by Mark Johns and Steve Shultz

County: Wake.

Habitats: Pine forest, mixed pine-hardwood, upland oak-hickory, Swift Creek floodplain.

Key birds: *Summer:* Summer and Scarlet Tanager. *Year-round:* Brown-headed Nuthatch; Red-headed Woodpecker.

Best times to bird: Any time of the year; especially excellent during migration periods for neotropical migrants along Swift Creek.

About this site:

Hemlock Bluffs is a state nature preserve that is managed by the Town of Cary through a lease arrangement with the state of North Carolina. The bluffs, which harbor a disjunct population of Eastern hemlock, divide the preserve into upland areas with pines, mixed pine-hardwood and oak-hickory woodlands, and the floodplain along Swift Creek. Hurricane Fran in 1996 created many gaps in the canopy that now have regenerating vegetation, giving the preserve several patches of early successional habitat. Elevated observation platforms allow for good treetop-level birding, which is advantageous during spring migration. Well-marked trails allow access to all habitat types. Visitors must remain on marked trails at all times.

More than 130 bird species have been documented at Hemlock Bluffs Nature Preserve and at the Ritter Park area. Look around the nature center in the pine habitat for Brown-headed Nuthatches year-round. Check out the feeders for great looks at Ruby-throated Hummingbirds in summer and for Brown-headed and White-breasted Nuthatches, Red-bellied and Downy Woodpeckers, and other feeder birds year-round. During winter under the feeders and around the courtyard edges, look for Dark-eyed Juncos and White-throated Sparrows. Look for Summer Tanagers in the pines around the parking lot and nature center. The Swift Creek Loop Trail takes you through a brief stretch of mature oak and hickory woodlands with canopy gaps before you get to the bluffs, which can yield looks at Red-eyed and Yellow-throated Vireos and Scarlet and Summer Tanagers in summer. The gaps and associated snags offer a year-round attraction to woodpeckers, including the Red-headed Woodpecker.

Descend down the stairs to reach the Swift Creek Loop Trail. The trail follows Swift Creek on a raised boardwalk for the first part of the loop. Watch and listen for Wood Thrushes; Red-eyed and Yellow-throated Vireos; Summer and Scarlet Tanagers; Ovenbirds; Acadian Flycatchers; and Louisiana Waterthrushes. The boardwalk also offers good chances for close looks at Blue-gray Gnatcatchers and

The Swift Creek Loop Trail at Hemlock Bluffs. PHOTO: C. EDWARD DOMBROFSKI

Northern Parulas in summer, as well as neotropical migrants like Black-throated Green, Black-throated Blue, Blue-winged, Prothonotary, and Worm-eating Warblers and Northern Waterthrushes during migration. The back side of this loop is a good spot to check for Yellow-throated Warblers singing from the large pines, as well as roosting Barred and Great Horned Owls. In springtime, both Barred Owls and Red-shouldered Hawks are actively calling. Watch for Brown Creepers, Yellow-bellied Sapsuckers, and Hermit Thrushes along this loop in winter. In the summer the shrubs along the boardwalk near Swift Creek may yield such thicket-loving birds as Brown Thrashers, White-eyed Vireos, Gray Catbirds, and even Yellow-breasted Chats during migration. Thrush species (especially Veery, Hermit, and Wood) are common along this trail during migration. Waterbirds such as Belted Kingfishers year-round and Great Blue Herons in fall and winter are found along Swift Creek, and migrating shorebirds show up occasionally along the creek.

After finishing the Swift Creek Loop, return to the courtyard for access to Chestnut Oak Trail, another loop trail, about a mile in length, which winds through mature oak-hickory woodlands and mixed pine hardwoods. This is an excellent trail in summer for Ovenbirds; Red-eyed and Yellow-throated Vireos; Scarlet and Summer Tanagers; and Pileated Woodpeckers. In winter this is also an excellent place to search for Winter Wrens along the brushy areas near the trail and to watch for woodpeckers in winter. In winter, with patience, it is possible to see seven species of woodpeckers in a single day along this trail.

Ritter Park offers similar species found along the Swift Creek Loop Trail at Hemlock Bluffs. This greenway is an excellent spot for warblers in April and early May, with almost two dozen species on a good day. The additional open areas and fields around Ritter Park and parts of the greenway near Regency Park offer chances for Eastern Bluebirds, American Robins, Eastern Phoebes, and even foraging swallows and Chimney Swifts. Eastern Wood-Pewees and Eastern Kingbirds both are possible along this trail and its many openings and edges, especially during migration. The brushy areas along parts of the greenway can yield Common Yellowthroats year-round and often are good spots to watch for Indigo Buntings during spring migration and Palm Warblers in winter. Red-tailed and Red-shouldered Hawks and Barred, Great Horned, and Eastern Screech-Owls have nested along this greenway. The best time to bird Ritter Park is in the morning.

Swift Creek Bluffs has similar north-facing bluffs like those at Hemlock Bluffs. To get to Swift Creek Bluffs, turn right out of the Hemlock Bluffs parking lot and proceed to the first light, Penny Road, and turn left. Proceed a few miles and turn left onto Holly Springs Road. Go downhill for about a quarter mile to the small parking lot on the left before the bridge. The parking lot is just after the power plant access road.

The Swift Creek Bluffs property is owned by the Triangle Land Conservancy and consists of a narrow riparian corridor along the south side of Swift Creek and the adjacent bluffs. A single footpath with short branching side trails provides visitor access. The trail follows the gently meandering Swift Creek for almost half a mile before ending at a steep bluff that blocks foot traffic. The footpath can become very muddy after heavy rains. Swift Creek Bluffs does not attract any species that cannot be seen or heard at Hemlock Bluffs. This site is not usually busy, however, and offers birders access to a pleasant riparian corridor that remains largely undiscovered by the general public. Recent timber harvests adjacent to the property may yield early successional species.

Other key birds: *Summer:* Louisiana Waterthrush; Ovenbird; Yellow-throated and Red-eyed Vireo; Yellow-throated Warbler; Northern Parula; Wood Thrush; Gray Catbird; Blue-gray Gnatcatcher; Acadian Flycatcher. *Winter:* White-throated Sparrow; Dark-eyed Junco; Yellow-bellied Sapsucker; Hermit Thrush; Brown Creeper; Winter Wren; Yellow-rumped Warbler; Ruby and Golden-crowned Kinglets. *Year-round:* White-breasted Nuthatch; Pileated Woodpecker; Hairy Woodpecker; Pine Warbler; American Goldfinch; Eastern Bluebird; Belted Kingfisher; Barred Owl.

Nearby opportunities: Historic Yates Mill County Park is a 574-acre ecological research area for North Carolina State University. The park includes Wake County's last remaining gristmill with an adjoining millpond. Wood Duck nest boxes are maintained and monitored for productivity.

Lake Benson Park was established by the Town of Garner to preserve a small undeveloped area on the north shore of Lake Benson. The park is a combination of rolling open grassy areas and woodlands.

Additional details for these sites are available online at the Carolina Bird Club Web site, www.carolinabirdclub.org.

Directions: The Hemlock Bluffs Nature Preserve is located at 2616 Kildaire Farm Road in Cary, which is about 1 mile south of the Kildaire Farm Road and Tryon Road intersection. The preserve entrance is well marked with a large sign. Ritter Park is off West Lochmere Drive. From Hemlock Bluffs turn left and proceed down the hill toward the Kildaire Farm Road–Tryon Road intersection. Turn left at the first traffic light onto West Lochmere Drive and proceed about a quarter of a mile, and then turn left at the signed Ritter Park entrance. The greenway is accessed from the first parking area on the left after entering the park.

Access: Some trails at Hemlock Bluffs are wheelchair-accessible, and the Swift Creek Greenway along Swift Creek at Ritter Park is accessible.

Bathrooms: Available at Hemlock Bluffs when nature center is open.

Hazards: Biting and stinging insects, venomous snakes.

Nearest food, gas, and lodging: Cary.

Nearest camping: More than a thousand campsites for tents and RVs are available in the Jordan Lake State Recreation Area at Crosswinds Campground, Parkers Creek, and Poplar Point.

DeLorme map grid: Page 40, D1.

North Carolina Travel Map grid: H2.

For more information: Hemlock Bluffs Nature Preserve and Ritter Park, Town of Cary, (919) 387–5980; www.townofcary.org/depts/ prdept/parks/hemlock.htm. Hemlock Bluffs Nature Preserve is open from 9:00 A.M. to about sunset daily. Specific closing hours are posted at the gate and trailhead. Swift Creek Bluffs, Triangle Land Conservancy, (919) 833–3662; www.tlc-nc.org.

18 William B. Umstead State Park

by John Gerwin

County: Wake.

Habitats: Pine forest, mixed pine-hardwood, upland oak-hickory, several small lakes, floodplains of Crabtree, Sycamore, and Reedy Creeks.

Key birds: *Summer:* Hooded and Kentucky Warbler; Summer and Scarlet Tanager. *Winter:* Red-breasted Nuthatch; Red Crossbill; Pine Siskin; *Year-round:* Brown-headed Nuthatch.

Best times to bird: Good opportunities year-round and excellent during migration periods.

About this site:

William B. Umstead State Park is administered by the North Carolina Division of Parks and Recreation and consists of two sections, known as Crabtree Creek and Reedy Creek. Together they total 5,381 acres. Most of the forested areas contain trees sixty-plus years old. Hurricane and tornado activity since the early 1990s has created numerous patches of open, regenerating vegetation. Nineteen miles of hiking trails and about 11 miles of bridle trails provide access to most of the park.

Pileated Woodpeckers can be found along Loblolly Trail and around the lakes. Look for them and American Goldfinches, Eastern Phoebes, and Yellow-throated Warblers around Reedy Creek Lake and the nearby bridge over Sycamore Creek. Yellow-throated Warblers, Louisiana Waterthrushes, Northern Parulas, and Acadian Flycatchers can be found along any of the creeks. Look for Yellow-throated Vireos, Hooded Warblers, Red-headed Woodpeckers, and Scarlet Tanagers above the Company Mill Site along the Company Mill Trail, and check Inspiration Trail for Scarlet Tanagers and Hooded Warblers. Kentucky Warblers have been found nesting along Inspiration Trail and Loblolly Trail just south of Reedy Creek Lake. Worm-eating Warblers have been found along Sal's Branch Trail, adjacent to Umstead Parkway. Blue-headed Vireos have nested near Sycamore Lodge and may be found at various spots in the southern section.

Summer Tanagers, Ovenbirds, Wood Thrushes, White-breasted Nuthatches, Red-bellied Woodpeckers, and Yellow-billed Cuckoos are found throughout the park in appropriate habitats. Look for Brown-headed Nuthatches in mature pine at any time of year and Red-breasted Nuthatches and, rarely, Red Crossbills in winter. The southeast section between Ebenezer Church and Reedy Creek Road access points has been good for these species in past years. Fox Sparrows, although uncommon, can be expected anywhere in forested areas of the park in winter. Various species of waterfowl have been found on the three lakes during migration and winter seasons, with occasional shorebirds on exposed mud banks. The power line right-of-way gets quite weedy at times and can be very good for sparrows in win-

More than any other species of North American woodpecker, the Pileated Woodpecker relies on insects common to dead trees and fallen logs as a food source.
PHOTO: BILL DUYCK

ter and Indigo Buntings, Common Yellowthroats, and White-eyed Vireos in spring and summer, and sometimes Yellow Warblers in the section by Big Lake. Fall migration can be quite good for warblers, vireos, and thrushes.

Other key birds: *Summer:* Yellow-billed Cuckoo; Acadian Flycatcher; Northern Rough-winged Swallow; Wood Thrush; Louisiana Waterthrush; Ovenbird; Yellow-throated and Blue-headed Vireo. *Winter:* Sharp-shinned Hawk; Yellow-bellied Sapsucker; Brown Creeper; Ruby and Golden-crowned Kinglet; Hermit Thrush; Winter Wren. *Year-round:* American Woodcock; Cooper's Hawk; woodpeckers.

Nearby opportunities: Lake Crabtree County Park is located near the Raleigh-Durham International Airport in Wake County. The park consists of 215 forested acres adjacent to a 520-acre impoundment. Very little of the park is inaccessible to birders on foot, and many of

the pathways are wheelchair-accessible. A three-story enclosed observation tower provides protection from the wind as well as an excellent vantage point from which to view the lake. Additional details for this site are available online at the Carolina Bird Club Web site, www.carolinabirdclub.org.

Directions: Umstead State Park is located between Raleigh and Durham, with the south part essentially in Raleigh. It is adjacent to Raleigh-Durham International Airport, which results in it being noisy at times because of airplane traffic. The two main access points to the Park are the Reedy Creek entrance from Harrison Avenue, off Interstate 40 (southwest side), and the Crabtree Creek entrance, off of U.S. Highway 70 (northeast side).

Access: Numerous roads within the park are either paved or hard-packed dirt and are suitable for wheelchairs. Picnic areas are also wheelchair-accessible.

Bathrooms: Park office, picnic and camping areas.

Hazards: Poison ivy, venomous snakes, and ticks.

Nearest food, gas, and lodging: Raleigh and Durham.

Nearest camping: A family campground in the park has twenty-eight sites for tents and trailers. The campground is open from March 15 to December 15.

DeLorme map grid: Page 40, B1.

North Carolina Travel Map grid: H2.

For more information: William B. Umstead State Park, (919) 787–3033; www.ils.unc .edu/parkproject/visit/wium/home.html. The park opens at 8:00 A.M. and closes at dusk daily during the year. The park office is accessed from the Crabtree Creek entrance. Trail maps and picnic areas are available at the Reedy Creek and Crabtree Creek entrances.

⑲ Falls Lake State Recreation Area

by Brian Bockhahn

Counties: Wake and Durham.

Habitats: Bottomland hardwoods, pine, mixed deciduous and scrub forests, field habitats, natural and artificial sandy areas, wetland, lake and stream habitats.

Key birds: *Summer:* Broad-winged Hawk; Chuck-will's-widow; Whip-poor-will; Eastern Kingbird; Cliff Swallow; Hooded Warbler; Scarlet and Summer Tanager. *Winter:* Horned Grebe; Greater Scaup; Hooded Merganser; Loggerhead Shrike. *Year-round:* Bald Eagle; Red-headed Woodpecker; Brown-headed Nuthatch.

Best times to bird: Year-round.

About this site:

Falls Lake Recreation Area was developed by the U.S. Army Corps of Engineers to control damaging floods and to supply a source of water for surrounding communities. The area consists of a 12,000-acre lake surrounded by 26,000 acres of land and consists of seven individual parks managed by the North Carolina Division of Parks and Recreation. An admission fee of $5.00 per car is charged daily from Memorial Day through Labor Day and on weekends and holidays in April, May, and September.

The best place to view Bald Eagles at Falls Lake is Rollingview State Recreation Area. Turn onto Baptist Road and head north toward Rollingview Recreation Area and Marina. Baptist Road ends at the park. Once you enter the park, turn right for the marina, and stay straight to get out to the point. The B-loop fishing pier in the campground is a great place to scope the lake for ducks, loons, and grebes. Look for American Wigeons, Gadwalls, Buffleheads, and Greater and Lesser Scaup. During migration look for Caspian and Forster's Terns and a variety of shorebirds at the boat beach, and for Black-throated Green and Blackpoll Warblers and Rose-breasted Grosbeaks on the point. In the evening scan across the lake to Sandling Beach and watch the sky as thousands of Ring-billed and Herring Gulls return from a nearby landfill during winter to roost on the lake each night.

Sandling Beach occupies the eastern side of the widest part of Falls Lake, resulting in good opportunities to view waterbirds and migrants. The entrance is located off Highway 50, almost 2 miles north of the main bridge at Falls Lake. Turn left into the park. Winter is the best time to scan the lake for waterfowl. Mixed duck flocks, loons, grebes, and mergansers should be easily seen by scanning the lake. Spring brings a variety of shorebirds and often Caspian Terns to the swim beach. Look for Indigo Buntings in the fields and Eastern Kingbirds, Great Crested Flycatchers, and Ospreys along the shoreline. Bald Eagles and Wild Turkeys can be seen reliably throughout the year.

The Bald Eagle is a year-round resident of the Coastal Plain and Piedmont regions of the state that also frequents Falls Lake. PHOTO: HARRY SELL

The Highway 50 Boat Ramp Recreation Area is located off Highway 50 just north of the bridge at Falls Lake. Almost 2 miles north on Highway 50 is the Beaverdam State Recreation Area. Continue another 2 miles north, and then turn right onto Old Weaver Road to the Old Weaver Causeway. Parking is available on the causeway and at the intersection of Old Beaverdam Road. The Old Weaver Causeway has good flocks of waterfowl in winter. Look for American Kestrels along the power lines, Bonaparte's and other gulls on the causeway, and Logger-head Shrikes near the fields by the road. Listen for American Woodcocks in the field northwest of that intersection. During the summer watch for Cliff and Barn Swallows, which nest under the bridge, and for Orchard Orioles on the east side. Walk to the north end of the causeway for Cedar Waxwings, Red-headed and Pileated Woodpeckers, herons, and egrets. The pine stands and fields along Old Beaverdam Road harbor Eastern Screech-Owls and both Chuck-will's-widows and Whip-poor-wills. Wild Turkeys and many hawk species can be seen through-out the park. From Highway 50 Boat Ramp Recreation Area you can access the spillway in winter to watch ducks, mergansers, and Bald Eagles. Loons and Red-breasted and Common Mergansers are occasionally seen with the Hooded Mer-gansers. At the boat ramp look for Great Egrets and Solitary and Spotted Sandpipers in spring and fall and Horned Grebes in winter.

Wild Turkeys are abundant at both Holly Point and adjacent Shinleaf Recreation Areas, which are located in the southeast end of Falls Lake. This section of the lake is very narrow and resembles the river the lake once was. Holly Point has a large amount of shoreline access throughout the campground, and Shinleaf is a 2-mile peninsula surrounded by the lake. Both are off New Light Road, with the New Light Road Bridge in between. Shinleaf can be reached by taking Highway 98 east from the intersection of Highways 98 and 50. Drive 1.5 miles to the first stoplight and turn left onto New Light Road, and after half a mile look for the sign for Shinleaf Recreation Area. To reach Holly Point Recreation Area, continue for another 1.5 miles. The park will be on your right.

New Light Road Bridge is a good place to view Bald Eagles, Ospreys, winter gulls, and, in summer, Cliff and Barn Swallows, which nest under the bridge. From the bridge, walk northwest through a small field to a small beaver-dammed creek for Louisiana Waterthrushes and Pileated Woodpeckers. Spring and fall migrants can be seen in all areas of both parks. The area around the boat ramp at Holly Point has been particularly productive for warbler fallouts when the weather is right. During the summer watch for Broad-winged Hawks and Eastern Kingbirds. Red-headed Woodpeckers are present year-round.

Woodpecker Ridge has good habitat diversity and produces excellent birding opportunities. This area is accessed off of Highway 50 just north of the main bridge over the lake. Park by the WOODPECKER RIDGE MANAGEMENT AREA sign across from the Highway 50 Boat Ramp Recreation Area and enter the area by walking to the right of the sign. This area is excellent for a variety of warblers, vireos, and other spring migrants. Cavity nesters abound in the many snags created from prescribed burning. Look for Red-headed Woodpeckers and Brown-headed Nuthatches in the pines.

Other key birds: *Summer:* Osprey; Fish Crow. *Winter:* Great Black-backed Gull; Winter Wren; Cedar Waxwing; waterfowl and sparrows.

Nearby opportunities: Durant Nature Park, north of Raleigh, offers two lakes, streams, and 5 miles of hiking trails to scenic overlooks and through woodland wildflower meadows. The park encompasses 237 acres, making it the largest land-based park in the Raleigh system. More than 160 species of birds have been recorded in the park. Additional details for this site are available online at the Carolina Bird Club Web site, www.carolinabirdclub.org.

Directions: Falls Lake is approximately 10 miles north of Raleigh and 12 miles east of Durham. The park office is located on Highway 50, 1 mile north of the intersection with Highway 98, just before the bridge over the lake.

Access: Parking lots and restrooms at most facilities.

Bathrooms: At most sites except Woodpecker Ridge.

Hazards: Venomous snakes, biting and stinging insects, poison ivy.

Nearest food, gas, and lodging: Raleigh and Durham.

Nearest camping: Holly Point has 153 camping sites, 89 of which have electrical hookups for RVs.

DeLorme map grid: Page 40, A2.

North Carolina Travel Map grid: H2.

For more information: Falls Lake State Recreation Area, (919) 676–1027; www.ils.unc .edu/parkproject/visit/fala/home.html. Most sites of the recreation area are open from 8:00 A.M. to dusk daily throughout the year.

20 Eno River State Park

by Joshua S. Rose and Colleen Bockhahn

County: Durham.

Habitats: Floodplain hardwood forest with patches of meadow.

Key birds: *Summer:* Broad-winged Hawk; Summer and Scarlet Tanager; Blue Grosbeak;

Indigo Bunting. *Year-round:* Brown-headed Nuthatch.

Best times to bird: Early summer and migration.

About this site:

The Eno River winds its way through Durham County, along a corridor of parklands forming a lush green barrier on the north side of the main populated areas of the city of Durham. Historic mills in varying levels of restoration dot the river. The Eno River State Park is the centerpiece of preservation efforts, more than 2,800 acres of mostly hardwood forest winding along the river. Down the river is the Penny's Bend Nature Preserve, owned by the U.S. Army Corps of Engineers but managed for rare plant species by the North Carolina Botanical Garden.

One hundred and fifty-five bird species have been recorded for Eno River State Park, including thirty species of warblers, six vireos, seven thrushes, and ten sparrows. Of all of the locations along the Eno River, Few's Ford may be the best for birding. A meadow near the parking area usually has Prairie Warblers, Brown

Blue Grosbeak singing on territory. PHOTO: HARRY SELL

Thrashers, and Indigo Buntings singing during the breeding season. The trails down toward the river are good for Northern Parulas and Blue-gray Gnatcatchers in summer. A bridge across the river is a good vantage point to scan for Green Herons, Spotted Sandpipers, Belted Kingfishers, and Yellow-billed Cuckoos. The woodlands on the far side have Red-eyed Vireos and Scarlet Tanagers. Anywhere along here may have sparrows, mostly White-throated, in winter. Cox Mountain has been used as a vantage point for hawk watching, with modest numbers of Broad-winged Hawks during migration. Barred Owls and Red-shouldered Hawks are the most common and reliable resident raptors.

The loop trail around Penny's Bend can be easily walked in a couple of hours. A shortcut trail runs through an upland meadow in the middle of the property and can save time, but at the cost of skipping some of the best riparian habitat. Penny's Bend does not normally host many migrants, but it has all the regular winter residents, including White-throated Sparrows and Ruby and Golden-crowned Kinglets, and plenty of breeding species such as Acadian Flycatcher, Ovenbird, and Northern Parula. The meadows host mainly Eastern Bluebirds. American Woodcocks have been flushed in the woods.

Other key birds: *Summer:* Green Heron; Wood Thrush; Acadian Flycatcher; vireos. *Winter:* Blue-headed Vireo; Cedar Waxwing; Brown Creeper. *Year-round:* Wood Duck; woodpeckers.

Nearby opportunities: Occoneechee Mountain State Natural Area, located off of Interstate 85 at exit 164, is a satellite park of Eno River State Park. Occoneechee Mountain, at 867 feet in elevation, is the highest elevation between Hillsborough and the coast. Broad-winged Hawks nest on the steep edges of the mountain. Additional details for this site are available online at the Carolina Bird Club Web site, www.carolinabirdclub.org.

Directions: From I-85 through Durham, take Roxboro Street, U.S. Highway 501 Business, north and take a right on Old Oxford Highway. The parking area for Penny's Bend Nature Preserve is on the left side of Snowhill Road, a left turn just after Old Oxford crosses the Eno. Return to I-85 and drive south to the Cole Mill Road to its end for the Few's Ford access. Eno River State Park opens at 8:00 A.M. and closes at dusk.

Access: The visitor center at Few's Ford has wheelchair-accessible facilities.

Bathrooms: Visitor center at Few's Ford and Occoneechee Mountain State Natural Area.

Hazards: None.

Nearest food, gas, and lodging: Durham and Hillsborough.

Nearest camping: Few's Ford and Occoneechee Mountain State Natural Area.

DeLorme map grid: Page 39, A6/7.

North Carolina Travel Map grid: H1.

For more information: Eno River State Park and Occoneechee Mountain State Natural Area, (919) 383-1686; www.ils.unc.edu/parkproject/visit/enri/home.html. Penny's Bend North Carolina Botanical Garden, (919) 962-0522; www.enoriver.org/eno/pennys bend.htm.

Duke Forest

by Jeffrey S. Pippen

Counties: Durham and Orange.

Habitats: Pine forest, mixed pine-hardwood, variously aged regenerating areas, upland oak-hickory, New Hope Creek riparian corridor.

Key birds: *Summer:* Great Crested Flycatcher; Hooded Warbler; Summer and Scarlet Tanager; Blue Grosbeak; Indigo Bunting. *Year-round:* Brown-headed Nuthatch; Red-headed Woodpecker.

Best times to bird: Year-round.

About this site:

Duke Forest is owned by Duke University and comprises nearly 8,000 acres of recovered farmlands and patches of forest purchased during and since the mid-1920s. The forest is sectioned into six divisions spanning four counties. Since the Duke Forest is an active teaching and research facility for Duke University, including its forestry program, regular timber harvests occur and alter the habitat. Research is ongoing, so visitors should use only designated access points and trails.

The Shepherd Nature Trail is a 1-mile, self-guided loop trail that goes over several hills and small, intermittent streams. Beginning at a rustic old picnic table under some tall oaks, listen for mixed flocks of Carolina Chickadees, Tufted Titmice, and woodpeckers, vireos, thrushes, nuthatches, and warblers that may be found with them. The trail quickly winds down to a stream and then ascends through various mixed hardwoods and pines. Mixed flocks of migrants are usually found in these areas at the appropriate season. Migrants that have been seen here include Rose-breasted Grosbeaks and a variety of warblers and thrushes. In summer look for Hooded Warblers along the trail. Continue along the trail to a series of steps and then pass through a large clear-cut regeneration area. Other breeding species include Red-headed Woodpecker, Great Crested Flycatcher, Brown-headed Nuthatch, Indigo Bunting, and Summer and Scarlet Tanagers. American Woodcocks may be seen or heard from December into March. Cooper's and Sharp-shinned Hawks are occasionally seen in this vicinity every summer but are more common in winter. The trail eventually joins a wide gravel road and passes by a tall loblolly pine stand, where Blue-headed Vireos may be found year-round but easily missed. Shortly the trail turns to the right off the gravel road and winds a few hundred yards through more mixed pine and hardwoods and ends at a modern picnic shelter about 50 yards from the rustic old table where it began.

Most of the trail at Gate 26 in the Korstian Division wanders through mixed oak-hickory and riparian forest. A 2003 clear-cut at the beginning of the trail could be expected to offer a variety of early succession birds over the next few years. Several hundred yards from the beginning, the trail splits. The right fork is the three-quarter-mile Slick Hill Fire Trail that leads to a stand of loblolly pines and an older clear-cut. In the breeding season look among the brambles and saplings for Carolina and House Wrens, Eastern Bluebirds, Hooded and Prairie Warblers, Eastern Towhees, Yellow-breasted Chats, and Blue Grosbeaks. Scan along the edges for Blue-gray Gnatcatchers, Scarlet and Summer Tanagers, and Indigo Buntings. In autumn large flocks of blackbirds including Common Grackle, Red-winged Blackbird, and Brown-headed Cowbird often cruise through these areas. In winter look for accipiters, Ruby and Golden-crowned Kinglets, Eastern Blue-birds, and various sparrows including Song and Fox. The forested portion of the trail is a good place in winter for Yellow-bellied Sapsuckers, Brown Creepers, kinglets, and Hermit Thrushes. Northern Flickers and Downy, Hairy, Red-headed, Red-bellied, and Pileated Woodpeckers are found here all year. Backtrack to the

Red-headed Woodpeckers are found in open mature woods.
PHOTO: HARRY SELL

original fork in the trail and take the left fork, which is the Laurel Hill Fire Trail. This trail leads to a nice rhododendron bluff overlooking New Hope Creek. In the breeding season, look and listen for Yellow-billed Cuckoos, Acadian Flycatchers, Wood Thrushes, Northern Parulas, Ovenbirds, Louisiana Waterthrushes, and tanagers. During migration, many species of thrushes and warblers may be seen in the vegetation along the creek.

Other key birds: *Summer:* Yellow-billed Cuckoo; Acadian Flycatcher; Prairie Warbler; Ovenbird; Louisiana Waterthrush; Yellow-breasted Chat. *Winter:* Winter Wren; Brown Creeper.

Nearby opportunities: Johnston Mill Nature Preserve consists of 295 acres. It is one of Triangle Land Conservancy's public-access properties and is considered one of Orange County's most important natural areas. Additional details for this site are available online at the Carolina Bird Club Web site, www.carolinabirdclub.org.

Directions: To reach the Shepherd Nature Trail from Interstate 85, take U.S. Highway 15-501 South, exit 174B, to exit 107, Duke University and Highway 751. On Highway 751 go 1.3 miles northwest. Pull off at the second gravel area on the right after Constitution Drive. This is Duke Forest Gate C. Hike past the gate, and you will find the trailhead near the rustic old picnic table less than 100 yards from the highway. At the trailhead is a wooden box with maps and a description of the Shepherd Nature Trail. The Korstian Division is also reached from Highway 751. From US 15-501 Bypass take Highway 751 approximately 200 yards northwest and turn left at the roundabout onto Erwin Road. Continue for 3.3 miles and turn right at the stoplight onto Whitfield Road. Pull off to the right onto the gravel area after 0.6 mile, being careful not to block the gate. Duke Forest is open only during daylight hours.

Access: Not accessible for persons with disabilities.

Bathrooms: None available.

Hazards: Venomous snakes, biting and stinging insects, poison ivy.

Nearest food, gas, and lodging: Durham and Chapel Hill.

Nearest camping: Eno River State Park.

DeLorme map grid: Page 39, A7.

North Carolina Travel Map grid: H2.

For more information: Office of Duke Forest, Duke University, (919) 613-8013; www.env.duke.edu/forest.

22 Mason Farm Biological Reserve

by Will Cook

County: Orange.

Habitats: Fields, mature oak-hickory forest, stream, riparian forest, beaver impoundments.

Key birds: *Summer:* Eastern Kingbird; American Redstart; Hooded, Prothonotary, and Kentucky Warbler; Blue Grosbeak; Indigo Bunting; Summer and Scarlet Tanager.

Best times to bird: Spring, fall, and winter are excellent.

About this site:

Mason Farm has long been the most popular birding spot in Chapel Hill. It is close to town, loaded with birds, and the main loop is a flat, easy hike. This 367-acre sanctuary has large open fields, extensive oak-hickory woods, a creek, beaver marshes, and lots of great brushy areas.

The main section of the reserve is the Big Oak Woods Trail. Drive past the gate and look for the concrete ford crossing Morgan Creek on the right. Turn right, drive over the ford, and park on the other side in the parking area. The parking area is often loaded with birds, so check it carefully. Continue on foot past the gate, sign the guest register, and check the sightings log. The main trail is a level gravel road, which takes you past weedy fields and thickets on the left and low woods on the right. Both sides of the trail abound with birds. When you get to the fork in the road, turn left. The trail continues through brushy areas between fields and is often loaded with White-throated Sparrows in winter. King Rail have nested in the ditch on the left, and Northern Waterthrushes often use it as a stopover during migration. Good numbers of Fox Sparrows are here in winter. To the left is a short side road that goes straight between fields to the creek. It is usually well worth exploring if you have time. If you turn left from the side road and follow the straight row of planted trees (no trail) to the left, you will get back to the parking lot. This area is outstanding for seeing the twilight aerial displays of American Woodcocks in January and February.

Continue following the main trail as it turns to the right. This route takes you past a large open field on the left and a brushy border on the right, usually packed with birds. The trail enters the lowland forest of tall hardwoods. On the left is a semiopen area and on the right mature forest, called the Big Oak Woods, which is home to Kentucky Warblers. The trail takes another sharp bend to the right and enters a swampy area, known as Siler's Bog. During winter the wet field on the left is great for Swamp Sparrows. Check the tips of the dead trees for Olive-sided Flycatchers in migration.

After leaving the swampy area, you continue past areas of field and forest, which usually harbor smaller numbers of the birds already seen, though Eastern Bluebirds are more plentiful on this side thanks to bluebird boxes. About halfway through the back section of the loop, a trail off to the left goes up into some drier woods. This one-way trail eventually leaves the reserve but is worth exploring for a short distance for Ovenbirds and Hooded Warblers, which are rarely found along the main loop. Continue on the main trail to complete the loop. Total length of this loop is about 2 miles.

For the field north of Morgan Creek, park near the concrete ford on the north side of Morgan Creek but instead of crossing the creek, continue straight on foot to the end of the road and past a gate. Follow the gravel trail, with field on the left and thicket and forest on the right, until it dead-ends at a swamp, and then retrace your steps. One-way distance is about a mile. The field is great for sparrows in winter and has Orchard Orioles in spring. Common Yellowthroats and Orange-crowned Warblers are possible in winter. The adjacent trees are good for American Redstarts, Prothonotary Warblers, and migrants in spring. In summer look near the swamp for Northern Rough-winged Swallows and Green Herons.

The Prothonotary Warbler is one of the two North American cavity-nesting warblers.
PHOTO: JEREMY POIRIER

Other key birds: *Summer:* Acadian Flycatcher; Northern Parula; Yellow-breasted Chat; Orchard Oriole. *Winter:* Wilson's Snipe; American Woodcock; Fox Sparrow; Rusty Blackbird; Purple Finch.

Nearby opportunities: Before leaving this area consider returning to the North Carolina Botanical Garden to visit. Check out both the gardens as well as the birds that visit them.

Directions: To access Mason Farm, you will need to obtain a permit and gate card from the North Carolina Botanical Garden (NCBG) before visiting. Annual and day passes are available ($5.00 deposit) at the North Carolina Botanical Garden's Totten Center. Take US 15-501 Bypass around Chapel Hill. After the intersection of Highway 54 and before Manning Drive, turn left on Old Mason Farm Road and look for the brown NC Botanical Garden sign. If you need a permit, turn right into the NCBG parking lot; otherwise continue on this road until you see Finley Golf Course.

Just before the road makes a sharp turn to the left, turn right into what looks like a parking lot behind the building at the corner. Follow the edge of the parking lot, and turn right when you get to the practice green. After continuing a short distance, bear right again, just past the little cemetery, to the entrance. Mason Farm is open from dawn to dusk daily year-round.

Access: Totten Center facilities are wheelchair-accessible; trails at Mason Farm are not.

Bathrooms: At Totten Center.

Hazards: Biting insects in the summer.

Nearest food, gas, and lodging: Chapel Hill.

Nearest camping: Chapel Hill.

DeLorme map grid: Page 39, B6.

North Carolina Travel Map grid: H2.

For more information: North Carolina Botanical Garden, (919) 962-0522; www.ncbg .unc.edu.

㉓ Pee Dee National Wildlife Refuge

by Judy Walker

Counties: Anson and Richmond.

Habitats: Bottomland hardwood forest, upland pine forest, croplands, old fields, beaver ponds, open water, mixed pine-hardwood forest.

Key birds: *Summer:* Chuck-will's-widow; Whip-poor-will; Prothonotary, Hooded, and Kentucky Warbler; Grasshopper Sparrow; Indigo Bunting; Blue Grosbeak. *Winter:* Snow Goose; Sedge Wren; sparrows. *Year-round:* Bald Eagle; Brown-headed Nuthatch; Red-headed Woodpecker.

Best times to bird: Spring and fall migration and winter.

About this site:

The refuge straddles the Pee Dee River and is part of the Savannah–Santee–Pee Dee ecosystem. It contains 8,843 acres of natural area, including 3,000 acres of contiguous bottomland hardwood forest along Brown Creek, 1,200 acres of upland pine forest, and a 4,300-acre mosaic of croplands, old fields, moist soil units, and mixed pine-hardwood forests. The refuge is interlaced with 50 miles of trails and roads. A refuge map and other information are available at the main entrance.

Peak populations of waterfowl in the fall and winter can exceed 8,000 birds. The refuge's bird list contains 207 species, with 94 species breeding. Winter sparrows abound in the thousands of acres of open fields, marshy areas, and thickets.

Wildlife Drive is a 2-mile loop accessed from the refuge main entrance on U.S. Highway 52. It provides a good cross section of refuge habitats. In winter be prepared for an onslaught of Red-headed Woodpeckers along the impoundment road. Wood Ducks are easily heard along this road but not always seen. The flooded field edges host large numbers of Song and Swamp Sparrows and an occasional Lincoln's Sparrow. The first stretch from the gate to Sullivan Pond passes fields of native grasses. In the spring the fields are full of bluebirds, Blue Grosbeaks, Eastern Meadowlarks, and Indigo Buntings. At the Sullivan Pond parking area, a quarter-mile loop trail on the left side of the road goes through a deciduous forest, along Brown Creek, and then back through open fields. Walk this trail for Prothonotary, Hooded, and Kentucky Warblers and Louisiana Waterthrushes. Return to the parking area and follow the road as it descends a small hill through a hardwood forest into Sullivan's impoundment. Open fields on the right are flooded in the fall for wintering waterfowl. The loop continues around this impoundment and ascends into an upland pine forest. At the parking area for an observation blind, Wildlife Drive turns left and ends at US 52, half a mile south of the main entrance. If you go straight you will return to the refuge main entrance.

The Green Tree Reservoir Trail is about 2 miles long. From the main entrance go south on US 52 for about a mile. Turn left onto Pleasant Grove Church Road (labeled SR 1650, for State Road 1650, on the refuge map). Travel 0.9 mile to a gated road on the left. It is easy to miss this gate, which is just before the intersection with SR 1648. Sometimes the first half mile of the road behind the gate is open to drive. Be sure not to block the gate when it is closed. In spring this trail is a haven for migrating warblers, including Golden-winged and Swainson's Warblers. During the summer watch for Prothonotary, Hooded, Kentucky, and Yellow-throated Warblers; Louisiana Waterthrushes; Common Yellowthroats; Northern Parulas; Acadian Flycatchers; and Barred Owls. During most winters this is a great place for Wood Ducks and Rusty Blackbirds.

Ross's Pond can best be reached from the refuge headquarters by driving north on US 52. Go 1.7 miles and turn right onto SR 1636, Ross Road. Drive down this gravel road for 1.8 miles and take the right fork for 0.4 mile to Ross's Pond. During summer evenings listen for Chuck-will's-widows, Whip-poor-wills, and Common Nighthawks. In winter the harvested fields are a magnet for sparrows such as Savannah, Chipping, and Field. Lark and Henslow's Sparrows and Smith's Longspurs have also been found here. Check the brushy areas for Fox Sparrows.

To reach Gaddy's Covered Bridge and the Beaver Pond from the refuge headquarters, travel north on US 52 for 2.6 miles to State Road 1634, Grassy Island Road. Turn right onto SR 1634 and go about 2 miles. Turn left at the intersection of SR 1634 and SR 1627. About 50 yards from the intersection, turn right onto the unnamed refuge road. The Beaver Pond is just past the kiosk. In winter look for Ring-necked and Wood Ducks. Red-headed Woodpeckers are also fairly common here in winter, as are a variety of sparrows. The upland pine forest in summer is good for Brown-headed and White-breasted Nuthatches, Pine Warblers, Summer Tanagers, and an occasional Blue-headed Vireo. Around the beaver pond and along Thoroughfare Creek at the covered bridge is excellent habitat for migrating and breeding warblers such as Prothonotary and Hooded Warblers. Return to the kiosk. Turn left and go another 0.8 mile to the parking area for Gaddy's Covered Bridge. The bridge serves as a blind for viewing the beaver pond. The quarter-mile trail to the bridge is wheelchair-accessible. The trail continues another quarter mile beyond the bridge to the Low Grounds.

To drive to the Low Grounds, return to your car and continue on the road for another 0.2 mile to a T intersection. Turning left will take you to an old silo and access to the Low Grounds, an area adjacent to the Pee Dee River that is cultivated by local farmers in spring and summer. Once the crops have been harvested, large areas are flooded for wintering waterfowl. A scope is a must for viewing waterfowl. The best time to see the thousands of ducks is at either sunrise or sunset. Fourteen species of dabbling ducks are common to abundant. The majority of the Canada Geese are migratory, and a few Snow Geese have appeared the last few winters. The Low Grounds is also the most likely place to see Bald Eagles. In the winter the Low Grounds can also host thousands of Common Grackles and Red-winged

Blackbirds. The area around Thoroughfare Creek can be very good in the spring and fall for warblers and other neotropical migrants. Look for Prothonotary and Kentucky Warblers close to the road.

To reach Arrowhead Lake from the Low Grounds, return to the intersection with SR 1634. Continue going straight for 0.8 mile to where an unnamed refuge road comes in from the right. In winter look for Sedge Wrens at this intersection. Drive until you come to where the road ends at the big oak. Park and walk to the left along the path through an open field to Arrowhead Lake. This area consists of a variety of habitats. Typical early successional species such as Field and Grasshopper Sparrows, Eastern Meadowlarks, Indigo Buntings, Blue Grosbeaks, Prairie Warblers, and Yellow-breasted Chats are common. During the summer look for Summer Tanagers, Brown-headed Nuthatches, and Pileated Woodpeckers. Spectacular flights of Tree Swallows and Red-winged Blackbirds can be seen in the fall and winter. In winter the area is teeming with a variety of sparrows including White-throated, Field, Chipping, Song, Swamp, Savannah, and Fox. Look for Sedge Wrens in the sedge grass near the big oak. Bald Eagles and other raptors regularly soar over this area.

A flock of Snow Geese. PHOTO: HARRY SELL

Other key species: *Summer:* Prairie Warbler; Yellow-breasted Chat. *Winter:* Tree Swallow; waterfowl and sparrows.

Nearby opportunities: Morrow Mountain State Park is in the Uwharrie Mountain Range of North Carolina's Piedmont region. It is comprised of 4,742 acres, and elevations vary from 280 to 936 feet above sea level. The park has over 6 miles of shoreline along Lake Tillery, an impoundment of the Yadkin–Pee Dee River system. Additional details for this site are available online at the Carolina Bird Club Web site, www.carolinabirdclub.org.

Directions: Located 5 miles north of Wadesboro on US 52, Pee Dee National Wildlife Refuge is an easy drive from Charlotte, Winston-Salem, Greensboro, and Chapel Hill. From Charlotte take U.S. Highway 74 east to Wadesboro and turn north on US 52. From Winston-Salem take US 52 south through Albemarle and Ansonville.

Access: The refuge is accessible by car. The quarter-mile trail to Gaddy's Covered Bridge is wheelchair-accessible.

Bathrooms: At refuge headquarters.

Hazards: None.

Nearest food, gas, and lodging: Wadesboro.

Nearest camping: Morrow Mountain State Park.

DeLorme map grid: Page 71, A5.

North Carolina Travel Map grid: G3.

For more information: Pee Dee National Wildlife Headquarters, (704) 694–4424; http://peedee.fws.gov.

24 Charlotte-Mecklenburg Area

by Jeff Esely, Don Seriff, Sudie E. Daves,
Taylor Piephoff, and Louise Barden

County: Mecklenburg.

Habitats: Upland hardwood forest, mixed pine-hardwood forest, pine forest, floodplain, Piedmont Prairie, shrubland.

Key birds: *Summer:* Osprey; Broad-winged Hawk; Cliff Swallow; Eastern Kingbird; Grasshopper Sparrow; Summer and Scarlet Tanager; Indigo Bunting; Blue Grosbeak. *Winter:* Snow Goose; Loggerhead Shrike; American Pipit; Vesper Sparrow. *Year-round:* Red-headed Woodpecker; Brown-headed Nuthatch.

Best times to bird: Year-round.

About this site:

The Division of Natural Resources manages eleven nature preserves protecting over 5,200 acres of natural communities. Three are described here—McDowell Nature Preserve, Cowan's Ford Wildlife Refuge, and Latta Plantation Nature Preserve—with additional information about other birding sites provided later in this book.

McDowell Nature Preserve, encompassing over 1,100 acres, contains relatively large expanses of various second-growth forest habitats in a variety of successional stages. The preserve contains moderate to steep topography and is drained by several small streams, which feed into the adjacent Lake Wylie. The 140-acre McDowell Piedmont Prairie restoration area, with a variety of early successional habitats ranging from prairie to shrubland, is located in the northeast corner of the preserve. Nearly 160 species have been documented at McDowell Nature Preserve. Any of the various hiking trails in the southern half of the preserve offer good birding opportunities. These trails run predominantly through forested habitats, and often along steep slopes.

No excursion to the McDowell Nature Preserve would be complete without visiting the Piedmont Prairie Restoration in the northeast corner. This site may be accessed from a small parking area off of Shopton Road West, approximately 1.5 miles north of York Road. Due to its relatively large size, McDowell Prairie provides excellent year-round birding opportunities and often attracts rare or unusual birds. During winter and migration periods, species such as Loggerhead Shrike, Northern Harrier, American Kestrel, Savannah and Vesper Sparrow, Sedge Wren, and Bobolink may be found. In summer look for breeding species such as Grasshopper Sparrow, Eastern Meadowlark, Eastern Kingbird, Northern Bobwhite, Orchard Oriole, Yellow-breasted Chat, Prairie Warbler, Blue Grosbeak, and Red-winged Blackbird, as well as various swallows including Barn, Cliff, and Northern

The American Pipit, a winter resident, prefers plowed or open fields. PHOTO: HARRY SELL

Rough-winged. As this restoration area is currently in its initial phases, the habitat is constantly changing. However, the management of McDowell Prairie is focused on maintaining a mosaic of early successional habitats for plant and wildlife species.

Cowan's Ford Wildlife Refuge is a 668-acre peninsula surrounded by the Catawba River. Cowan's Ford Wildlife Refuge was the first site in North Carolina to receive designation as a North Carolina Important Bird Area by the National Audubon Society. Birding is permitted along the 2-mile entrance road and at the observation platform viewing area at the end of the road. Most of the birds can be seen from these areas. There have been 206 species of birds documented at the wildlife refuge. More than fifty species of neotropical migrants can be commonly seen moving through each spring and fall. Viewing from the parking area and from the covered observation platform is good all year. Twenty-two species of waterfowl visit the viewing ponds during the winter and can be observed using binoculars or spotting scopes. More than twenty species of shorebirds visit the mudflats and shoreline of the viewing ponds, along with nine species of wading birds and thirteen species of raptors. The fields host a variety of grassland species including Grasshopper, Savannah, Le Conte's, Vesper, Clay-colored, White-crowned, and Swamp Sparrows and American Pipit during the winter.

Latta Plantation Nature Preserve is part of the Mountain Island Lake Important Bird Area. A prairie restoration site of about twenty-five acres harbors several rare plants. The preserve has 16 miles of well-marked trails through various habitats,

NORTH CAROLINA'S IMPORTANT BIRD AREAS (IBAs) PROGRAM

The threat of long-term population declines of neotropical migrant song-birds, shorebirds, seabirds, wading birds, and others is well known. Although factors that cause declines are complex, there is a broad consensus among scientists that habitat degradation and loss are major factors affecting breeding grounds, migratory stopovers and pathways, and wintering areas.

An essential step in conserving bird habitats is to identify places that provide the greatest habitat value and support significant populations or an exceptional diversity of birds. These Important Bird Areas (IBAs) are essential strongholds of avian abundance and diversity.

IBAs are identified according to standardized, scientifically defensible criteria based on numbers of birds or assemblages of birds regularly occurring at particular locations. Once nominated, a site undergoes strict review by a technical committee comprised of the state's leading experts on birds. Once approved by the technical committee, the site is designated an IBA.

A listing of the state's IBAs has recently been produced by Audubon, North Carolina. It presents a complete listing of those sites known to be vital to maintaining bird populations, diversity, and habitats in North Carolina. This listing will be a blueprint for bird conservation in North Carolina.

Other sites will continue to be evaluated as we learn more about the birds and their habitats across North Carolina. Audubon NC plans a complete review and update of North Carolina's IBAs every five years. Important Bird Areas is an exciting program for Audubon and North Carolina. It is one of the most important efforts undertaken in recent years to conserve birds and their habitats in our state.

For information on IBAs, go online and check www.ncaudubon.org.

---

along streams, and along Mountain Island Lake. Many warblers, thrushes, grosbeaks, and other species are typically seen during spring and fall migration. All of the forested trails offer good birding opportunities. Try the mixed hardwood forests off the Beechwood Trail and the Treasure Tree Trail during migration to find Black-throated Blue, Worm-eating, Yellow-throated, and Black-and-white Warblers and Swainson's Thrushes. During the summer check for Acadian Flycatchers, Louisiana Waterthrushes, Ovenbirds, Wood Thrushes, and Red-eyed Vireos. The Hill Trail leads across the power line right-of-way and along the eastern edge of the Piedmont Prairie restoration site. Summer birds include Prairie Warblers, Yellow-breasted Chats, Blue Grosbeaks, Indigo Buntings, Brown Thrashers, White-eyed Vireos, Common Yellowthroats, and Field Sparrows.

Other key birds: *Summer:* Prairie Warbler; Yellow-breasted Chat; Orchard Oriole. *Winter:* Brown Creeper; Le Conte's and Clay-colored Sparrow.

Nearby opportunities: Reedy Creek Park and Nature Preserve, located in the northeast part of the county, encompasses 727 forested acres including seven hiking trails with remote sections often void of people. Evergreen Nature Preserve is located in the eastern area of Charlotte. The preserve has had 120 recorded species. Additional details for these sites are available online at the Carolina Bird Club Web site, www.carolinabirdclub.org.

Directions: McDowell Nature Preserve is adjacent to Lake Wylie in the southwest corner of Mecklenburg County. From Charlotte, take Interstate 77 south to exit 90 (Carowinds Boulevard). Turn right onto Carowinds Boulevard and go approximately 2.5 miles to Highway 49 (York Road). Turn left onto York Road and go approximately 5.0 miles to the park entrance on the right. Maps of the preserve are available at the nature center.

Cowan's Ford Wildlife Refuge is reached by taking exit 37 off Interstate 85. Go north on Beatties Ford Road for approximately 8.5 miles to Neck Road. Turn left onto Neck Road. Continue on Neck Road for approximately 4 miles. At the Y in the road take the left fork; continue straight until reaching the refuge parking lot.

To reach Latta Plantation Nature Preserve, take I–77 north to exit 16B, Sunset Road West. Travel on Sunset Road West to the second stoplight, about half a mile and turn right onto Beatties Ford Road. Continue on Beatties Ford Road for approximately 5 miles to Sample Road. Turn left onto Sample Road and continue through the nature preserve's gates, and take the first right after the speed bump into the Latta Plantation Nature Center parking lot.

Access: Primarily by foot. Wheelchair-accessible facilities are available at McDowell Nature Preserve and Latta Plantation Nature Center.

Bathrooms: At McDowell Nature Preserve and Latta Plantation Nature Center.

Hazards: None.

Nearest food, gas, and lodging: Charlotte.

Nearest camping: McDowell Nature Preserve.

DeLorme map grid: McDowell Nature Preserve, page 57, D1; Cowen's Ford and Latta Plantation, page 57, B/C5.

North Carolina Travel Map grid: McDowell Nature Preserve, H2; Cowen's Ford and Latta Plantation, F3.

For more information: Mecklenburg County Park and Recreation Department, (704) 598–8857; www.co.mecklenburg.nc.us/ Departments/park+and+rec/home.asp. Mecklenburg Audubon (additional local birding sites): http://meckbirds.org/birdingspots/ county.htm.

25 Greensboro Municipal Reservoirs

by Dennis Burnette

County: Guilford.

Habitats: Large municipal reservoir crossed by several causeways and surrounded by mixed pine-hardwood forest.

Key birds: *Summer:* White Ibis; Indigo Bunting. *Winter:* Horned Grebe; Hooded Merganser; Canvasback. *Year-round:* Bald Eagle; Brown-headed Nuthatch.

Best times to bird: Very good to excellent in fall and winter, fair in summer.

About this site:

The City of Greensboro maintains three municipal reservoirs: Lake Townsend, Lake Brandt, and Lake Higgins. Together the reservoirs comprise a total area of over 2,600 acres. Lake Townsend, the largest of the three, has numerous car-accessible overlooks from which the lake and surrounding wooded shore may be observed. Lake Brandt, a large boomerang-shaped body of water, is the second largest. Not much of Lake Brandt is accessible by road, but a system of trails provides access for hikers. Lake Higgins, the smallest and westernmost of the three, is a 280-acre reservoir. It has a shallow marsh at the southwest end and a dam at the northeast end.

Because of its size, Lake Townsend offers several good birding overlooks accessible by car. If coming from Greensboro on Church Street, the lake will soon be on both sides of the road. The overlooks will be obvious from either a southern or a northern approach. The most popular place to park is easily identified at the south end of the causeway.

On the western side of the causeway is a wide, relatively shallow cove at the base of the dam for nearby Lake Jeannette. When the water is low, old stumps provide perches for Double-crested Cormorants, as well as herons and egrets in late summer. White Ibises use this area when the water is shallow enough. A scope will be helpful here in sorting out the waterfowl. In some years when the water is deeper, this site may attract Redheads and Canvasbacks. Northern Shovelers, Green-winged and Blue-winged Teal, Buffleheads, and Lesser Scaup are often common.

Return south on Church Street toward Greensboro 2 miles to Lee's Chapel Road and turn left. Proceed 0.9 mile to Yanceyville Street and turn left again. Drive north about 2 miles to the first overlook where water can be seen on both sides of the causeway. Many of Guilford County's unusual sightings come from this site, particularly in late fall and winter. At the north end of the causeway, the shallow inlet often attracts Great and Snowy Egrets in late summer. On the other side of the road, look for American Coots; Common Loons; Pied-billed and Horned Grebes; and Hooded and Red-breasted Mergansers. Gulls usually loaf in huge flocks in the middle of the lake, where a scope is useful for sorting out the Herring

The Horned Grebe is a fairly common winter resident of coastal areas and inland lakes and is usually seen alone or in small flocks. PHOTO: HARRY SELL

and Bonaparte's from the abundant Ring-billed Gulls. Caspian, Common, and Forster's Terns are possible in migration.

The access points at each end of Lake Brandt not only offer different views of the lake but also provide different birding experiences. At the Strawberry Road Access, birding is done by walking a trail and along the marshy edge of the lake to see species that are attracted to weedy and brushy habitats, in addition to waterbirds. Immediately to the right of the parking lot is a small marshy inlet surrounded by dense shrubs and small trees that often produces interesting birds. Across the road is wet woodland. One strategy is to walk back toward the U.S. Highway 220 intersection from the parking lot, checking the trees, undergrowth, and mudflats for birds. Look for Wood Ducks and Great Blue Herons all year, Green Herons in summer, Great Egrets in late summer, warblers during migration, and a variety of small passerines. A wooden footbridge crosses the creek, and the trail continues north for a distance on a dead-end road, so hikers will have to retrace their steps.

Return to the parking area and enter the Lake Brandt Greenway. In about 200 yards the trail forks. Take the trail on the left, the Piedmont Trail, which goes 3 miles (one way). The trail leads along the north shore of the lake through overgrown fields and woodlands, eventually terminating at Lake Brandt Road. In summer watch for Indigo Buntings, Eastern Towhees, Yellow-breasted Chats, and various sparrows. Watch for Bald Eagles and other raptors soaring overhead. In fall and winter a few ducks, grebes, and loons, as well as gulls and terns, are possible.

The Lake Brandt Marina office is situated on a hill that provides a good vantage point to look west and southwest down the two arms of the boomerang-shaped lake. When the marina gate is closed, park in the gravel parking lot outside the gate and walk in. While this site may be birded with binoculars, a scope is best to look for waterfowl. Late fall and winter usually offer abundant waterfowl including Ruddy Ducks and Pied-billed Grebes. Lesser Scaup and Ring-necked Ducks are not uncommon. Ring-billed and Bonaparte's Gulls are attracted to the dam, and sometimes large rafts of gulls are seen on the northern arm of the lake. Occasionally, a Bald Eagle may be seen perched or soaring.

The dock at the Lake Higgins Marina provides a good panoramic view of the northeastern two-thirds of the lake, including the dam. In winter the deeper water attracts diving ducks, such as Ruddy and Ring-necked Ducks, and Buffleheads. Look for rafts of Hooded Mergansers and a few Green-winged Teal in the coves. Often there is a Bonaparte's Gull flying around in winter among the Ring-billed Gulls. Around the lawn and pine trees behind the marina buildings, check for Tree Swallows, Brown-headed Nuthatches, and other passerines.

Other key birds: *Summer:* Great Egret; Green Heron; Tree Swallow; Yellow-breasted Chat. *Winter:* Bufflehead; Common Loon; Eared Grebe; Red-breasted Merganser; Brown Creeper.

Nearby opportunities: Bog Garden is a small artificial wetland along a creek that feeds into an artificial lake in a residential section adjacent to Friendly Shopping Center in Greensboro. There is a half-mile elevated boardwalk through the garden. Additional details for this site are available online at the Carolina Bird Club Web site, www.carolinabirdclub.org.

Directions: Lake Townsend is north of Greensboro and may be reached from Greensboro by going north either on Church Street or on Yanceyville Street. To get to Strawberry Road Access at Lake Brandt, travel north on US 220/Battleground Avenue 0.2 mile past Hamburg Mill Road to Strawberry Road.

The Lake Higgins Marina is located at 4235 Hamburg Mill Road on the northern edge of Greensboro. From Greensboro go north on Battleground Avenue (US 220) for about 6.8 miles north of Wendover Avenue; watch on the left side of the road for the Lake Higgins dam and on the right side for the open water of nearby Lake Brandt. Continue north about 0.3 mile to the first intersection, Hamburg Mill Road, and turn left. Go about 0.4 mile to the entrance gate of the marina on the left.

Access: By car and foot. No facilities accessible for people with disabilities.

Bathrooms: At Lake Higgins Marina.

Hazards: Traffic along causeway.

Nearest food, gas, and lodging: Greensboro.

Nearest camping: Privately owned campgrounds in Greensboro.

DeLorme map grid: Lakes Townsend, Higgins, Brandt, page 17, D7.

North Carolina Travel Map grid: G1.

For more information: City of Greensboro Parks and Recreation Department, (336) 373-2574; www.ci.greensboro.nc.us/leisure/lakes/index.html.

26 Salem Lake

by Doug DeNeve

County: Forsyth.

Habitats: Reservoir, mixed pine-hardwood, upland hardwood, freshwater marsh.

Key birds: *Summer:* Great Crested Flycatcher; Eastern Kingbird; Prothonotary Warbler. *Win-* *ter:* Horned Grebe; Canvasback; Hooded Merganser. *Year-round:* Brown-headed Nuthatch.

Best times to bird: Winter during extremely cold weather.

About this site:

Salem Lake is a 365-acre municipal water source for the city of Winston-Salem and surrounding Forsyth County. There is a wooded buffer zone around the lake that provides good habitat for a variety of birds. A small marina and fishing pier are located near the dam at the western end of the lake. Over the years a number of rarities have been spotted here, including such species as Sabine's Gull, Black and Gull-billed Terns, White-winged Scoter, and Olive-sided Flycatcher. More routinely, a quick scan of the lake from the parking area is always a good start. In winter look for Buffleheads, Ring-necked Ducks, American Coots, and Pied-billed Grebes. Bonaparte's Gulls, Horned Grebes, Canvasbacks, Common Loons, Lesser Scaup, and Hooded Mergansers are frequent visitors. The trail above the paved parking area is a good place to look for flycatchers such as Eastern Phoebes, Eastern Kingbirds, and Great Crested and Acadian Flycatchers in the summer, and a good place for Eastern Bluebirds and Brown-headed Nuthatches any time. The loop trail along the north side of the lake between the dam and the iron footbridge is especially good for songbirds. At the east end of the lake, there is a marsh where you may find ducks in winter, Prothonotary Warblers in summer, and Great Blue Herons and Belted Kingfishers year-round.

The lake is closed, but still accessible, during Thanksgiving weekend and from Christmas through New Year's Day. The visitor center, with concessions and bait shop, is open approximately from dawn to dusk, with specific hours changing throughout the year. The paved parking area above the marina is a good place to set up a spotting scope and scan the lake in winter. A 7-mile trail around the lake provides easy access to most birding areas. It takes you along the lakeside through a variety of habitats. You'll also find a few pocket marshes along the way, especially at the heads of the several bays in the lake. The loop trail crosses Salem Creek just below the dam and is sometimes flooded. If you want to hike the entire loop and are planning to start on the south side of the lake, be sure to check this area first to make sure you can get across and instead of having to backtrack the full 7 miles to return to your car.

Brown-headed Nuthatches are residents of open pine forest in coastal and many Piedmont areas. PHOTO: HARRY SELL

Other key birds: *Summer:* Purple Martin; Barn and Northern Rough-winged Swallows. *Winter:* Bufflehead; Ring-necked Duck; American Coot; Pied-billed Grebe; Bonaparte's Gull; Common Loon; Lesser Scaup.

Nearby opportunities: Tanglewood Park is a 1,100-acre, multiple-use county park nestled against the Yadkin River. It is best known for its two championship golf courses, but it also includes hiking and horseback riding trails, conference facilities, and picnic shelters. Reynolda Gardens is a magnet for migrants. Twenty-nine warbler, six vireo, and four thrush species have been recorded here. Additional details for these sites are available online at the Carolina Bird Club Web site, www.carolina birdclub.org.

Directions: From U.S. Highway 421/Business Interstate 40, exit at Martin Luther King Jr. Drive south toward Winston-Salem State University (WSSU). From U.S. Highway 52, exit at Stadium Drive and drive east 1 block to Martin Luther King Drive. Go south on Martin Luther King Drive past WSSU, and turn left onto Reynolds Park Boulevard and continue east for 1.8 miles. At the point where the road narrows to two lanes, turn left onto Salem Lake Drive. This road ends at the parking areas for the lake.

Access: Marina parking area accessible by car, other areas by foot.

Bathrooms: Marina.

Hazards: None.

Nearest food, gas, and lodging: Winston-Salem.

Nearest camping: Pilot Mountain State Park.

DeLorme map grid: Page 36, A4.

North Carolina Travel Map grid: F1.

For more information: Winston-Salem Recreation and Parks, (336) 727–2063; www.city ofws.org/recreation.

Riverbend Park and Lower Lake Hickory

by Dwayne Martin

Counties: Catawba and Alexander.

Habitats: Pine forest, mixed hardwood-pine, upland oak-hickory, small wetlands, Catawba River floodplain, Lake Hickory shoreline.

Key birds: *Summer:* Broad-winged Hawk; Eastern Kingbird; Cliff Swallow; Scarlet Tan-ager; Indigo Bunting. *Winter:* Hooded Merganser; Greater Scaup; Pine Siskin. *Year-round:* Bald Eagle; Ruffed Grouse; Brown-headed Nuthatch; Loggerhead Shrike.

Best times to bird: Late summer through late winter.

About this site:

Riverbend Park is a 400-acre park owned and operated by Catawba County. It includes a mile of shoreline on the Catawba River just below Lake Hickory. There are 12 miles of trails in the park, most of which are easy to moderate. Riverbend Park is open Friday through Monday during daylight hours. You must sign in at the kiosk near the park office upon arrival. There are two boat accesses on lower Lake Hickory that are excellent for birding.

More than 160 bird species have been observed at Riverbend Park since it was opened in the summer of 1999. Begin by looking around the office area. Check the feeders for American Goldfinches, Northern Cardinals, Mourning Doves, and Song Sparrows. In winter look for Purple Finches, Dark-eyed Juncos, and, under the feeders, Fox Sparrows. In summer watch for Red-eyed Vireos, Indigo Buntings, and Eastern Kingbirds around the park office and for Cliff, Barn, and Northern Rough-winged Swallows and Purple Martins.

Walk or drive down to the lower parking area next to the river. Look for Cedar Waxwings and Brown-headed Nuthatches between the parking lot and the canoe access area. In summer watch for Eastern Kingbirds, Orchard Orioles, Northern Parulas, Red-eyed Vireos, and Scarlet Tanagers. Along the river trail look for Bald Eagles, Great Blue Herons, Belted Kingfishers, and Wood Ducks. All six of the eastern swallow species can be found over the water in early spring. During the winter months look for Hooded Mergansers, Lesser Scaup, Ring-necked Ducks, Green-winged Teal, and Northern Shovelers. The river trail is also the best area for neotropical migrants.

Other trails in the park go through upland and pine forest. A variety of year-round species can be seen on these trails, including Wild Turkeys, woodpeckers, and Ruffed Grouse. On the back side of the green trail next to the cow pasture, check the trees and fences for Loggerhead Shrikes and Brown Thrashers. Sharp-shinned, Cooper's, and Broad-winged Hawks and Barred Owls can be seen along the upland trails.

Seen here together are both Greater and Lesser Scaup. PHOTO: HARRY SELL

Oxford Access is a great place during migration for waterfowl and land birds. Waterfowl include Buffleheads, Lesser and Greater Scaup, and Hooded and Red-breasted Mergansers. The Surf Scoter is a regular visitor here, and occasionally Black Scoters show up. In late summer, Black, Common, and Forster's Terns are possible. Thousands of gulls can be seen here in winter. Most are Ring-billed and Bonaparte's, with a few Herring Gulls mixed in. On the peninsula itself Great Blue Herons, Pine Warblers, Brown-headed Nuthatches, Eastern Bluebirds, and Bald Eagles are likely year-round.

At Dusty Ridge Access area, most of the same birds can be found as at Oxford. The Common Loon is known to overwinter in this part of the lake. Some of the rarer species have been found in this area.

Other key birds: *Winter:* Bufflehead; Northern Shoveler; Red-breasted Merganser; Surf Scoter; Brown Creeper; Rusty Blackbird.

Nearby opportunities: Hickory's Park system encompasses three parks: Hickory City and Geitner Parks, which are on Lake Hickory and heavily wooded, and Glenn Hilton Park, which has a 150-yard boardwalk through a wooded,

wetland area. Additional details for this site are available online at the Carolina Bird Club Web site, www.carolinabirdclub.org.

Directions: For Riverbend Park take Interstate 40 exit 131. Go north on Highway 16 for approximately 8 miles. The park entrance is on the right. To get to Oxford Access area, take Highway 16 north from I-40 for approximately

7.5 miles. Turn left onto St. Peter's Church Road and go 0.1 mile and turn right onto Claude Road. Proceed 0.5 mile to the entrance on the right. For Dusty Ridge Access area, take Highway 16 north from I-40 for approximately 8.0 miles across the Catawba River Bridge and then take the first road on the right, Wayside Church Road. At the stop sign turn right, go about 0.2 mile, and then turn left onto Rink Dam road. Follow this road for approximately 1.5 miles and the turn left onto Poly Bowman Road. Go another 0.2 mile or so and turn right onto Deal Farm Lane. The entrance to the access is just ahead on the right.

Access: The observation platform on the river is wheelchair-accessible.

Bathrooms: At the park office.

Hazards: Venomous snakes, biting and stinging insects.

Nearest food, gas, and lodging: Hickory.

Nearest camping: Privately owned campgrounds in Hickory.

DeLorme map grid: Page 34, C3.

North Carolina Travel Map grid: E2.

For more information: Catawba County Riverbend Park, (828) 256–9157; www.catawba countync.gov/depts/parks/rbndmain.asp.

Mountains

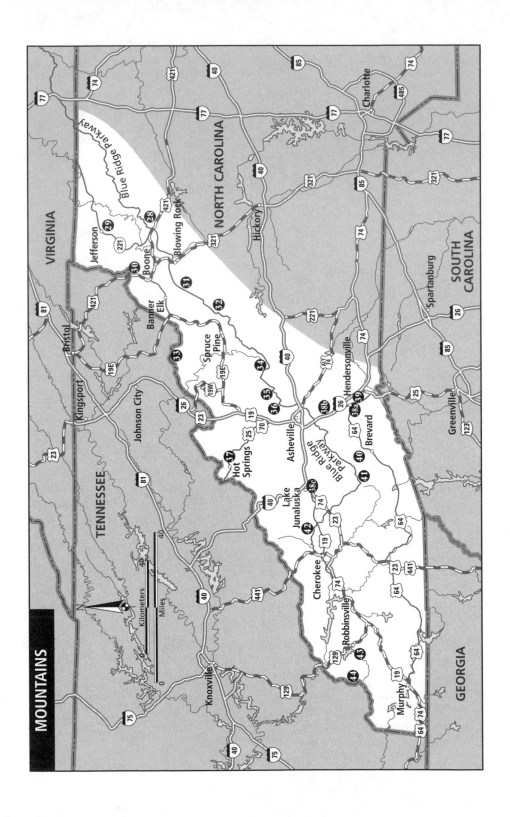

(28) Blue Ridge Parkway North

by Curtis Smalling

Counties: Ashe and Wilkes.

Habitats: Cove and oak-pine forest, white pine stands, and early successional habitat.

Key birds: *Summer:* Veery; Cerulean, Worm-eating, Hooded, Black-throated Blue, Black-throated Green, and Kentucky Warbler; American Redstart; Rose-breasted Grosbeak;

Scarlet Tanager. *Winter:* Common Raven; Red-breasted Nuthatch; Ruffed Grouse.

Best times to bird: Spring migration is best, but during breeding season Cerulean Warblers and a large variety of other neotropical migrant breeders are possible from May through July. Fall migration is good.

About this site:

This section of the Blue Ridge Parkway, milepost 280 north to EB Jeffress Park at milepost 265, runs very close to the escarpment with the terrain steep and the south- and east-facing coves providing some excellent birding opportunities. The more disturbed areas support a lot of white pine stands and meadows adding to the bird species mix. Milepost 270 just south of the Laurel Fork Overlook usually hosts Cerulean Warblers, making it one of the more reliable spots along the parkway for this elusive warbler. Most of the overlooks in this part of the parkway also make for decent areas to watch for fall migrating hawks.

Milepost 270 can be a great stop on a spring morning. In early to mid-May, up to twenty-two species of warbler have been seen here on a good morning, and the steep terrain allows for treetop-level views. Check the overlook, before and after the rock face area, for Kentucky Warblers, Indigo Buntings, Eastern Towhees, and other shrub- and thicket-loving species. The deep cove in the curve of the parkway normally host three vireo species, as well as Scarlet Tanagers and Rose-breasted Grosbeaks. Listen for Ruffed Grouse on the mountain above you and Wild Turkeys gobbling below.

EB Jeffress Park is an excellent stop for mid- to high-elevation species. This park has nice hiking trails including the Cascades Trail, a moderate 1.2-mile loop to the head of Cascades Falls. The oak-pine forest along the crest of the Blue Ridge supports an occasional Worm-eating Warbler and good numbers of Black-and-white Warblers. Other neotropical migrants are plentiful here in the breeding season. During spring and fall migration, this trail can be very productive.

At EB Jeffress Park stop in the picnic area parking lot and check the surrounding pine trees and forest across the parkway for Canada Warblers, Red-breasted Nuthatches, and Golden-crowned Kinglets. A half dozen warbler species are regulars here, including Hooded, Black-and-white, Black-throated Blue, and Black-throated Green Warblers; American Redstarts; and Ovenbirds. Also listen for Veeries and Wood Thrushes. Cedar Waxwings are usually present, and Common Ravens are

Black-throated Blue Warblers often place nests low in shrubs or evergreen rhododendrons.
PHOTO: BILL DUYCK

occasionally seen soaring over the escarpment. Dark-eyed Juncos will be every-where at anytime of the year. The Cascades Trailhead is immediately to the left of the restroom facility and follows the ridge before dropping off to the top of the falls. Some visits yield Worm-eating Warblers, although they typically breed down slope another 500 to 1,000 feet from the falls. As you continue on around the Cascades Loop, you should encounter Canada Warblers, Dark-eyed Juncos, and Scarlet Tanagers along the creek.

Other key birds: *Summer:* Eastern Wood-Pewee; Blue-headed, Red-eyed, and Yellow-throated Vireo; Wood Thrush; Black-and-white Warbler; Ovenbird. *Year-round:* White-breasted Nuthatch; Hairy and Pileated Woodpecker; Dark-eyed Junco.

Nearby opportunities: Doughton Park is a 6,000-acre park situated along the top of the Blue Ridge escarpment and the Blue Ridge Parkway from mileposts 246 to 238. The park provides access to a wide variety of habitats,

including open grassy fields, dry slopes, cove hardwoods, and mixed forest. Additional details for this site are available online at the Carolina Bird Club Web site, www.carolinabird club.org.

Directions: Begin this tour from the point where U.S. Highway 421 crosses the Blue Ridge Parkway. Go north on the parkway. At milepost 271 look for a grassy pull-off on your right just before you reach a large rock face on your left. This area is the core of the Cerulean

Warbler territories and should be birded patiently in the morning, especially in early May.

Access: By car and foot. Facilities at Doughton Lodge are wheelchair-accessible.

Bathrooms: EB Jeffress Park restroom facilities from May through September.

Hazards: Venomous snakes on trails.

Nearest food, gas, and lodging: Doughton Park at milepost 240.

Nearest camping: Doughton Park.

Delorme map grid: Page 14, D1.

North Carolina Travel Map grid: E1.

For more information: Blue Ridge Parkway, (828) 295-7591.

29 New River

by Curtis Smalling

Counties: Ashe, Alleghany, and Watauga.

Habitats: Agricultural fields, pastureland, shrubby fields, riparian zones, mixed forest, wetlands.

Key birds: *Summer:* Alder, Willow, Least, and Great Crested Flycatcher; Black-billed Cuckoo; Warbling Vireo; Yellow and Golden-winged Warbler; Baltimore Oriole. *Fall and spring:* Bald Eagle. *Winter:* Vesper Sparrow.

Best times to bird: Year-round.

About this site:

Averaging only 2,000 feet in elevation, the New River hosts a variety of species that are uncommon in other parts of the northwest corner of the state. The New River basin is largely agricultural and disturbed with open fields, shrubby fields, and associated wetlands. Interspersed are cliffs and drainage areas containing forest coves, bluffs, and dense rhododendron stands that shelter forest species. The shrubby fields and wetland areas host wide variety of wintering birds and uncommon migrants such as waterfowl and shorebirds. Many species reach their southern range limits in the New River valley. These include the first southern range expansion records of breeding Tree Swallows in 1979, breeding Savannah Sparrows, and possibly Spotted Sandpipers breeding along the river. Birds along the river are generally easy to view, and many of the nonpublic sections of the river are easily birded from the roadside. Many of the roads are not heavily traveled and have frequent pull-offs. The upper section, between the U.S. Highway 221 access and the Alleghany access, is the best area for Warbling Vireos. Willow Flycatchers are common along the entire course, and Least Flycatchers generally occur in pockets of high density. Alder Flycatchers are sometimes heard in drainages associated with the river. They may also be found the upper (southern) end of the river toward Todd (Virginia) and Watauga County.

Check the large stands of sycamore for orioles and Warbling and Yellow-throated Vireos. Linear riparian areas with willow and alder are good spots to check for Yellow Warblers and Willow Flycatchers, while more forested areas are usually home to Great Crested Flycatchers and Northern Parulas. Pastures and agricultural areas host Red-winged Blackbirds, Eastern Meadowlarks, Indigo Buntings, and other open country birds. The Northern Rough-winged Swallow tends to be a colonial nester along the river, using the exposed mudbanks creating by flooding. Also, watch for Barn and Tree Swallows.

In winter carefully scan the river for wintering and migrant waterfowl such as American Black Ducks, Wood Ducks, and mergansers. In spring and late summer check for Great Egrets and Spotted and Solitary Sandpipers, which are regulars

The Baltimore Oriole is a fall and spring migrant and also breeds in central and northern mountain areas. PHOTO: HARRY SELL

along the river. Ospreys and Bald Eagles are also regular visitors in April and early fall. At the Alleghany access, located at the extreme northern end of the river, look for Golden-winged and Prairie Warblers. Blue-winged Warblers are occasionally seen here in the summer, and Brewster's Warbler hybrids are possible, especially along the north fork of the river. In winter dense wetland and shrub areas near the river often attract large numbers of wintering and migrating sparrows, including good numbers of Swamp and White-throated Sparrows. Others seen with regularity, especially in November and March, include Savannah, White-crowned, Vesper, and an occasional Lincoln's Sparrow.

Numerous outfitters provide float trips with multiple areas to put in and take out, making for short or long trips. This is often the best way to bird the river. The river is often shallow and slow, allowing ample time for bird identification.

Other key birds: *Summer:* Northern Rough-winged, Tree, and Barn Swallow; Northern Parula; Prairie Warbler; Orchard Oriole. *Winter:* American Black and Wood Duck; Savannah, White-crowned, and Lincoln's Sparrow.

Directions: To get to the New River State Park, take Wagoner Road Access, located 8 miles southeast of Jefferson by following Highway 88 from the intersection with Highway 16. Proceed 1.2 miles on Highway 88 and turn on SR 1590. The park is at the end of this road. If coming from Jefferson, follow US 221 for 8 miles and then follow the park signs to your right.

Access: Many of the areas are accessible by car.

Bathrooms: At New River State Park.

Hazards: Flash flooding.

Nearest food, gas, and lodging: Jefferson and West Jefferson, approximately 10 miles from New River State Park.

Nearest camping: New River State Park.

DeLorme map grid: Page 14, ABC1&2.

North Carolina Travel Map grid: D1.

For more information: New River State Park, (336) 982-2587; www.ils.unc.edu/parkproject/visit/neri/home.html.

30 Amphibolite Mountains and Elk Knob Game Land and State Natural Area

by Curtis Smalling

County: Watauga.

Habitats: Northern hardwood forest, balds, open country and other early successional habitat.

Key birds: *Summer:* Broad-winged Hawk; Yellow-bellied Sapsucker; Least Flycatcher; Veery; Canada, Chestnut-sided, Black-throated Blue, and Golden-winged Warbler (including Brewster's hybrids); Rose-breasted Grosbeak; Indigo Bunting; Scarlet Tanager; Vesper Sparrow. *Winter:* Golden Eagle; Horned Lark; Lincoln's Sparrow. *Year-round:* Ruffed Grouse; Common Raven; Red-breasted Nuthatch.

Best times to bird: Excellent opportunities during spring and fall migration and breeding season. Visit the gap of Rich and Snake Mountains early on fall mornings for neotropical migrant fallouts. Excellent hawk migration from September through November.

About this site:

The Amphibolite Mountains of northwestern North Carolina form a large chain containing some ten peaks stretching from Rich Mountain near Boone in the south to Mount Jefferson and Phoenix Mountain in the north. Most of the area is privately owned, with roadside birding opportunities. There are, however, several public lands including Mount Jefferson State Park, the Nature Conservancy's Bluff Mountain and Peak preserves, Elk Knob State Natural Area, Elk Knob Game Land, and Howard's Knob Park. Access to some of these is limited (Nature Conservancy properties) or seasonal (Howard's Knob Park). Two areas are especially noteworthy and have year-round access: the Elk Knob Game Land and the newly established Elk Knob State Natural Area. These areas consist of large tracts of largely northern hardwood forest. The game land includes one of the largest early successional areas in the region. Balds also occur on Rich Mountain and just north of Elk Knob at Long Hope; the elevations in this area range from about 4,000 to 5,555 feet to the top of Elk Knob.

Elk Knob Game Land can be a very productive area for early successional, open country, high-elevation birds, as well as a good variety of forest species. During the breeding season look and listen especially for Golden-winged Warblers. The area at the first wooden gate, described later in the directions, typically has birds very close to the road. Cross over the gate and follow the path. Least Flycatchers are especially common here and on the other side of the gap. The Chestnut-sided Warbler is another common breeder here. In this area also look for Common Yellowthroats, Gray Catbirds, Field Sparrows, and Indigo Buntings. From the clearing you should hear Veeries, Scarlet Tanagers, and Rose-breasted Grosbeaks in the nearby woods.

Vesper Sparrows are found on grassy balds in the mountains. PHOTO: HARRY SELL

During migration this small, open area attracts many migrants. The morning flights in September can be especially impressive, particularly around the headwaters of Meat Camp Creek, the small stream you cross on the path. Nashville, Blue-winged, Worm-eating, Mourning, and Tennessee Warblers all are found with regularity here each fall. Most migrants in the fall are passing westerly through the gap from daybreak until about 9:00 A.M. If there is a strong headwind for them, they tend to pile up here on the leeward side of the mountain. Migrating Rose-breasted Grosbeaks, Cedar Waxwings, American Robins, and Scarlet Tanagers can be numerous in early October. For more forest birds, continue on this path up the side of the mountain until the game land ends. Head west through the woods until you enter the cleared portions of the where you should be able to look down on your vehicle in the gap.

After returning to your car, drive into the gap itself and look for more Golden-winged Warblers; the area to your left is Rich Mountain. Just west of the gap, as many as three Brewster's Warbler hybrids have been found in recent years. This area is also one of the best places in North Carolina for Vesper Sparrows, which stay until mid-October. The Grasshopper Sparrow is also an occasional breeder here, and Horned Larks are sporadically reported. Common Ravens are seen in the gap year-round. The autumn hawk migration is often very good, and Golden

NORTH CAROLINA PARTNERS IN FLIGHT

Partners in Flight was created in 1990 and is a dose of preventative medicine designed to save species and habitats before they become endangered. A major goal of this voluntary program is to maintain populations of all types of birds, especially neotropical migrants that breed in temperate North America and then migrate to spend our winter in the New World tropics.

This important initiative brings together government and nongovernment agencies, conservation organizations and groups, academia, and industry at the federal, state, and local levels. It also includes numerous Latin American participants. Biologists, educators, and policy makers from all of these groups are working cooperatively to help keep bird populations stable and conserve or improve the breeding, wintering, and migration habitats they need.

In North Carolina, the Partners in Flight program seeks to improve and increase communication, cooperation, and collaboration among concerned partners and individuals to further bird conservation throughout the state, the region, and the Americas. PIF was born in North Carolina in 1993, and the program in this state is supported and coordinated by the North Carolina Wildlife Resources Commission.

In North Carolina, the Partners in Flight initiative has involvement on many levels. Federal involvement includes the U.S. Fish and Wildlife Service, National Park Service, Department of Defense, U.S. Army Corps of Engineers, and Forest Service, among others, with state level participation featuring agencies such as the North Carolina State Parks System, North Carolina Natural Heritage Program, North Carolina Museum of Natural Sciences, and Division of Forest Resources. Other conservation partners include the Nature Conservancy, Audubon North Carolina, and local land trusts. In addition, private industry and dozens of universities and colleges add to the versatility of this program. Finally, concerned citizens are important for grassroots participation throughout the state.

The North Carolina Partners in Flight Steering Committee and State Working Group is heavily involved with all facets of the program and coordinates production of a biennial newsletter and other educational and outreach materials. There are many volunteer opportunities available on all scales. To learn more about Partners in Flight in North Carolina, visit the NC PIF Web site, www.faculty.ncwc.edu/mbrooks/pif.

Eagles have been seen regularly during the winter. Visit the gap during the spring and fall migrations for good looks at a number of neotropical migrants. From late October into November, check hedgerows and wet areas for migrating sparrows. Vesper Sparrows linger into October, and Lincoln's, Fox, White-crowned, White-throated, Swamp, Song, Field, Savannah, and Chipping Sparrows are typical.

During migration continue roadside birding through the gap west until you reach mile 3.5 at the end of the game land on your right. Look for Chestnut-sided and Golden-winged Warblers, Least Flycatchers, and Vesper Sparrows through this section during the breeding season. The Northern Bobwhite is a possibility as well as Ruffed Grouse and Wild Turkeys.

At Elk Knob State Natural Area, spend a few minutes at the wooden fence entrance listening for Field and Vesper Sparrows, Indigo Buntings, and Gray Catbirds. Common Yellowthroats and Golden-winged Warblers are also present just 0.1 to 0.2 mile farther on Meat Camp Road. Common Ravens nest on the craggy side of Snake Mountain and are usually present year-round.

Drive or walk this flat road for half a mile or so through a second-growth hardwood forest. This is a good area for Black-throated Blue and Hooded Warblers, Ovenbirds, and Red-eyed and Blue-headed Vireos. Rose-breasted Grosbeaks, Scarlet Tanagers, Wood Thrushes, and Veeries are plentiful. Ruffed Grouse and Wild Turkeys are common.

Follow the Jeep–ATV (all-terrain vehicle) trail to the top of the mountain. Be aware that it is a fairly strenuous climb. As the canopy shortens listen for Canada and Black-throated Blue Warblers and Veeries. During the breeding season be alert for Yellow-bellied Sapsuckers, Dark-eyed Juncos, and Red-tailed and Broad-winged Hawks. Near the top of the mountain, on the east and southern facing slopes, is a large heath bald with low shrubs. This area hosts Gray Catbirds, Eastern Towhees, Chestnut-sided Warblers, and Indigo Buntings. At the top listen for Red-breasted Nuthatches and Golden-crowned Kinglets. The large grassy area in view to the northeast is Long Hope Bald, and at the base is a small stand of spruce fir forest. Breeding birds found there include Magnolia Warblers and Northern Saw-whet Owls.

Other key birds: *Summer:* Ruby-throated Hummingbird; Gray Catbird; Wood Thrush; Red-eyed and Blue-headed Vireo; Ovenbird. *Winter:* Cooper's and Sharp-shinned Hawk; Lincoln's Sparrow. *Year-round:* Wild Turkey; Pileated and Hairy Woodpecker; Dark-eyed Junco.

Nearby opportunities: Meat Camp Creek Environmental Studies Area is a 9.5-acre wetland that is privately owned but available for use. Bounded on two sides by Meat Camp Creek,

this riparian corridor attracts many migrants in spring and fall. More than 130 species of birds have been seen here. Valle Crucis Community Park is a true community park, with an active board and volunteer base that keep it well maintained. The bird diversity of the park is due to the wide variety of habitats surrounding it. Woods, the Watauga River, a small pond and associated cattail marsh, agricultural areas including row crop, hayfields, nursery areas, and suburban yards all combine to make birding reliably good. Additional details for these sites are available online at the Carolina Bird Club Web site, www.carolinabird club.org.

Directions: From the intersection of Highway 194 North and U.S. Highway 421 North in Boone, proceed north on Highway 194 for 4.3 miles and then turn left onto Meat Camp Road (State Road 1340). Continue on Meat Camp Road for 3.7 miles and then turn left on gravel Rich Mountain Road (State Road 1300). At 0.7 mile you enter the Elk Knob Game Land. At a wooden gate on the left in the first major clearing, park on the side of the road to access a trail to the upper parts of Rich Mountain to the gap at 2.6 miles. Park in the gap and access Rich and Snake Mountains by crossing either side of the road.

For the Elk Knob State Natural Area, stay on Meat Camp Road (SR 1340) for 5.3 miles until you reach the gap between the Snake Mountain on the left and Elk Knob on the right. Proceed through a gate in the wooden fence on the right, and travel this road until it splits to a Jeep trail at 5.7 miles. Go straight ahead to reach the top of Elk Knob, or bear left through a northern hardwood forest.

Access: Some access by car. Most areas require walking.

Bathrooms: In Boone.

Hazards: Avoid the game land during hunting seasons, but if you go, wear blaze orange!

Nearest food, gas, and lodging: Boone.

Nearest camping: Privately owned campgrounds in Boone.

DeLorme map grid: Page 13, C6.

North Carolina Travel Map grid: D-E, 1.

For more information: North Carolina Wildlife Resources Commission, (919) 733-7291; www.ncwildlife.org/pg04_HuntingTrapping/pg 4a.htm. The Nature Conservancy, http://nature.org/wherewework/northamerica/states/northcarolina/preserves.

31 Moses Cone and Julian Price Memorial Parks

by Curtis Smalling

County: Watauga.

Habitats: Hemlock coves, oak forest, regrowth in extensive apple orchards.

Key birds: *Summer:* Yellow-bellied Sapsucker; Alder Flycatcher; Veery; Chestnut-sided, Black-throated Blue, Black-throated Green, Black-burnian, Hooded, and Canada Warbler; Winter Wren. *Winter:* Northern Saw-whet Owl. *Year-round:* Common Raven; Red-breasted Nuthatch; Brown Creeper; Red Crossbill; Pine Siskin.

Best times to bird: Year-round.

About this site:

Moses Cone Memorial Park was formed from the estate of textile magnate Moses Cone and includes 25 miles of 2 percent grade carriage trails and the manor house, which is now a craft center. Moses Cone Park includes Bass and Trout Lakes. Julian Price Memorial Park—named for the founder of the Jefferson Standard Life and Pilot Life Insurance Companies—also includes a medium-size lake. Together they comprise over 7,500 acres of a diverse landscape. From the parking lot for Trout Lake, follow the hiking trail that emerges from the woods at the end of the lot. Once on the trail turn left and follow the well-marked carriage trail around the lake. This first section is excellent for Yellow-bellied Sapsuckers, Winter Wrens, Eastern Wood-Pewees, Brown Creepers, Red-breasted Nuthatches, and Blackburnian, Canada, and Black-throated Blue Warblers. When you reach the hemlocks, listen for Golden-crowned Kinglets, Veeries, Wood Thrushes, and Scarlet Tanagers. In summer check for Wood Ducks on the lake. During migration you may find a variety of waterfowl including Ring-necked Ducks, Pied-billed Grebes, and Hooded Mergansers.

A short side trip to the Sims Pond Overlook at milepost 295.3 just north of the Sims Creek Bridge might yield Northern Saw-whet or Barred Owls in the huge hemlocks around the parking area. Saw-whets are usually present in winter.

Bass Lake is best accessed from U.S. Highway 221 South about a mile from Blowing Rock. Look for the access road on your right just past the MOSES CONE MEMORIAL PARK sign. The trail around the lake is productive year-round. Red Crossbills have been regularly found year-round here, with breeding occurring in the area. Listen for them flying over and using the hemlocks and Norway spruces on the ends of the lake. Yellow-bellied Sapsuckers are common around the lake and along the trails leading up to the manor house. During the summer look for Pine

A view of the Moses Cone estate. PHOTO: C. EDWARD DOMBROFSKI

Siskins; Red-breasted Nuthatches; Canada, Blackburnian, Black-throated Blue, Black-throated Green, and Chestnut-sided Warblers; Northern Parulas; and Louisiana Waterthrushes. During migration many species of waterfowl and shore-birds use the lake, including Common Loons, Ruddy Ducks, Buffleheads, and Spotted and Solitary Sandpipers. In recent years the island in the middle of the lake has supported a breeding pair of Great Blue Herons, presumably the highest elevation record in the state.

To reach Price Park Picnic Area and Bog, continue on the Blue Ridge Parkway to milepost 296.5 and enter the Price Park Picnic Area. Behind the first comfort station is the Boone Fork Trailhead. Follow the trail, bearing right at the fork, and proceed about 300 yards to the Boone Fork Bog area. This area supports a variety of open habitat species such as Common Yellowthroats, American Woodcocks, Gray Catbirds, Chestnut-sided Warblers, and Carolina Wrens. During most years Alder Flycatchers are present in the bog. Migration can be great here, with numerous species in good numbers. Many of the species found at Bass and Trout Lakes can also be found by following the Boone Fork Trail for its complete 5 miles. After visiting the bog area, return to your car and continue to Price Lake. During migration periods check the lake for waterfowl.

Other key species: *Summer:* Wood Duck; Golden-crowned Kinglet; Louisiana Waterthrush; Common Yellowthroat; American Woodcock; Gray Catbird; Wood Thrush.

Nearby opportunities: Grandfather Mountain is the world's only privately owned International Biosphere Preserve. Encompassing some 3,000 acres, this southern terminus of the Blue Ridge Mountains hosts a large variety of breeding birds. At 5,964 feet above sea level, the mountain is high enough to support extensive spruce fir forest and the birds that depend on that habitat. Additional details for this site are available online at the Carolina Bird Club Web site, www.carolinabirdclub.org.

Directions: These two parks are contiguous and are located close to Boone and Blowing Rock. The parks are located between mileposts 293 and 300 on the Blue Ridge Parkway. For the Trout Lake area, take U.S. Highway 221 south from Blowing Rock for approximately 2 miles to the intersection with the Blue Ridge Parkway. Take the entrance road, but make an immediate left before reaching the parkway. This road runs under the parkway.

Stay to the left at the fork and take an immediate right along a small paved access road to the Trout Lake parking area. If traveling the parkway, access US 221 at milepost 294.6, and then take the first right and circle back under the parkway to follow the previous directions.

Access: Most areas are accessible only by footpaths.

Bathrooms: Restrooms are now available year-round at the Moses Cone Craft Center Carriage House, but hours are limited. Portable toilets are provided at Price Park Picnic Area and Bass Lake year-round.

Hazards: None.

Nearest food, gas, and lodging: Blowing Rock and Boone.

Nearest camping: Julian Price Memorial Park.

DeLorme map grid: Page 13, D6.

North Carolina Travel Map grid: E1.

For more information: National Park Service, 199 Hemphill Knob Road, Asheville, NC 28803-8686; (828) 295-7591; www.nps.gov/blri.

32 Linville Gorge and Surrounding Area

by Clyde E. Sorenson

Counties: Burke, Avery, McDowell, and Caldwell.

Habitats: Hardwood forest, dry pine forest, Eastern hemlock forest, rhododendron thickets, mountain streams.

Key birds: *Summer:* Broad-winged Hawk; Black-billed Cuckoo; Chuck-will's-widow; Whip-poor-will; Red-headed Woodpecker; Least Flycatcher; Louisiana Waterthrush; Yellow, Chestnut-sided, Blackburnian, Kentucky, Canada, Hooded, Swainson's, Black-throated Green, Black-throated Blue, and Worm-eating Warbler; American Redstart; Summer and Scarlet Tanager; Rose-breasted and Blue Grosbeak; Indigo Bunting; Orchard and Baltimore Oriole. *Winter:* Brown Creeper. *Year-round:* Ruffed Grouse; Peregrine Falcon; Common Raven; Winter Wren; Brown-headed Nuthatch; Red Crossbill.

Best times to bird: Good opportunities year-round; neotropical migrants plentiful along Mortimer Road and other Forest Service roads in spring; raptor migration during the fall.

About this site:

Linville Gorge and the wilderness area that surrounds it are among the most spectacular natural features in the eastern United States. The gorge, formed by the Linville River and starting at the Linville Falls, runs for about 15 miles to the head of Lake James. Elevations in the Linville Gorge area range from nearly 4,000 feet on the highest portions of the ridges to just over 1,500 feet near Lake James. The gorge itself and much of the land around it constitute Linville Gorge National Wilderness Area. Access into the wilderness area itself is by foot only. The topography of the area is extremely rugged, and journeying any great distance into the gorge should be given some careful consideration. There are, however, many areas in the vicinity of the gorge that offer excellent birding opportunities. Everything that can be seen in the roadless portions of the wilderness area can also been seen in areas with easier access.

The gorge runs roughly from north to south. The first 7 miles or so of Highway 181 from Morganton run through a typical Piedmont landscape with homes, scattered farm fields, and small woodlots. Through this area be vigilant for raptors, including Red-tailed, Cooper's, and Broad-winged Hawks soaring over the fields and woods. About 7 miles out of Morganton, Highway 181 will start climbing the flank of the mountains; much of the land on both sides of the road for the next 15 miles is part of the Pisgah National Forest. Watch for Ruffed Grouse on the sides of the road as you climb.

Approximately 14.5 miles from the U.S. Highway 64 Business intersection in Morganton, about 2 miles beyond the intersection of Highway 181 and the Brown Mountain Road, look on the right for the small gravel road leading to the parking area for the Upper Creek Falls. From this parking lot you can access two trails, one leading to the Lower Falls, about a thirty-minute walk, and the other leading to the Upper Falls, about a fifteen-minute walk. Both descend through mature hardwood forest with a well-developed understory of rhododendron and mountain laurel in places. In spring both trails can be excellent for warblers, including Black-throated Green, Black-throated Blue, and Worm-eating, among many others. The torrent at the bottom of the trails, Upper Creek, usually harbors Louisiana Waterthrushes in summer. One may make a circuit of the area by descending the lower trail, following the creek upstream to the Upper Falls, and returning to the parking area on the upper trail. Allow at least two hours for this walk, and be careful; the creek portion of the trail requires repeated crossings of the stream and is extremely rugged.

Returning to the parking lot and continuing on Highway 181, you will enter the tiny community of Jonas Ridge. Look for Mortimer Road to the right. A side trip down this road in early May could be well worth your while. To do this side

Male Hooded Warblers are most likely to be seen when they are singing. PHOTO: HARRY SELL

trip, turn on Mortimer Road and follow it through a residential area for about 2 miles. You will come to a fork in the road with a small church; take the right, gravel fork—this is still Mortimer Road, but it is not well marked at this intersection. Within a mile or so, you will enter national forest land, and for the rest of your descent, approximately 10 miles, you will be in heavily forested country and should drive slowly with the windows open. Near the top of the forest section, Blackburnian, Black-throated Green, Black-throated Blue, Worm-eating, and Kentucky Warblers, Ovenbirds, and other warbler species are abundant for most of the road's length, as are Scarlet and Summer Tanagers, Red-eyed and Yellow-throated Vireos, and Acadian and possibly Least Flycatchers. Two Forest Service access points along the road provide hiking access to the valley of Lost Cove Creek; the second is shorter, a twenty-five-minute walk to the stream at Hunt Fish Falls and less strenuous than the first. Hiking the trails will probably not add much to your list, with the possible exception of Ruffed Grouse and Louisiana Waterthrushes when you get to the creek. Continue on to the tiny community of Mortimer and follow Winchester Road to the right and then Brown Mountain Road to return to Highway 181 and Morganton, or backtrack to Highway 181 and Jonas Ridge.

Continuing on Highway 181 from Jonas Ridge, you will encounter the Blue Ridge Parkway in approximately 1 mile; Highway 181 parallels the parkway for approximately 2 miles from here. To the north on the parkway from this intersection is Grandfather Mountain and its high-altitude spruce fir forests. To the south from this point, you can access the Linville Falls Campground.

Just before Highway 181 meets the Blue Ridge Parkway, it intersects Highway 183 on the left. From this intersection a number of interesting birding areas can be accessed. One of the more interesting from both birding and scenic points of view is a trip along Wiseman's View Road, Old Highway 105, also known as the Kistler Memorial Highway. This dirt road follows the razor-backed ridge bordering the southwestern side of Linville Gorge. To get to Wiseman's View Road, turn left on Highway 183 and follow signs for the Linville Falls overlooks. Soon after you get on Wiseman's View Road, you will come to a parking area and access to the Linville Falls overlooks. Park here and probe the trails in the area. Part of this area is old-growth hemlock of impressive size. You can also access this area from the parkway south of its intersection with Highway 181. In and around the hemlock groves at the appropriate times of the year, you should have no trouble finding Red-breasted Nuthatches, Brown Creepers, Least Flycatchers, and possibly Red Crossbills or Ruffed Grouse. Watch for soaring raptors, Turkey and Black Vultures, Common Ravens, and possibly Peregrine Falcons from the overlooks. After leaving the parking area, you may continue on Wiseman's View Road toward the southeast. The road is narrow, very rough, and steep in places, but there are several interesting overlooks and thickets along the route that may yield warblers, sparrows, and other passerines. Grouse or turkeys can also be expected anywhere along the road. This road, if you continue on it, will carry you to Lake James.

Approximately 4 miles south of the intersection with Highway 181 on U.S. Highway 221, just beyond the small town of Crossnore, is the North Carolina Department of Forestry training facility and tree nursery. A fir seed nursery on the site frequently attracts Red Crossbills, and it is relatively easy to build a substantial list of warblers and other migrants at the site in spring and fall.

Other key birds: *Summer:* Yellow-billed Cuckoo; Louisiana Waterthrush; Yellow-throated Vireo. *Winter:* Great Horned and Eastern Screech-Owl; White-crowned Sparrow. *Year-round:* Cooper's and Sharp-shinned Hawk.

Nearby opportunities: South Mountains State Park is North Carolina's largest state park with over 40 miles of trails. Elevation ranges from 1,200 feet along the Jacob's Fork River to 3,000 feet on Buzzard's Roost along the western edge of the park. The park is filled with a streams and tumbling brooks. The most visited area is High Shoals Falls, where the Jacob's Fork River takes an 80-foot plunge over bare rock. South Mountains State Park is located south of Morganton. Additional details for this site are available online at the Carolina Bird Club Web site, www.carolinabirdclub.org.

Directions: The main thoroughfare on the eastern flank of the wilderness area is Highway 181, which runs from Morganton to the small communities of Pineola and Linville. To reach Highway 181 from Interstate 40, take exit 105 toward Morganton. You will be on Highway 18. At approximately 2.5 miles from the interstate in Morganton, Highway 18 will intersect US 64 Business; continue straight through this intersection and you will be on Highway 181. Set your trip meter to 0 at the intersection with Business 64. Several interesting birding sites are located along Highway 181. Many of the trails into the gorge itself, apart from those in the vicinity of Linville Falls at the head of the canyon, are poorly marked and maintained.

Access: Much of the birding can be done from the road. Trails are not accessible for people who have difficulty walking.

Bathrooms: Linville Falls Campground.

Hazards: Venomous snakes; extremely rugged terrain on some trails.

Nearest food, gas, and lodging: Crossnore (limited lodging) and Morganton.

Nearest camping: Linville Falls Campground has sites for fifty tents and twenty trailers. Facilities include water and flush toilets with sink, but no showers or hookups.

DeLorme map grid: Page 33, B4.

North Carolina Travel Map grid: D2.

For more information: U.S. Forest Service–Pisgah National Forest–Grandfather Ranger District, Route 1, Box 110-A, Nebo, NC 28761; (828) 652-2144; www.cs.unca.edu/nfsnc/recreation/linville.pdf.

㉝ Roan Mountain

by Curtis Smalling

Counties: Avery (North Carolina) and Carter (Tennessee).

Habitats: Grass balds, heath balds, spruce fir forest, rhododendron gardens, mixed hardwoods-conifers, cove hardwoods, northern hardwoods.

Key birds: *Summer:* Broad-winged Hawk; Alder, Willow, and Least Flycatcher; Veery; Magnolia, Canada, Chestnut-sided, Golden-winged, Black-throated Blue, Black-throated Green, Hooded, Kentucky, and Worm-eating Warbler; Ovenbird; Scarlet Tanager; Vesper Sparrow; Rose-breasted Grosbeak. *Year-round:* Northern Saw-whet Owl; Red-breasted Nuthatch; Brown Creeper; Black-capped Chickadee; Red Crossbill.

Best times to bird: Year-round opportunities, with best variety during spring and fall migration, when migrants stream through Carver's Gap.

About this site:

The Roan Highlands sit on the border of North Carolina and Tennessee and form the highest of the Unaka Mountains at 6,286 feet. Roan Mountain has several striking features, including the world's largest grassy bald complex, which stretches for miles from Carver's Gap to Big Yellow Mountain. The natural rhododendron gardens, or heath balds, covering over 600 acres are the most extensive in the country. The 800 acres of spruce fir forest and additional diversity of habitats yield a high diversity of breeding, migrating, and wintering bird species. The four major habitats of the area— mixed hardwood forests, spruce fir, grassy bald, and heath bald—are treated separately.

As you approach the highlands from either side of the mountain, you will pass through mixed forest containing some hemlock and cove hardwoods at midelevations, which change over to northern hardwoods above 4,000 feet. Roadside birding and birding at the state park, picnic grounds, and pull-offs should yield good numbers of forest species such as Scarlet Tanager; Rose-breasted Grosbeak; and Black-throated Blue, Black-throated Green, Black-and-white, Hooded, Kentucky, and Worm-eating Warblers. Golden-winged Warblers are found from about 3,000 to 4,800 feet in old clearings on both sides of the mountain as well as in the gaps along the Appalachian Trail. Most of the eastern woodpeckers can be found in the forests along the mountain, along with Blue-headed, Yellow-throated, and Red-eyed Vireos. Also check for Willow Flycatchers along streams at lower elevations and Acadian and Least Flycatchers at low and mid-elevations.

From Carver's Gap, at the state line, you can access the dense areas of spruce fir forest on the west and north faces of the mountain. Take the Appalachian Trail from the parking lot south toward Roan High Knob. During the breeding season Hermit Thrushes, Magnolia and Canada Warblers, Golden-crowned Kinglets,

Brown Creepers, and Pine Siskins are common. Red Crossbills are a possibility at any time of year. Also listen and look for newly reintroduced Black-capped Chickadees. Listen for Northern Saw-whet Owls here as well, especially in spring during the active calling period. Some years Ruby-crowned Kinglets and Purple Finches are found during summer.

The extensive grassy balds are also accessed from Carver's Gap. Head north on the Appalachian Trail up to Round Bald for breathtaking views of Grandfather Mountain to the east and the Black Mountains to the south. Look and listen for Dark-eyed Juncos, Vesper Sparrows, and Chestnut-sided Warblers throughout the balds. Gray Catbirds, Indigo Buntings, Barn Swallows, Chimney Swifts, and Eastern Towhees are also common. Snow Buntings will turn up on the balds from November through February some years. Golden Eagles visit, and Common Ravens are usually present. Golden-winged Warblers and Alder Flycatchers are usually easier to find in the gaps or low spots between the prominent knobs. Look closely in the thickets in these slightly wetter and protected areas. Golden-winged Warblers seem to be more plentiful toward Yellow Mountain and Big Yellow Mountain. The bald

View of Round Bald (5,826 feet) from Carver's Gap parking area. PHOTO: KAREN BEARDEN

areas and especially those low gaps can be very exciting and rewarding during migration seasons as hundreds of warblers and other migrants pour through. Warbler migration can also be exceptional at Carver's Gap as well, especially in the shrubby areas just below the gap on the North Carolina side of the mountain.

The natural rhododendron gardens—heath balds—provide excellent views at a number of species, with the added benefit of paved paths and wheelchair accessibility. The gardens are in the Carver's Gap area. Often crowded on weekends, the best days are usually fall mornings during the week. Early successional species such as Chestnut-sided and Canada Warblers, Gray Catbirds, Indigo Buntings, Dark-eyed Juncos, and Eastern Towhees are plentiful. The edges yield spruce fir residents including Golden-crowned Kinglets and Winter Wrens. Chimney Swifts, Barn Swallows, and Red-tailed, Cooper's, and Broad-winged Hawks often are seen.

Other key birds: *Summer:* Hermit Thrush; Ovenbird; Black-and-white and Mourning Warbler. *Winter:* Snow Bunting. *Year-round:* Hairy Woodpecker; Golden-crowned Kinglet; Dark-eyed Junco.

Directions: From Linville take North Carolina Highway 181 to Newland, then North Carolina Highway 194 to Elk Park, then U.S. Highway 19E to the Town of Roan Mountain, Tennessee. Turn left on Tennessee Highway 143 to Roan Mountain State Park or continue on to Carver's Gap at the state line. Carver's Gap may also be accessed from the North Carolina side by leaving Spruce Pine and taking North Carolina Highway 226 for 9.4 miles to Bakersville, and then following North Carolina Highway 261 to for 12.9 miles to Carver's Gap, where the road becomes TN 143.

Access: Roan Mountain State Park (Tennessee), the Appalachian Trail, and Cherokee National Forest facilities give good access to all areas, especially for mobility-impaired visitors in the rhododendron gardens area.

Bathrooms: At Roan Mountain State Park.

Hazards: None.

Nearest food, gas, and lodging: Roan Mountain State Park; food and lodging at Bakersville.

Nearest camping: Roan Mountain State Park.

DeLorme map grid: Page 32, A3; page 12, 3D.

North Carolina Travel Map grid: D1.

For more information: Roan Mountain State Park, (800) 250-8620; www.state.tn.us/environment/parks/roanmtn.

34 Mount Mitchell State Park

by Simon Thompson

County: Yancey.

Habitats: Spruce fir forest in higher reaches of the park. Northern hardwood forests dominate at elevations below 4,500 feet.

Key birds: *Summer:* Northern Saw-whet Owl; Yellow-bellied Sapsucker; Alder and Willow Flycatcher; Brown Creeper; Winter Wren; Veery; Magnolia, Chestnut-sided, Black-throated Green, Blackburnian, and Canada Warbler; Red Crossbill; Pine Siskin. *Year-round:* Common Raven; Red-breasted Nuthatch.

Best times to bird: The warmer months are the best for birding, and both spring and fall migrations can be profitable.

About this site:

Mount Mitchell rises above the adjacent Blue Ridge Parkway to an elevation of 6,684 feet. Mount Mitchell State Park encompasses 1,469 acres of predominantly red spruce and Fraser fir forest. The modern-day flora and fauna are quite different from those of the past. Extensive logging and fires destroyed much of the original forest, but the forested slopes still hold a unique selection of plants and animals more typical of Canada. The forests near the peak do not look healthy. The slopes are carpeted with the skeletons of dead firs. The dieback of the spruce fir system may be a result of a combination of air pollution and a balsam woolly adelgid infestation. The adelgid, a nonnative insect, attacks and kills fir trees, with mature trees most affected.

Typical breeding birds of the park include Common Ravens, Brown Creepers, Dark-eyed Juncos, Winter Wrens, and Red-breasted Nuthatches. Red Crossbills can be found as well, although they are more likely to be heard calling as they fly over the treetops. Spending time at either dawn or dusk during the summer months should also enable you to hear the ethereal song of the Hermit Thrush. Also present in the hardwood forest and adjacent spruce fir forest is the Northern Saw-whet Owl. The bell-like hoots can usually be heard on a spring night, but due to the owl's very small size, it can be very hard to see.

The Mountains-to-Sea/Buncombe Horse Range Trail offers the prospect in spring of breeding Magnolia Warblers, found in open areas in past years. This trail leads through a mix of spruce fir forest and open shrubby areas. From the entrance to the park drive half a mile on Highway 128. The trail entrance is on the right side of the road. Shortly after entering the trail, it will fork. Take the left fork. It is 3.8 miles to Camp Alice, a former logging camp. The trail continues for many miles.

The easiest trail to bird is the Commissary Trail, which can be good for high-elevation bird species in spring and migrating songbirds in fall. This mostly level trail goes through a fairly open area. The trailhead can be found behind the ranger station on Highway 128 about 1.7 miles from the Blue Ridge Parkway. Walk behind (to the right of) the ranger station along the old road. The trail continues for about 1 mile and connects with the Camp Alice Trail ending at the remnants of Camp Alice.

The Balsam Nature Trail winds through thickets and remnant spruce forest where Winter Wrens, Gray Catbirds, and Veeries can be observed. The trailhead can be found at the end of Highway 128 about 4.3 miles from the park entrance at the Blue Ridge Parkway. The Nature Trail forms a 0.75-mile loop. It can be accessed from the parking lot or from the Mount Mitchell tower area. This trail is also rated easy.

Another good trail is the Old Mitchell Trail, which climbs to the peak of the mountain. Both Golden-crowned Kinglets and Pine Siskins are often seen on this walk. Another short hike to the peak offers excellent views on a clear day. Remember that the weather can change rapidly, so wear or carry rain gear and warm clothing.

From early September through mid-October, Ridge Junction Overlook on the Blue Ridge Parkway is one of the best spots in the Blue Ridge to see migrating warblers, thrushes, grosbeaks, and more. After birding the park return to the Blue Ridge Parkway, turn left on the parkway, and go about 50 yards north. Over the past few years more than twenty-five different species of warblers have been seen at this spot, including Blackburnian, Magnolia, Mourning, and Cerulean Warblers. Other species include Broad-winged and Sharp-shinned Hawks; Swainson's, Wood,

Mount Mitchell towers as the highest point east of the Mississippi River. PHOTO: KAREN BEARDEN

Gray-cheeked, Hermit, and even Bicknell's Thrushes; Blue-headed and Philadelphia Vireos; Rose-breasted Grosbeaks; Scarlet Tanagers; and many more. This is also one of the most reliable spots in the mountains to find Red Crossbills. The best way to enjoy this spot is to dress in layers and arrive early in the morning.

To reach the Bald Knob Ridge Trail, continue north on the parkway to reach the trailhead, which is about 0.4 mile north of the junction with Highway 128 (just after milepost 355). Park in the small gravel area on the left side of the road. Bald Knob Ridge Trail provides access to some of this area's best birds. The trail goes through mature stands of spruce fir and is excellent for Veeries, Hermit Thrushes, Red-breasted Nuthatches, Brown Creepers, Winter Wrens, Blackburnian and Black-throated Green Warblers, Blue-headed Vireos, Golden-crowned Kinglets, Dark-eyed Juncos, Ruffed Grouse, and sometimes Red Crossbills. The trail is 2.8 miles, or 5.6 miles round-trip. When you reach Forest Service Road 472, you will need to turn around and retrace your steps to return to the parking lot.

Other key birds: *Summer:* Golden-crowned Kinglet; Hermit Thrush; Blue-headed Vireo. *Year-round:* Dark-eyed Junco.

Nearby opportunities: A little more than an hour away from Mount Mitchell State Park, Lake James State Park encompasses 605 acres along the southern shore of a 6,510-acre lake by the same name. Bald Eagles may be present year-round. Lake James State Park is located in Burke and McDowell Counties, 5 miles northeast of Marion on Highway 126. For additional information call the park office at (828) 652-5047 or visit http://ils.unc.edu/parkproject/ncparks.html.

Directions: Mount Mitchell State Park is located at milepost 355.4 on the Blue Ridge Parkway. From Asheville take the parkway north for approximately 33 miles. If coming from the east, the closest access is to take Highway 80 north from Marion until it intersects the parkway and then travel south on the parkway for about 10 miles.

Access: Ridge Junction Overlook is accessible by car.

Bathrooms: Mount Mitchell restaurant and concession area.

Hazards: Sudden changes in weather.

Nearest food, gas, and lodging: Restaurant at Mount Mitchell; nearest gas and lodging in Marion, approximately 25 miles.

Nearest camping: Mount Mitchell State Park. A nine-site campground (tents only) is open throughout the year, depending on the weather conditions during the colder months.

DeLorme map grid: Page 32, D1.

North Carolina Travel Map grid: D2.

For more information: Mount Mitchell State Park, 2388 State Highway 128, Burnsville, NC 28714; (828) 675-4611; www.ils.unc.edu/parkproject/visit/momi/home.html. Park is open from 8:00 A.M. to 6:00 P.M. November through February, 8:00 A.M. to 7:00 P.M. March and October, 8:00 A.M. to 8:00 P.M. April and September, 8:00 A.M. to 9:00 P.M. May through August. It is closed on Christmas Day.

35 Big Ivy, Craggy Gardens, and Balsam Gap

by Marilyn Westphal

County: Buncombe.

Habitats: Rich cove forest, hardwood and mixed pine-hardwood forests, areas of old growth with an extensive herbaceous layer, mountain streams.

Key birds: *Summer:* Veery; Black-throated Green, Black-throated Blue, Blackburnian, and Canada Warbler; Scarlet Tanager; Indigo Bunting; Rose-breasted Grosbeak; Red Crossbill. *Year-round:* Common Raven; Ruffed Grouse; Winter Wren; Red-breasted Nuthatch; Brown Creeper.

Best times to bird: Excellent from late April through early June. Birding remains good into later June at the higher elevations.

About this site:

Big Ivy refers to a kidney-shaped region in the Craggy Gardens that forms the headwaters of the Ivy River. This is a dense, cove-hardwood forest with a well-developed herbaceous layer, myriad wildflowers in spring, fast-flowing streams, numerous waterfalls, and areas of old growth forest. Elevation ranges from 2,200 feet to over 5,000 feet. Higher-elevation areas include sections in the spruce fir zone. Several hiking trails intersect the area, and they can also be interesting birding hikes, but it is extremely important to stay on the trail. It is easy to get lost in this dense forest. It is important to note that weather conditions can change greatly from lower to higher elevations. Where it may be warm and calm at lower elevations, it may be cool, foggy, and windy at higher elevations.

The Big Ivy area is one of the most beautiful areas of the Pisgah National Forest. This rich cove forest has sections of old growth and a thick herbaceous layer. The Coleman Boundary Road crosses streams in the upper part of the Ivy River watershed several times and passes several waterfalls. The range in elevation from the lower part of the road to the upper provides a variety of bird species.

Spring is the best time of year to visit the area when neotropical migrants are present. From Barnardsville take Dillingham Road to the entrance to the Pisgah National Forest. Along Dillingham Road, Yellow Warblers are fairly common. At 3.6 miles from the beginning of Dillingham Road, Stony Fork Road turns to the right. Stay on Dillingham Road another 1.3 miles to Coleman Boundary Road (Forest Road 74). At 0.4 mile from the entrance to the Coleman Boundary Road, you will see the picnic grounds on the right. Acadian Flycatchers and Northern Parulas are common in this area, and Wild Turkeys are possible. At the lower elevations for approximately 1 to 2 miles, listen and watch for Black-and-white and Black-throated Blue Warblers and Ovenbirds. Continue along Coleman Boundary

Road. From mid-April through May at the lower elevations, Red-eyed Vireos, Wood Thrushes, Ovenbirds, and Black-throated Blue, Black-throated Green, Black-and-white, and Blackburnian Warblers are common. About 6 to 7 miles up the road, at higher elevations, Canada Warblers, Veeries, Golden-crowned Kinglets, Red-breasted Nuthatches, Winter Wrens, Rose-breasted Grosbeaks, Dark-eyed Juncos, and Brown Creepers are present. Blue-headed Vireos, Scarlet Tanagers, and many species of woodpeckers may be seen at all elevations. Watch for Ruffed Grouse and Wild Turkeys crossing the road.

At 7.7 miles up the forest road there will be an old but well maintained gated logging road on the left. Note that there are other logging roads going off to the left before this as well, so it is important to watch mileage. This logging trail goes along under the edge of the Blue Ridge Parkway for about 7 miles and is a good birding trail. It is not a circular trail, so the distance you walk up the trail will be the distance you must hike back. Most of the warblers and high-elevation birds previously mentioned can be found along this rather open trail. Because it is more open, Chestnut-sided Warblers are possible. Dark-eyed Juncos frequently nest along the embankment at the edge of the road. Ruffed Grouse are often seen. Continue up the trail as far as you like, but if you are trying to cover the entire Big Ivy area in one day, it is best to turn back within a mile or so.

Return to Coleman Boundary Road and continue driving up the road for another 1.2 miles until the road ends at a parking area. There is a trail that leads off from the end of this parking area that goes about half a mile to Douglas Falls. This is another high-elevation trail with similar high-elevation species, although they may be more difficult to see because the trail is forested.

To continue birding the Big Ivy area, drive back down the Coleman Boundary Road to Dillingham Road and turn left at Stony Fork Road about 1.2 miles from the beginning of the pavement. Warblers are numerous on this road, with special-ties being Canada, Black-throated Blue, and Blackburnian. Also expect to find Rose-breasted Grosbeaks in good numbers. It is about 5 miles from the beginning of the gravel road to the entrance on the Craggy picnic area, which is located on the Blue Ridge Parkway. Black-throated Green and Canada Warblers and Blue-headed Vireos are fairly common in this area, and Red-breasted Nuthatches can often be heard. Dark-eyed Juncos are common at all of these higher-elevation areas.

Drive to the Blue Ridge Parkway and turn left. The road comes out near mile-post 370. Continue north on the Blue Ridge Parkway. The Craggy Gardens Visitor Center will be on the left after the tunnel. There is a trail that leads through the rhododendron thickets to the picnic area. Chestnut-sided Warblers are common in this area. Continue north on the Blue Ridge Parkway to the overlook just past milepost 360 at Balsam Gap. This area is in the spruce fir zone. At the parking area check the tops of the trees for Red Crossbills, as they can often be found passing over this area, especially from April through June. Pine Siskins also frequent the

The Red-breasted Nuthatch is a fairly common resident in the spruce fir zone of the mountains and is an irregular winter resident throughout the state. PHOTO. BILL DUYCK

area, and on most spring days Red-breasted Nuthatches can often be heard. The Big Butt Trail begins at the southern end of the parking area at this overlook, follows the ridgeline, and is moderate to easy for the first couple of miles. It offers excellent birding and wildflower opportunities. Where the trail begins there appear to be two trails, one on the left that goes downhill and another on the right that is more level. Take the left trail that goes downhill. The other trail is short and enters private property.

The Big Butt Trail goes through areas of mixed hardwood and spruce, fir, and hemlock where high-elevation species are common. Black-throated Green and Blackburnian Warblers are common along the trail as well as Blue-headed Vireos, Red-breasted Nuthatches, Veeries, Winter Wrens, and Golden-crowned Kinglets. Also expect Hairy Woodpeckers and Brown Creepers, and listen for Common Ravens, Pine Siskins, and Red Crossbills flying overhead. The trail continues for a total of about 7 miles and ends at the Cane River gap. It becomes more difficult after the first couple of miles, but for those who enjoy a vigorous hike, it can be very rewarding. You may surprise a few Ruffed Grouse and possibly even a black bear along the trail, so use caution. Yellow-bellied Sapsuckers have also been found during breeding season at some locations along this trail. It is not a loop trail, however, and it will be necessary to retrace your steps to return to the car. The quickest way to return to Asheville from this location is on the Blue Ridge Parkway.

Other key birds: *Summer:* Ovenbird; Wood Thrush; Acadian Flycatcher; Hermit Thrush. *Year-round:* Golden-crowned Kinglet; Pileated and Hairy Woodpecker; Dark-eyed Junco.

Nearby opportunities: Crabtree Meadows Recreation Area (Blue Ridge Parkway milepost 339.5) marks the last stretch of the parkway through the Blue Ridge Mountains before it turns westward into the Black, Craggy, Pisgah, and Balsam Mountains. The loop trail to the falls offers the possibility of a variety of spring migrants and breeding birds during the spring and early summer as well as excellent views of wildflowers.

Directions: This is a large area that can be approached from various directions. From Asheville take Highway 19/23 north to Barnardsville Road (Highway 197) and head toward Barnardsville. Drive about 7 miles. Turn right onto Dillingham Road, which is just after the Barnardsville post office on the left. Dillingham Road will continue as a paved road until it ends at the Coleman Boundary Road. In winter there may be a gate across the road if snow or ice prevents passage.

The area is also accessible from the Blue Ridge Parkway. This section of the Craggy Mountains includes the parkway from the Craggy Gardens picnic area to Balsam Gap.

Suggested trails off the Blue Ridge Parkway include Big Butt at the Balsam Gap overlook and Craggy Gardens. Also, from the Craggy Gardens picnic area, Coleman Boundary Road can be reached by following Stony Fork Road opposite the entrance to the picnic area down to Dillingham Road and turning right.

Access: Some areas are accessible by car, but the rugged trails are unsuitable for anyone who has difficulty walking.

Bathrooms: Public restrooms at Craggy Gardens Visitor Center and Craggy Gardens picnic area.

Hazards: Weather can change rapidly.

Nearest food, gas, and lodging: Restaurant available at Mount Mitchell, other services in the Asheville area.

Nearest camping: Mount Mitchell State Park, Blue Ridge Parkway milepost 355.4. The nine-site family campground is open throughout the year.

DeLorme map grid: Page 31, D7.

North Carolina Travel Map grid: D2.

For more information: Pisgah National Forest, P.O. Box 2750, 160A Zillicoa Street, Asheville, NC 28802; (828) 257–4200; www.cs.unca.edu/nfsnc.

36 Blue Ridge Parkway from Craven Gap to Lane Pinnacle

by Charlotte Goedsche

County: Buncombe.

Habitats: Mainly south-facing somewhat dry slope with mixed oak/hickory/poplar forest and some exposed rock

Key birds: *Summer:* Cerulean, Blackburnian, Worm-eating, Black-throated Blue, Kentucky, Chestnut-sided, and Hooded Warbler; American Redstart; Scarlet Tanager; Rose-breasted Grosbeak; Yellow-bellied Sapsucker. *Year-round:* Ruffed Grouse.

Best times to bird: Spring and summer for neotropical migrants and mountain breeding specialties. In winter the parkway is sometimes closed, especially the stretch northeast of the Weaverville exit.

About this site:

This section of the Blue Ridge Parkway generally runs along the southeastern slopes of the Great Craggy Mountains a few hundred feet below the ridgeline. The elevation of this section of the parkway varies from 3,080 feet to 3,880 feet. The best and most accessible birding sites in this area are Tanbark Ridge Overlook at milepost 376.8 and Bull Creek Valley Overlook at milepost 373.8. The overlooks and several vistas offer good treetop-level birding, but the vistas must be accessed on foot.

The best approach is to traverse this route from south to north, beginning by parking at the pull-off just off the parkway at Craven Gap. You may hear Cerulean or Black-and-white Warblers, Wood Thrushes, and Scarlet Tanagers from the pull-off. You can now either walk the Mountains-to-Sea Trail or bird the parkway. Walk to the parkway and turn left. Kentucky Warblers are possible in the woods near the Mountains-to-Sea trailhead or near the trailhead on the opposite (downhill) side of the parkway. Walk a few hundred feet along the downhill side of the road to the vista for Worm-eating and Hooded Warblers. Chestnut-sided Warblers often sing from the trees along the edge of the vista.

Drive north half a mile to Tanbark Ridge Overlook for another opportunity for most of the same species as at Craven Gap, although Kentucky and Worm-eating Warblers are less likely here. Continue 1.1 miles north, and park at the pull off at the Weaverville exit. Walk to the downhill side of the parkway for Blackburnian Warblers, Scarlet Tanagers, and Rose-breasted Grosbeaks in the canopy. Cerulean, Hooded, and Black-and-white Warblers are likely here as well.

For a somewhat different assemblage of birds, drive another 1.1 miles north, park at the pull off before the entrance to Tanbark Ridge Tunnel, and listen for Acadian Flycatchers from the creek after the second week of May, as well as Blue-headed Vireos and Black-throated Blue and possibly Black-throated Green War-blers. Bull Creek Valley Overlook at milepost 373.8 provides another good chance for Cerulean and Kentucky Warblers. This is the most reliable spot for Rose-breasted Grosbeaks on this section of the parkway. Wood Thrushes and Scarlet Tan-agers are fairly reliable here, as are Hooded and Chestnut-sided Warblers and Hairy, Pileated, and Red-bellied Woodpeckers. An area less than 0.2 mile north along the parkway is the most reliable for American Redstarts, Wood Thrushes, Scarlet Tan-agers, and Eastern Wood-Pewees. Listen and look for Blue-headed and Yellow-throated Vireos; Yellow-bellied Sapsuckers; and Cerulean, Blackburnian, and Black-and-white Warblers.

Lane Pinnacle Overlook at milepost 372.0 affords a safe opportunity to turn around for those wishing to return to Asheville. It also is worth checking out for breeding Northern Rough-winged Swallows, Dark-eyed Juncos, Scarlet Tanagers, Rose-breasted Grosbeaks, Yellow-billed Cuckoos, and Black-throated Blue War-blers.

The Mountains-to-Sea Trail between Craven Gap and Rattlesnake Lodge often allows closer views of birds, especially of Ovenbirds and Worm-eating Warblers,

Worm-eating Warblers are summer residents of dry slopes in the mountains. PHOTO: BILL DUYCK

than does the parkway. All the aforementioned birds between Craven Gap and Tanbark Ridge Tunnel can be seen or heard from the trail. If you don't have time to hike the entire distance (4.0 miles each way), you can either walk the Craven Gap–Ox Creek segment (1.8 miles) or the Ox Creek–Rattlesnake Lodge segment (2.2 miles). In either case, you can simply retrace your steps, or make a loop by returning to your point of departure via the parkway.

Other key birds: *Summer:* Black-and-white Warbler; Ovenbird; Wood Thrush; Blue-headed and Yellow-throated Vireo; Yellow-billed Cuckoo; Eastern Wood-Pewee; Acadian Fly-catcher; Northern Rough-winged Swallow. *Year-round:* White-breasted Nuthatch; Pileated and Hairy Woodpecker; Barred Owl; Ruffed Grouse; Wild Turkey.

Nearby opportunities: Bent Creek Recreation Area is located off the Blue Ridge Parkway immediately south of Asheville at the exit for Highway 191. During the summer months check the area for a variety of birds, including Yellow-throated Warblers and White-eyed and Yellow-throated Vireos. For additional information contact the Office of the National Forest Supervisor by calling (828) 257-4200.

Directions: This section of the Blue Ridge Parkway lies northeast of Asheville and stretches from Craven Gap at milepost 377.3 to Lane Pinnacle Overlook at milepost 372.0. This area is most quickly accessed by taking the parkway north from U.S. Highway 70 in east Asheville (Oteen). To reach US 70, use exit 7 on Interstate 240. The parkway can also be reached from U.S. Highway 74A just southeast of the I-40/I-240 interchange in east Asheville.

Access: Tanbark Ridge Overlook has a sidewalk that is wheelchair-accessible.

Bathrooms: Craggy Gardens picnic area at milepost 364.5; Folk Arts Center at milepost 382.0.

Hazards: Heavy traffic on the parkway during some seasons and holidays.

Nearest food, gas, and lodging: Restaurants can be reached by exiting the parkway at milepost 382.6 onto US 70 or exiting at milepost 377.4 (Craven Gap) and taking Webb Cove Road (the gravel road on the right) for 2.9 miles.

Nearest camping: Crabtree Meadows at milepost 340 has seventy-one tent and twenty-two trailer campsites. Asheville has a number of private campgrounds.

DeLorme map grid: Page 31, D6-7.

North Carolina Travel Map grid: D2.

For more information: Blue Ridge Parkway, (828) 298-0398; www.nps.gov/blri/pphtml/planyourvisit.html. Information, maps, and books are available at the Craggy Gardens Visitor Center at milepost 364.5 (open May though October) and the Folk Arts Center at milepost 382.0.

37 Max Patch Road and Environs

by Bob Olthoff

Counties: Haywood and Madison.

Habitats: Grassy balds, old fields, pastureland, hardwoods and mixed conifer-hardwood forests, streams, rhododendron thickets.

Key birds: *Summer:* Broad-winged Hawk; Ruffed Grouse; Great Crested and Least Flycatcher; Eastern Kingbird; Winter Wren; Veery; Golden-winged, Yellow, Chestnut-sided, Hooded, Canada, Black-throated Blue, Black-throated Green, Blackburnian, and Worm-eating Warbler; American Redstart; Grasshopper Sparrow; Scarlet Tanager; Rose-breasted and Blue Grosbeak.

Best times to bird: Early in the day from mid-April through June for migrants and breeding birds.

About this site:

Max Patch Road represents a mix of old fields, hillsides and pastureland, fast-moving streams, a grassy bald, and mixed forests, culminating in Max Patch Bald. Elevation ranges from 1,900 feet at the Interstate 40 end of Cold Springs Road to 4,629 feet at Max Patch Bald. Max Patch Road traverses Pisgah National Forest, and the Appalachian Trail crosses the road. Prior to reaching the national forest, the road winds its way through farmland, hilly pastureland, old fields, and second-growth forest. The unusual topography attracts an interesting variety of species. This is one of the best areas in western North Carolina to see Golden-winged Warblers and Least Flycatchers on the breeding grounds. A wide variety of other neotropical migrants can also be found. There are several trails; some of them are strenuous in sections. Contact the Pisgah National Forest for additional trail information. Please do not trespass on private property. Birds can be seen from Max Patch Road. Drive cautiously—this is a narrow, winding mountain road used frequently by logging trucks. The loop described subsequently covers 58 miles and takes several hours to bird thoroughly.

Take Highway 209 north 5 miles to Silver Cove Road. Go about 150 yards, and check the fields on the left for Willow Flycatchers, Eastern Kingbirds, and Orchard Orioles. Grasshopper Sparrows have nested on the hillside farther back on the left side. Continue 1 mile on Highway 209 to School House Road on the left and look for Yellow-breasted Chats, Blue Grosbeaks, and Willow Flycatchers. Travel an additional 5 miles (you will now be on Max Patch Road), and check the hillside on left for Golden-winged and Chestnut-sided Warblers. Travel 2 more miles to where the gravel road starts. Least Flycatchers, Yellow Warblers, and Common Yellowthroats are commonly found here. Continue an additional mile, and the next mile will be the heart of Golden-winged Warbler territory. Scan the hillside on the left and listen for Golden-winged, Yellow, and Chestnut-sided Warblers; American

Redstarts; Common Yellowthroats; Least Flycatchers; House Wrens; Northern Bobwhites; and Red-tailed and Broad-winged Hawks. Alder Flycatcher have also recently been present.

Continue for the next mile, stopping and listening for Golden-winged Warblers on the left. On the right listen and look for Black-throated Blue Warblers, Scarlet Tanagers, Rose-breasted Grosbeaks, and Eastern Wood-Pewees. The habitat through this area changes from mixed wood- and pastureland to mainly forest. Stop just before the next intersection. Worm-eating Warblers, American Redstarts, and Dark-eyed Juncos should be present. Next stop should be 2 miles up the road. Look for Rose-breasted Grosbeaks, Blue-headed Vireos, Dark-eyed Juncos, and Chestnut-sided, Black-throated Blue, and Blackburnian Warblers in this area. One mile farther up Max Patch Road, these same six species should be present, as well as Yellow-throated Vireos and possibly Broad-winged Hawks. For the next mile look for Great Crested Flycatchers and Northern Parulas, and watch for Ruffed Grouse near the road.

The next stop is the Max Patch trailhead for the Appalachian Trail, where the habitat changes to a large, open, grassy bald, and the bird species change as well.

The Yellow Warbler is a summer resident and one of the earliest to begin its fall migration.
PHOTO: HARRY SELL

Northern Bobwhites, Eastern Meadowlarks, Field Sparrows, and Barn and Northern Rough-winged Swallows are usually present. At 4,629 feet, this is the highest point on this trip. Continuing past Max Patch Bald down the other side of the mountain for about half a mile, there will be a small trout pond followed by a rhododendron thicket on the right. Birds generally present in this area in spring include Canada, Black-throated Blue, and Chestnut-sided Warblers; Winter and House Wrens; and Broad-winged Hawks. The trout pond is opened to the public and offers a nice spot to enjoy a break or picnic before proceeding.

At this point turn around and come back down Max Patch Road to Cold Springs Road on the right. Travel down Cold Springs Road about 1 mile and park where you can on the right. Listen for Hooded and Black-throated Green Warblers and Acadian Flycatchers. This is a narrow, winding road, so drive carefully and watch for logging trucks. Two miles farther down turn left into a picnic area and park in the parking area. The Harmon Den Horse Camp is located a bit farther along this road. The road to the camping area is often gated, but you can park along side the road and walk into the camp, where public restrooms are available.

Return to Cold Springs Creek Road and continue another mile. As you continue down this road, listen for Louisiana Waterthrushes and Acadian Flycatchers along the stream on the left. Three miles farther on you will reach I–40 at exit 7 (Harmon Den) and the end of the trip. The entire loop for this trip is 58 miles.

Other key birds: *Summer:* Yellow-billed Cuckoo; Yellow-throated and Blue-headed Vireo; Wood Thrush; Cedar Waxwing; Yellow-throated Warbler; Ovenbird; Louisiana Waterthrush; Common Yellowthroat; Yellow-breasted Chat; Eastern Meadowlark; Orchard Oriole.

Nearby opportunities: See Site 38.

Directions: From Asheville or coming west on I-40, take exit 24 to Highway 209. Take Highway 209 north to Ferguson's Store. Stay to the left at Ferguson's, which is Max Patch Road (Highway 209 will turn right). Bear right at the next fork (after new bridge) and continue on Max Patch Road. Coming east on U.S. Highway 19 or Highway 23/74, take the exit to Highway 209 North. An alternate route would be to take exit 15 (Fines Creek) from I-40 to Fines Creek Road to Max Patch Road. Exit 24 is recommended for birds such as Willow Flycatchers, Common Yellowthroats,

Yellow-breasted Chats, Blue Grosbeaks, and possibly Grasshopper Sparrows.

Access: Most of the area is accessible by car, but often pull offs are narrow.

Bathrooms: Harmon Den Horse Camp and Ferguson's Store.

Hazards: Narrow, winding roads.

Nearest food, gas, and lodging: The only food and gas available along the route is at Ferguson's Store. More services are available along I-40 and in Waynesville.

Nearest camping: Several private campgrounds in Waynesville.

DeLorme map grid: Page 30, C3.

North Carolina Travel Map grid: C2.

For more information: Pisgah National Forest, P.O. Box 2750, 160A Zillicoa Street, Asheville, NC 28802; (828) 257-4200; www.cs.unca .edu/nfsnc.

38 Lakes of the Southern Mountains

by Marilyn Westphal and Bob Olthoff

Counties: Buncombe, Henderson, and Haywood.

Habitats: Weedy marsh and three small to medium-size lakes surrounded by residential areas, parks, industry, and a conference center.

Key birds: *Winter:* Horned Grebe; Hooded and Red-breasted Merganser; Greater Scaup.

Migration: White Ibis; Snowy Egret; Little Blue Heron.

Best times to bird: Winter and early spring.

About this site:

Each lake has its own particular characteristics, and each has certain species that are more likely to be found. Lake Julian is about a mile long and about 0.3 to 0.5 mile wide. Compared with other lakes in the area, Lake Julian is much deeper and much warmer in winter (it never freezes over), since it is used as coolant for a coal-fired power plant. In fact, in winter it is best to bird this area in the afternoon because thick fog frequently shrouds the lake in the morning. Lake Junaluska, which is about the same size as Lake Julian, is mostly shallow. Lake Osceola is about 0.5 mile long and 0.1 mile wide. Lake Osceola is the smallest and the shallowest of the three lakes, with weeds at the surface in about a third of the lake. Nearby Four Seasons Marsh is not a lake but a weedy marsh that is about 0.3 mile long and 0.1 mile wide.

Visiting all of these sites in one day, while possible, may be a challenge since it is over 40 miles from Lake Osceola and Four Seasons Marsh in Hendersonville to Lake Junaluska near Waynesville. If, however, you want to visits all four sites in one trip, start with either Lake Junaluska or the Hendersonville lakes and marsh, and save Lake Julian for last because of the likelihood of fog in the mornings.

In winter the species on Lake Osceola most frequently found include the Pied-billed Grebe, Canada Goose, Mallard, Ring-necked Duck, Gadwall, and Ruddy Duck. Less frequent but still present at times during the winter are American Wigeons, Buffleheads, and Hooded Mergansers. When other ponds around are frozen, Northern Pintails and Green-winged Teal also appear. When most other smaller ponds and lakes are frozen, the sheer numbers of ducks and geese will often keep open the water in Lake Osceola's deepest cove. In March most of the ducks begin to leave, however. Horned Grebes appear at this time, and Ruddy Ducks can be seen in breeding plumage.

The marsh at Four Seasons Marsh provides good views of many ducks as well as some wading birds and other birds associated with water. The most common species found in winter include the Wood Duck and the Green-winged Teal, and

Members of the Carolina Bird Club looking for spring migrants at Beaver Lake Bird Sanctuary. PHOTO: KAREN BEARDEN

sometimes Gadwall, American Wigeon, Northern Pintail, and Hooded Merganser. This may be the best spot around to view large numbers of Wood Ducks. Four Seasons Marsh will freeze over in cold weather, but in late winter the area is very attractive to migrating dabbling ducks and may also attract migrating egrets and Sandhill Cranes. During postbreeding dispersal in June, Snowy and Great Egrets, Little Blue Herons, and White Ibises may also appear on the marsh. These are almost always immature birds.

Lake Junaluska is a good spot for viewing winter waterfowl. On an average winter day, Pied-billed Grebes, American Coots, Lesser Scaup, Hooded Mergansers, and Ring-necked and Ruddy Ducks should be seen. During inclement weather or immediately following, other birds that might be found are Horned Grebes, American Black and Wood Ducks, American Wigeons, Gadwalls, Northern Pintails, Green-winged Teal, Redheads, Buffleheads, and Red-breasted Mergansers. Others that appear from time to time are Common Loons, Blue-winged Teal, Northern Shovelers, Greater Scaup, and Common Goldeneyes.

Lake Julian is very different from the other lakes. It is much deeper, with few shallow areas. In late winter and early spring especially, you may find large numbers of waterfowl, particularly diving species. Rafts of Redheads, Common Loons, Pied-billed Grebes, Buffleheads, Ring-necked Ducks, Blue-winged Teal, and Lesser

Scaup occur, but these birds are more frequent some years than others. The lake also attracts Horned Grebes, Ring-billed and Bonaparte's Gulls, Forster's Terns, and on occasion Caspian Terns. Large numbers of Double-crested Cormorants often are seen on the transmission tower in the water near the dam. Migrating waterfowl rarely stay more than a day or two. The best time to check the lake is during poor weather when migrating waterfowl are forced down. Timing is everything at Lake Julian.

Other key birds: *Winter:* Pied-billed Grebe; American Coot; Bufflehead; American Black, Ring-necked, and Ruddy Duck; Gadwall; Blue-winged and Green-winged Teal; American Wigeon; Northern Pintail; Lesser Scaup; Northern Shoveler; Redhead; Common Gold-eneye. *Year-round:* Great Blue Heron; Wood Duck; Belted Kingfisher.

Nearby opportunities: Beaver Lake Bird Sanctuary consists of upland, wetland, and lakeside habitats in an urban setting. Elisha Mitchell Audubon Society, a chapter of National Audubon, owns half the ten-acre sanctuary. The sanctuary features a 3/8-mile boardwalk loop with two lake overlooks. Breeding species include Warbling Vireo, Yellow Warbler, and Orchard Oriole. Additional details for this site are available online at the Carolina Bird Club Web site, www.carolina birdclub.org.

Directions: To get to Lake Osceola, take Interstate 26 to the Hendersonville exit and drive into downtown Hendersonville on Four Seasons Boulevard (U.S. Highway 64). In about 2 miles, turn left on Church Street and drive 0.5 mile to Kanuga Road and turn right. Drive 0.2 mile to Willow Road just after the railroad tracks and turn right again. Take Willow Road about 0.9 mile and turn left on Lakeside. This will bring you down to the lake. To circle the lake, bear right at the fork and then turn left wherever possible on Lakeside.

To get to Four Seasons Marsh from Lake Osceola, return the way you came into town, except using King Street, the one-way mate of

Church Street. Turn right on Four Seasons Boulevard and follow the sign to I-26. Drive about 0.6 mile and pull over to the right on the shoulder of the road. The marsh will be below on the right.

Lake Junaluska is near Waynesville in Haywood County. From Asheville head west on Interstate 40 and take exit 27 onto U.S. Highway 19/23 heading west and drive 3.5 to 4.0 miles. Take exit 103 off of US 19/23 and head west on US 19. Travel about 1 mile. You will see Lake Junaluska on the right. Turn right at the main gate and follow North Lakeshore Drive to the swimming pool on Memory Lane. From the swimming pool return to North Lakeshore and continue following the road over a hill and across a bridge. Continue to follow the road, which becomes South Lakeshore Drive around the lake. This road will return you to US 19. If coming from points west on US 23/74, take the exit for U.S. Highway 276 north towards Maggie Valley. When US 276 intersects with US 19, turn right and travel 0.3 mile to the entrance to the Junaluska Assembly and turn left onto North Lakeshore Drive. Follow North Lakeshore Drive 0.2 mile to the swimming pool on Memory Lane.

Lake Julian is in southern Buncombe County. From Asheville take I-26 east to exit 37. Turn left onto Long Shoals Road and travel 1.1 miles. Turn right onto Overlook Road and travel 0.1 mile. The park entrance will be on the left. Drive into the park and walk along the edge from one bay to the other.

Access: All four sites are accessible by car.

Bathrooms: Only Lake Julian Park has restroom facilities.

Hazards: None.

Nearest food, gas, and lodging: Services are available near all four sites.

Nearest camping: Many private campgrounds and RV parks are located in and around Hendersonville, Asheville, and Maggie Valley.

DeLorme map grid: Lake Osceola and Four Seasons Marsh, page 53, C7; Lake Junaluska, page 52, A3; Lake Julian, page 53, B6.

North Carolina Travel Map grid: Lake Osceola and Four Seasons Marsh, D3; Lake Junaluska, C2; Lake Julian, C3.

For more information: Lake Julian Park, Buncombe County Parks and Recreation, 72 Gashes Creek Road, Asheville, NC 28805; (828) 684–0376; www.buncombecounty .org/governing/depts/parksalive/facilities/ parks/LakeJulian.htm.

39 Jackson Park

by Wayne K. Forsythe

County: Henderson.

Habitats: Creeks, ponds, bottomland, willow and alder thickets, meadows, mixed pine-hardwood, pines.

Key birds: *Migration:* Black-billed Cuckoo; Philadelphia and Warbling Vireo; Veery; Yellow, Chestnut-sided, Blackburnian, Canada, Hooded, Worm-eating, Connecticut, Mourning, Blue-winged, Black-throated Blue, Black-throated Green, Golden-winged, Kentucky, Cerulean, and Bay-breasted Warbler; American Redstart; Vesper Sparrow; Rose-breasted Grosbeak; Summer and Scarlet Tanager; Baltimore Oriole.

Best times to bird: Spring and fall migration, with fall migration being the best. Peak spring migration generally occurs the last week of April and first week of May. Peak fall migration generally occurs the second and third week of September.

About this site:

Jackson Park attracts an outstanding variety of migrating birds in spring and fall, the best times to bird in the park. To date, the park bird list contain a remarkable 196 species of birds. Jackson Park consists of 250 acres of diverse habitat located in downtown Hendersonville. The park is run by the Henderson County Parks and Recreation Department. There are several trails in the park.

Begin at the paved Nature Trail, which is about a quarter-mile loop. It proceeds through shrubby habitat as well as wet areas and meadows. This area can be good for warblers, flycatchers, tanagers, orioles, vireos, thrushes, sparrows, raptors, and waterbirds. The cut-through, a grass trail that connects a both ends to the Nature Trail, is very good for Orange-crowned Warblers in mid-October as well as Blue-winged and Golden-winged Warblers in mid- to late September. After finishing the Nature Trail, cross the road at the parking lot, make an immediate left, and walk about 75 yards to a trail on your right; you will see a chain between two posts. In fall this trail is excellent for Philadelphia Vireos, Rose-breasted Grosbeaks, tanagers, thrushes, and warblers. This trail, a grass path that runs alongside a creek through the shrubby habitat, was informally named the Warbler Trail after local birders saw twenty-two species of warblers one fall morning. Bird this trail to the end and return the way you entered.

When you reach the trailhead, make a left, walk about 75 yards, and make another left to what is known as the Bottomland Trail. This trail runs along a creek to the left and a mixed woodland slope on the right. This area can be good for thrushes, woodpeckers, and warblers. During migration Connecticut Warblers, Black-billed Cuckoos, and Gray-cheeked Thrushes have been seen here on many occasions. Follow this trail to an open field. Bird the edges on both sides where you exit the Bottomland Trail. Then, make a right and walk up the hill to the park office.

CITIZEN SCIENCE HELPS MONITOR BIRD POPULATIONS

Volunteers are the key to some of the most valuable bird monitoring programs in existence. Without "citizen science" efforts, our understanding of bird population numbers and trends would be lacking. Experienced birders play important roles in helping provide the information that allows natural resource managers to make decisions to help conserve birds and their habitats.

The Breeding Bird Survey (BBS), developed in 1965, is a long-term continental avian monitoring program designed to track the status and trends of the North American bird populations. The USGS Patuxent Wildlife Research Center and Canadian Wildlife Service jointly coordinate the BBS. During each breeding season, skilled participants collect bird population data along roadside survey routes. BBS data provide an index of population abundance that can be used to estimate population trends and relative abundances at various geographic scales. The U.S. Fish and Wildlife Service and Partners in Flight use BBS trends to help assess species management priorities.

Christmas Bird Counts (CBC) have been conducted by dedicated volunteers for more than one hundred years to help track winter bird trends. Participants include experienced birders who also help train beginning birders during the CBC surveys. CBC counts are held throughout North Carolina during winter and are an excellent way for birders to participate in a long-term monitoring effort.

Migration Monitoring is a Partners in Flight survey effort that helps gain information about birds during the spring and fall migration periods. Routes are run throughout the Southeast by experienced birders. In addition, one-day migration counts are held each spring and fall in North America. Volunteers also count birds at backyard feeders each winter via the Cornell Lab of Ornithology's Project FeederWatch program.

When facing the front of the administration building, walk to the yard area on the left side of the building. At the forest edge you will see Lieben's Loop Trail, a short loop trail through hardwoods. This trail is the best place in the park to look for Summer Tanagers and Red-headed Woodpeckers, which appear irregularly in spring and fall. In fall this trail is very reliable for Bay-breasted, Cape May, and Black-throated Green Warblers.

The Blue-winged Warbler is a rare to uncommon migrant throughout the state and sometimes an occasional breeder at a few sites in the mountains. PHOTO: HARRY SELL

Rails may also be seen in the park and are most often found along the ditch near the rear entrance of the park. When leaving the Nature Trail parking lot, turn right and drive about a quarter mile until you see the rear gate you would exit the park. Immediately before the gate, turn left and follow the pavement down the hill along the fence line a short distance. The road curves left. Just before the curve, park off to the right side. You will see a bench and an overgrown ditch, often full of water. Depending on water levels and vegetation, this area can be very good for Sora and Virginia Rail. The best times to find rails are in early November and in March and early April. This area can also be good for Willow Flycatchers.

Other key birds: *Summer:* Yellow-throated Vireo; Yellow-throated Warbler. *Winter:* Winter Wren. *Year-round:* Belted Kingfisher; Red-shouldered Hawk.

Nearby opportunities: Chimney Rock Park is a 1,000-acre private park. It is situated along the Blue Ridge escarpment, and the rocky cliffs rise from 1,000 feet on the valley floor to 2,200 feet on the mountain peaks. The cliffs look down to Lake Lure and into the Hickory Nut Gorge, and on a clear day the view from the top of the cliff is breathtaking. The unusual microclimates occurring in the park attract a wide variety of species, including Cerulean and Swainson's Warblers plus some that are more common at high elevations. Additional details for this site are available online at the Carolina Bird Club Web site, www.carolinabirdclub.org.

Directions: To access Jackson Park from Interstate 26, get off at exit 49B for Hendersonville. You will be on Four Seasons Boulevard (U.S. Highway 64 West). Go about 1 mile and you will see the signs for Jackson Park. At the traffic light at Harris Street, turn left onto Harris Street. Take Harris Street for about a quarter mile to the end and turn left onto Fourth Avenue. Continue about 0.2 mile to where you will enter Jackson Park. Drive across the small bridge and continue up the hill to the administration building parking lot on the left. To reach the park from downtown Hendersonville, head east on Fourth Avenue into Jackson Park and follow the previous directions.

Access: The paved Nature Trail is wheelchair-accessible.

Bathrooms: Two locations along the park road.

Hazards: None.

Nearest food, gas, and lodging: Hendersonville.

Nearest camping: Private campground and RV parks in the Hendersonville area.

DeLorme map grid: Page 53, C7.

North Carolina Travel Map grid: D3.

For more information: Henderson County Parks and Recreation, 801 Glover Street, Hendersonville, NC 28792; (828) 697–4884; www.hendersoncountync.org/depts/recreation.html. The official park hours are 7:00 A.M. to 11:00 P.M. daily.

40 Davidson River and Pink Beds

by Marilyn Westphal

County: Transylvania.

Habitats: Hardwood and mixed pine-hemlock forest, rocky cliffs, fast-flowing streams and waterfalls, rhododendron-laurel thickets.

Key birds: *Summer:* Yellow, Chestnut-sided, Black-throated Blue, Black-throated Green, Blackburnian, Worm-eating, Hooded, and Canada Warbler; American Redstart; Whip-poor-will; Broad-winged Hawk; Peregrine Falcon; Scarlet Tanager; Rose-breasted Grosbeak. *Winter:* Brown Creeper; Red-breasted Nuthatch; Winter Wren; Yellow-bellied Sapsucker. *Year-round:* Ruffed Grouse.

Best times to bird: Mid-April through early June during the morning hours.

About this site:

This section of the Pisgah National Forest provides outstanding spring birding in areas easily accessible by car as well as several excellent trails. Elevation ranges from 2,000 to over 4,000 feet and includes a variety of habitats. The area includes the Davidson River Campground, the Pisgah Forest Ranger Station, the Davidson River Fish Hatchery and Pisgah Center for Wildlife Education, Sliding Rock Recreational Area, Looking Glass Falls, Looking Glass Rock, the Cradle of Forestry in America, and the Pink Beds. There are also numerous pull-off areas and picnic tables along U.S. Highway 276 beside the Davidson River and Looking Glass Creek. Three gravel forest roads, one of which will be described in more detail later, lead away from US 276. Two of these roads return to US 276. Any of these roads can be a very rewarding experience, particularly for those who enjoy birding in the forest but may have difficulty with mountain hiking trails. These roads are usually in fair to good condition, but expect some rutted and washboard sections and some steep drop-offs along the edge. Drive carefully. For those who like to combine birding and hiking, numerous hiking trails begin at or cross US 276 or the other forest roads.

Neotropical migrants begin arriving in late March and early April. The Louisiana Waterthrush is generally the first warbler migrant to arrive, and the Davidson River is a popular breeding area for this species. Other early arrivals, such as Yellow-throated and Pine Warblers and Northern Parulas, can be found at low-elevation areas such as Sycamore Flats picnic area and the Pisgah Forest Visitor Center. By mid-April Blackburnian, Black-throated Blue, and Black-throated Green Warblers as well as Wood Thrushes, Whip-poor-wills, Broad-winged Hawks, and Red-eyed Vireos begin arriving and moving into the middle elevations. Blue-headed Vireos, generally a late March or early April arrival, begin moving into higher elevations by early to mid-April. By the end of April, almost all of the neotropical migrant breeding birds have arrived on their breeding areas at all elevations.

Follow US 276 from Highway 280. At 0.5 mile from the forest entrance on US 276, the Sycamore Flats picnic area will be on the left. This is a good spot for Northern Parulas, Yellow-throated Warblers, and Louisiana Waterthrushes. Continue west on US 276 to the Davidson River campground at 1.2 miles from the Highway 280, U.S. Highway 64, and US 276 intersection. The campground is sometimes a good area for spring and fall migrants. At 1.4 miles into the forest, the Pisgah Forest Visitors Center will be on the right. Check here for Northern Parulas and Pine and Yellow-throated Warblers.

At 5.2 miles from the forest entrance, the road to the Pisgah Forest Fish Hatchery and Pisgah Center for Wildlife Education turns off on the left. This quieter, less-traveled road offers easier birding than US 276, which it rejoins in about 8 miles, near the Cradle of Forestry. If you stay on US 276, you'll find numerous pull-offs and a parking area at Looking Glass Falls.

Peregrine Falcons may often be seen at the Davidson River and Devil's Courthouse sites.
PHOTO: HARRY SELL

Several pull-off areas along the road to the hatchery offer good birding. At 0.4 mile pull off at the trailhead for Looking Glass Rock Trail. Northern Parulas and Blackburnian Warblers are frequently seen in the treetops in the pines and hemlocks. Continue down the road to the fish hatchery. Along the way check for Blackburnian, Black-throated Green, Black-and-white, and Black-throated Blue Warblers, Northern Parulas, and Louisiana Waterthrushes. You may wish to visit the wildlife education center at this point.

Continue up the road, which becomes gravel and then divides. Take the right fork onto Forest Service Road 475B–Headwaters Road. This less-used road can be traveled at your leisure; stop as often as you like to listen for warblers, vireos, woodpeckers, Scarlet Tanagers, and Wood Thrushes. Watch for Broad-winged Hawks overhead. At 3.1 miles from the entrance to FS 475B, a small turnoff area on the right for a trail to the bottom of Looking Glass Rock provides a good place to stop and look for Peregrine Falcons. They have been breeding on the cliffs of Looking Glass Rock for several years and can sometimes be seen soaring. You may also choose to walk the trail toward Looking Glass Rock. This is a half-mile trail of medium difficulty.

Continue north on FS 475B, stopping occasionally to check for the many warblers, thrushes, and other songbirds that inhabit the mountain forest in spring. At about 6.7 miles from the beginning of FS 475B, the road will return to US 276. Turn left. In about 0.6 mile, you'll reach Forest Service Road 477, another quiet side road you may wish to explore. Otherwise, continue north (US 276 follows a northerly course after passing the fish hatchery) on US 276 for a short distance, passing the entrance to the Cradle of Forestry in America. About half a mile from FS 477, the Pink Beds will be on the right.

The Pink Beds is a large area of rhododendron, azalea, and mountain laurel thickets with rare mountain bogs and mixed hardwood-pine-hemlock forest. The trails that traverse the area are generally easy, although flooding caused by beaver dams in recent years has made some areas impassable at times. This area is ideal for Blackburnian Warblers, and the Pink Beds is one of the best places to find them in abundance. Black-throated Blue Warblers are common in the rhododendron thickets. Louisiana Waterthrushes can be found along the clear, cold headwaters of the South Mills River. Watch for Ruffed Grouse in the grassy areas and along the trails.

The complete Pink Beds Loop trail is 5 miles long and marked, although not always well, with orange blazes. You may choose to shorten the loop by taking the trail that cuts across the center of the loop. Be sure that you know which side of the loop you are on, however, as this cut-across trail continues for many miles in both directions, and you may end up far from the Pink Beds if you turn the wrong way. If you are going the correct way, you will cross a creek about halfway to the other side of the loop, and you should reach the other side of the loop in a few minutes. If you become confused, turn around and return the way you came.

Two more stops along US 276 may be of interest. The first at 0.4 mile past the Pink Beds, Forest Service Road 1206, Yellow Gap Road, turns off on the right. This gravel forest road can be fun to explore. It continues for about 13 miles, terminating at the Mills River Campgrounds on North Mills River Road. You can return to Interstate 26 this way by continuing down North Mills River Road for about 5 miles to Highway 280, turning left and continuing about 3 miles to I–26. This is a winding road with rough areas that cannot be traveled quickly and saves no time getting to I–26.

The last stop on US 276 is approximately 1.5 miles beyond the Pink Beds. This is the parking area at the end of the Buck Spring Trail. Cerulean Warblers have been reported on this trail about a quarter to a half mile from US 276. This trail continues for over 6 miles, passing the Pisgah Inn and ending at Buck Spring Gap. It is an excellent hiking trail for middle- to high–elevation species. A short distance farther up US 276, this half-day birding exploration ends at an entrance to the Blue Ridge Parkway. To return to Asheville you can either take the parkway northeast or return the way you came.

Other key birds: *Summer:* Ovenbird; Louisiana Waterthrush; Yellow-throated Vireo. *Winter:* Golden-crowned Kinglet; Hermit Thrush.

Nearby opportunities: The Hospital Fields area consists of county-owned old fields between Transylvania Community Hospital and Pisgah Forest Elementary School. The core of this site is a series of weedy fields threaded with ditches and wet hedgerows. The area has several intersecting paths of varying length, which provide easy walking and are wheelchair-accessible. Additional details for this site are available online at the Carolina Bird Club Web site, www.carolinabirdclub.org.

Directions: From I–26 exit 40 follow Highway 280 west toward Brevard. At the intersection of Highway 280, US 64, and US 276, turn right on US 276 west. The entrance to Pisgah National Forest is a few hundred yards west of the intersection. The highway continues about 15 miles to the Blue Ridge Parkway, the end of the trip described earlier, and then descends into Haywood County and Waynesville. The area can also be reached from the Blue Ridge Parkway by exiting at Wagon Road Gap. Coming from the north this exit is just past milepost 410. After exiting, turn left at the stop sign onto US 276 toward Brevard. From there follow the previous directions in "About this site" backward.

Access: Many of the stops are accessible by car.

Bathrooms: Restroom facilities are available at the Sycamore Flats picnic area, the visitor center, the Pisgah Center for Wildlife Education, and the Pink Beds.

Hazards: Gravel roads can be very muddy or slippery when wet.

Nearest food, gas, and lodging: Brevard.

Nearest camping: The Davidson River Campground is a full-facility campground. Many primitive Forest Service campsites are also available in the area.

DeLorme map grid: Page 53, C4.

North Carolina Travel Map grid: C3.

For more information: National Forest Service, Pisgah Ranger District, P.O. Box 2750, 160A Zillicoa Street, Asheville, NC 28802; (828) 257-4200; www.cs.unca.edu/nfsnc. The Cradle of Forestry in America is a fee area.

41 Devil's Courthouse and Black Balsam

by Marilyn Westphal and Reece Mitchell

Counties: Transylvania and Haywood.

Habitats: *At Black Balsam:* high-elevation (above 5,000 feet) mountain bald, partly grassy, partly heath, partly shrubby and low-growing spruce fir. *At Devil's Courthouse:* high-elevation rocky outcrop, 5,720 feet at the peak, spruce fir forest.

Key birds: *Summer:* Peregrine Falcon; North-ern Saw-whet Owl; Veery; Winter Wren; Brown Creeper; Rose-breasted Grosbeak; Chestnut-sided, Black-throated Blue, Black-throated Green, Blackburnian, and Canada Warbler; Alder Flycatcher. *Year-round:* Ruffed Grouse; Red-breasted Nuthatch; Pine Siskin; Common Raven.

Best times to bird: May through June.

About this site:

This area offers superb high-elevation birding, with excellent opportunities for some of the more sought-after species in North Carolina, including Peregrine Falcon, Alder Flycatcher, and Northern Saw-whet Owl. There are easy to moderate high-elevation hiking trails at Black Balsam and a short, more strenuous hike to the top of the rocky outcrop at Devil's Courthouse. Note that it can be much colder and windier at these high elevations, and they may be shrouded in fog while the lower elevations are clear and sunny. Be prepared for all types of weather.

Black Balsam has consistently been one of the best and most reliable spots in the mountains to get good looks at Alder Flycatchers, which usually arrive around the middle of May and can generally be heard singing through June. To get there take the Blue Ridge Parkway to milepost 420.2 and turn onto the road on the west side of the parkway that goes to Black Balsam. Drive this road for 1.2 miles to the end, stopping occasionally for Alder Flycatchers, mainly on the right side of the road. Other birds along this road include Common Yellowthroats, Golden-crowned Kinglets, Blue-headed Vireos, Canada and Chestnut-sided Warblers, and Cedar Waxwings.

When you reach the parking lot, park either at the end of the road or in the parking lot. The parking lot is often crowded on weekends because several excellent hiking trails cross here. As you face the restrooms from the paved parking area, look and listen for Alder Flycatchers in the shrubby area on your right. They often sing from the tops of the tallest shrubs or low trees. Walk along the right edge of the shrubby area down the wide trail. This is the Ivestor Gap Trail, which continues on several more miles. Alder Flycatchers and Common Yellowthroats can generally be found in this area. The high concentration of mountain ash and blueberries also make this a popular area for Cedar Waxwings. Golden-crowned Kinglets, Canada Warblers, Blue-headed Vireos, and chickadees are also commonly seen in this area.

Mark Johns (in the foreground with the hat) leads a North Carolina Partners in Flight bird identification workshop at Black Balsam. PHOTO: MARSHALL BROOKS

The chickadees may be Carolina–Black-capped hybrids, as they can often be heard singing the Black-capped song. Because they look alike, the only reliable way to verify such hybrids is through DNA testing.

Return to the parking lot and follow the Sam Knob Summit Trail past the restrooms and along the side of a spruce fir area where Red-breasted Nuthatches can be heard. Along the trail Canada and Chestnut-sided Warblers can often be found, and Veeries call from the hillside. The trail opens up and follows the bald up to the summit of Sam Knob. Hermit Thrushes occasionally have been heard along this trail, and Golden-winged Warblers have been seen. Back at the parking lot, the Flat Laurel Creek Trail, which goes off to the left, can also be productive for many high-elevation species. All of the trails from this parking lot can be fun hiking-and-birding trails. Most are very long, so you will need to plan for distance and time.

Devil's Courthouse is one of the most accessible locations in the mountains for viewing nesting Peregrine Falcons and hearing Northern Saw-whet Owls, which can sometimes be heard calling at dusk from the Devil's Courthouse parking area. The parking area is located at milepost 422.3 on the Blue Ridge Parkway. Elevation at the parking lot is 5,462 feet, and at the peak of Devil's Courthouse it is 5,720 feet. Peregrine Falcons have been nesting at this location since 1999. Nesting usually begins in February and egg laying in March. This part of the Blue Ridge Parkway, however, is often closed until April, making the area inaccessible by car.

The best time to view the young birds is during the first two weeks of June, when they will come onto the ledge to exercise their wings. They are also frequently fed during this period. To see the nest, park in the lot near the DEVIL'S COURTHOUSE sign and face the rocky outcrop directly in front of you. Look for a ledge that runs from left to right down the rock roughly parallel to the slope and about halfway between the trees on the left and the slope edge on the right. At the top of the ledge there is a rust-colored wash running down from the level area of the ledge. The nest is just above the wash. For best viewing a scope is advised.

Walk up the trail to the "courthouse" and look and listen for Golden-crowned Kinglets; Red-breasted Nuthatches; Winter Wrens; Brown Creepers; Blackburnian, Canada, and Black-throated Green Warblers; Blue-headed Vireos; and Pine Siskins.

The Northern Saw-whet Owl is regularly heard from Devil's Courthouse. April and May are generally the best months, but the bird may be heard at other times as well. The best opportunities to hear the owl is to arrive before dusk and stay through early evening. If you do not hear the owl calling from the courthouse area, try nearby parkway overlooks. The parking lot is also a great place to hear the Veery calling from the slopes and valleys at dusk.

Other key birds: *Summer:* Barred Owl; Golden-crowned Kinglet; Cedar Waxwing.

Nearby opportunities: For additional birding opportunities, see the site descriptions for Davidson River and Pink Beds (site 40) and Heintooga Spur Road and Nearby Parkway Locations (site 42).

Directions: Take the Blue Ridge Parkway to milepost 420.2 to reach Black Balsam and to milepost 422.3 to reach Devil's Courthouse. The best access points to the parkway that are near these areas are either Highway 215, which crosses the parkway at about milepost 423 and heads north, or Highway 276, which crosses at about milepost 412 and then heads south. Alternatively, you may get onto the parkway at any convenient entrance. Note that this section of the parkway is generally closed from the first snow until the end of March or early April.

Access: Some stops are accessible by car.

Bathrooms: Pit toilets at Black Balsam.

Hazards: Quickly changing weather conditions.

Nearest food, gas, and lodging: Food and lodging at the Pisgah Inn at Blue Ridge Parkway milepost 409; the Pisgah Inn is closed in winter. No gas available on this section of the parkway. All services available in Waynesville.

Nearest camping: Balsam Mountain Campground, with forty-two sites, on Heintooga Road Spur at Blue Ridge Parkway milepost 458.

DeLorme map grid: Page 52, C4.

North Carolina Travel Map grid: C3.

For more information: National Park Service, 199 Hemphill Knob Road, Asheville, NC 28801; (828) 298-0398; www.nps.gov/blri/index.htm. National Forest Service, Pisgah Ranger District, 1001 Pisgah Highway, Pisgah Forest, NC 28768; (828) 257-4200; www.cs.unca.edu/nfsnc.

42 Heintooga Spur Road and Nearby Parkway Locations

by Bob Olthoff

Counties: Haywood, Jackson, and Swain.

Habitats: Spruce fir and hardwood forests.

Key birds: *Summer:* Broad-winged Hawk; Ruffed Grouse; Black-billed Cuckoo; Northern Saw-whet Owl; Yellow-bellied Sapsucker; Least Flycatcher; Black-capped Chickadee; Brown Creeper; Winter Wren; Veery; Chestnut-sided, Black-throated Blue, Black-throated Green, Blackburnian, Hooded, Worm-eating, and Canada Warbler; American Redstart; Scarlet Tanager; Rose-breasted Grosbeak; Red Crossbill; Pine Siskin. *Year-round:* Common Raven; Red-breasted Nuthatch.

Best times to bird: From mid-April until the middle of October. Access to the site and the Blue Ridge Parkway in this area are closed during winter months.

About this site:

The Heintooga Spur Road intersects with the Blue Ridge Parkway around milepost 458. The Heintooga road travels first through parkway lands and then through the Great Smoky Mountains National Park and ends in 9 miles at the Balsam Picnic Area. Several trails in the Smoky Mountains section provide good birding hikes. The trailheads for the Rough Fork Trail and the Hemphill Bald Trail lead off at Polls Gap. About 2 miles beyond the signposted Black Camp, the Flat Creek Trail can be found on the left side of the road. It follows Flat Creek to its headwaters in the picnic grounds at the end of the Heintooga Spur Road. For those who prefer hiking to driving, the same species found along the road can be found along the trail.

Heintooga Spur Road, which includes spruce fir forests, provides a good mix of species found at higher elevations (3,800 to 5,400 feet) in North Carolina. Roadside stops and a bit of walking should result in a productive morning's birding. Approximately 0.1 mile after entering the road, stop at the gravel road on the right. Walk down this road for Red-breasted Nuthatches, Golden-crowned Kinglets, Blue-headed Vireos, and Blackburnian, Black-throated Blue, and Black-throated Green Warblers. Return to your car and continue on Heintooga Spur Road for 2 miles to Mile High Overlook (elevation 5,250 feet) and check for Common Ravens, Broad-winged Hawks, Black-billed Cuckoos, Northern Parulas, Chestnut-sided Warblers, American Redstarts, Ovenbirds, Scarlet Tanagers, and Rose-breasted Grosbeaks. As you drive along the road, watch for Ruffed Grouse and Wild Turkeys. Also watch for Cooper's and Red-tailed Hawks.

Drive 2 more miles to Black Camp Gap. Walk the field and the road. Summer species include Black-capped Chickadee; Least Flycatcher; Eastern Wood-Pewee;

House Wren; Veery; Black-billed Cuckoo; Northern Parula; Chestnut-sided, Black-throated Blue, and Black-and-white Warblers; Scarlet Tanager; and Rose-breasted Grosbeak. Shortly after Black Camp Gap, the road enters the national park. Drive another mile, and park on the left when you see cliffs on the right. This is an excellent location for Canada Warblers, Scarlet Tanagers, and Rose-breasted Grosbeaks. Other likely finds are Dark-eyed Juncos and Blue-headed Vireos.

Drive 2 miles farther up the road to Polls Gap, which starts the major spruce fir portion of the trip and provides one of the few locations in western North Carolina where Hermit Thrushes can be found during the breeding season. This loca-

The Yellow-bellied Sapsucker is an uncommon summer resident in the southern Appalachians and an uncommon winter resident throughout much of the state. PHOTO: BILL DUYCK

tion also offers the possibility of birds infrequently found breeding in the state: Yellow-bellied Sapsuckers, Least Flycatchers, Black-capped Chickadees, Brown Creepers, Veeries, Red Crossbills, and Pine Siskins. Also possible are Blue-headed Vireos; Common Ravens; Cedar Waxwings; Northern Parulas; Chestnut-sided, Black-throated Blue, Black-throated Green, Blackburnian, and Hooded Warblers; Scarlet Tanagers; and Rose-breasted Grosbeaks. For best results for this area, walk the road about half a mile in each direction from Polls Gap. Watch out for traffic on the road. Watch for Red Crossbills, Pine Siskins, Brown Creepers, Golden-crowned Kinglets, Blue-headed Vireos, Red-breasted Nuthatches, and Black-capped Chickadees along the road, and when possible, pull off and listen for Winter Wrens. Polls Gap is the trailhead for nine trails. If your are interested in birding any of the trails, check with the national park for trail information.

Two miles from Polls Gap, stop at the Balsam Mountain Campground for Red Crossbills, Pine Siskins, and Least Flycatchers. Northern Saw-whet Owls have been heard calling, in the spring, from the campground area. Heintooga Spur Road is considered a good location to hear or encounter other owls, including Eastern Screech-Owls, Great Horned Owls, and Barred Owls. A mile beyond the campground is the Balsam Picnic Area. Walking along the road should provide good views of Blue-headed Vireos, Black-capped Chickadees, Red-breasted Nuthatches, Golden-crowned Kinglets, Blackburnian and Chestnut-sided Warblers—and possibly Red Crossbills and Pine Siskins.

From here return to the parkway and turn right. Near milepost 459 pull off at Lickstone Gap Overlook. Look and listen for Black-billed Cuckoos; Yellow-bellied Sapsuckers; Least Flycatchers; Eastern Wood-Pewees; Yellow-throated, Blue-headed, and Red-eyed Vireos; Common Ravens; Brown Creepers; Winter Wrens; Veeries; Northern Parulas; Canada, Chestnut-sided, Black-throated Blue, Blackburnian, and Hooded Warblers; Scarlet Tanagers; and Rose-breasted Grosbeaks. Look also for these species at Bunches Bald Overlook slightly farther south and at Jenkins Ridge, 2 miles farther on. Watch for Broad-winged, Cooper's, and Sharp-shinned Hawks.

At Big Witch Gap, about a mile farther south, take the road on the right for about 200 yards and park. *Note:* Road conditions beyond that point can be extremely hazardous. Walk down the road on the left. Likely birds include Canada, Black-throated Blue, and Chestnut-sided Warblers. Watch for Black-billed Cuckoos and Yellow-bellied Sapsuckers. Take the trail up the hill for American Redstarts, Common Ravens, and Scarlet Tanagers. For this trip's final stop, return to the Blue Ridge Parkway and continue south a short distance to Big Witch Overlook. Check for Common Ravens, Least Flycatchers, Scarlet Tanagers, and Rose-breasted Grosbeaks. From here you can either go north on the parkway or exit at Soco Gap for Cherokee.

Other key birds: *Summer:* Cooper's Hawk; Hermit Thrush; Cedar Waxwing.

Nearby opportunities: Additional birding spots include parkway overlooks south of Heintooga Spur Road at Lickstone Ridge, Bunches Bald, Jenkins Ridge, and Big Witch Gap.

Directions: Take the Blue Ridge Parkway to milepost 458. Heintooga Spur Road, Black Camp Gap, is on the right.

Access: Many of the stops along this route are accessible by car.

Bathrooms: At Balsam Mountain Campground.

Hazards: Do not stray away from the trail. It is easy to become lost, and reception for cell phones is not dependable.

Nearest food, gas, and lodging: Maggie Valley and Cherokee.

Nearest camping: The National Park Service Balsam Campground, 8 miles from the parkway, has forty-six sites for tents and campers.

DeLorme map grid: Page 52, A1.

North Carolina Travel Map grid: C2.

For more information: Blue Ridge Parkway, National Park Service, 199 Hemphill Knob Road, Asheville, NC 28803-8686; (828) 456–9530; www.nps.gov/blri. Great Smoky Mountains National Park, 107 Park Headquarters Road, Gatlinburg, TN 37738; (828) 497–1900; www.nps.gov/grsm.

43 Stecoah Gap

by Simon Thompson

County: Graham.

Habitat: Cove forest.

Key birds: *Summer:* Golden-winged, Cerulean, Black-throated Green, Worm-eating, Kentucky, Black-throated Blue, Blackburnian, Hooded, and Chestnut-sided Warbler; American Redstart; Scarlet Tanager; Rose-breasted Grosbeak; Indigo Bunting. *Year-round:* Ruffed Grouse.

Best times to bird: Summer and migration.

Carolina Bird Club field-trip participants walk along a Forest Service road at Stecoah Gap.
PHOTO: KAREN BEARDEN

About this site:

Stecoah Gap is a cove forest at an elevation of 3,200 feet. The forest understory is mostly ephemeral herbs and wildflowers. The main trail is an easy walk along the Stecoah Gap Forest Service Road. In late April or early May, this area can produce a list that includes a large variety of warblers including Golden-winged, Cerulean, and Worm-eating Warblers. Scarlet Tanagers, Rose-breasted Grosbeaks, Indigo Buntings, and Wood Thrushes are present.

Other key birds: Black-and-white Warbler; Ovenbird; Blue-headed, Yellow-throated, and Red-eyed Vireo; Wood Thrush.

Nearby opportunities: Tulula Bog is the last remaining swamp-forest wetland complex in Graham County. Additional details for this site are available online at the Carolina Bird Club Web site, www.carolinabirdclub.org.

Directions: Stecoah Gap is situated where the Appalachian Trail crosses Highway 143, south of Fontana Lake and the Great Smoky Mountains National Park and 7 miles east of Robbinsville. A small parking area with a picnic table can accommodate about six cars. Park here and follow the APPALACHIAN TRAIL signs on the same side of the road as the parking area. The Forest Service road begins at the parking area.

Access: Not wheelchair-accessible.

Bathrooms: No facilities available at the site.

Hazards: None.

Nearest food, gas, and lodging: Robbinsville.

Nearest camping: Several private campgrounds in Robbinsville.

DeLorme map grid: Page 50, A2.

North Carolina Travel Map grid: D3.

For more information: Nantahala National Forest, U.S. Forest Service, (828) 257-4200.

44 Joyce Kilmer Memorial Forest and Cherohala Skyway

by Simon Thompson

County: Graham.

Habitats: Cove forests.

Key birds: *Summer:* Yellow-bellied Sapsucker; Veery; American Redstart; Kentucky, Black-throated Green, Black-throated Blue, Chestnut-sided, Canada, Hooded, and Swainson's Warbler; Brown Creeper; Winter Wren; Rose-breasted Grosbeak. *Year-round:* Common Raven.

Best times to bird: Summer; fall and spring migration.

About this site:

It is easy to spend a whole day in this area, starting out early by walking the trails at Joyce Kilmer Memorial Forest and then spending the rest of the day climbing high into the forests along the Cherohala Skyway. The skyway is a spectacular highway that winds through 15 miles of the North Carolina mountains, cresting above 6,000 feet before descending into the forests of Tennessee. The road traverses both the Cherokee and Nantahala National Forests, hence the name "Chero-hala." Several well-marked pullouts offer spectacular views, and several trails lead into the surrounding forests. Joyce Kilmer Memorial Forest is a 3,800-acre area of mainly cove hardwood forest with sections of magnificent old growth. Some trees are more than 20 feet in circumference and over 100 feet tall. The forest is part of the much larger Joyce Kilmer–Slickrock Wilderness Area. The most visited part of the Kilmer forest is the "figure 8" trail, which begins at the parking area. It is an easy trail, although there are many steps to climb. This 2-mile trail crosses Little Santeetlah Creek, winds up through rhododendron thickets, and eventually reaches the area of big trees.

At the lower elevations of the Cherohala Skyway look for a variety of warbler species including Black-and-white, Worm-eating, Kentucky, Black-throated Green, Black-throated Blue, Hooded, and Chestnut-sided Warblers; American Redstarts; and Ovenbirds; as well as Red-eyed and Yellow-throated Vireos. As you drive farther up the skyway, higher-elevation species begin to appear, including Rose-breasted Grosbeaks, Blue-headed Vireos, Canada and Blackburnian Warblers, Veeries, and even Yellow-bellied Sapsuckers, which probably nest in the higher reaches. Northern Rough-winged Swallows nest in the road embankments, and it is common to see Common Ravens overhead.

Due to the size of the trees in Joyce Kilmer Memorial Forest—the canopy is more than 100 feet above the forest floor—the birding can be a little challenging. Warblers are common, especially Ovenbirds and Blackburnian, Black-throated

Green, Black-throated Blue, Black-and-white, and Hooded Warblers. The songs of Wood Thrushes and Winter Wrens echoing through the cathedral-like atmosphere are breathtaking, and each stream seems to have a pair of Acadian Flycatchers. Cerulean and Swainson's Warblers have both been found within the forest, although they are not to be expected. Both Worm-eating Warblers and Louisiana Waterthrushes are more easily found along the access road, before you get to the Joyce Kilmer parking lot. Some birds more typical of higher elevations can also be found within this forest, especially Winter Wrens, Golden-crowned Kinglets, and Red-breasted Nuthatches.

The Swainson's Warbler is a local breeder in swamp forests of the Coastal Plain and in rhododendron and laurel thickets in the mountains. PHOTO: HARRY SELL

Other key birds: *Summer:* Blue-headed Vireo; Acadian Flycatcher; Wood Thrush; Golden-crowned Kinglet; Louisiana Waterthrush; Ovenbird.

Nearby opportunities: See Site 43.

Directions: From Robbinsville the approach to both sites involves taking U.S. Highway 129 to the north and in 1.5 miles turning left on Highway 143 (Massey Branch Road). Go about 5 miles to a stop sign. Turn right onto Kilmer Road and continue on Highway 143 for about 7.3 miles, to the top of Santeetlah Gap and the junction with the Cherohala Skyway. To go to the Joyce Kilmer Memorial Forest, bear right and go another 2.5 miles to the entrance. Turn left into the entrance. It is about half a mile to the parking area.

Access: Hiking trails at Joyce Kilmer are not accessible for persons who have difficulty walking.

Bathrooms: Restrooms are available at several locations along the Cherohala Skyway, although there are no gas stations or other amenities. Note that the skyway is popular with motorcyclists, and birders may want to avoid it on busy holidays or weekends.

Hazards: None.

Nearest food, gas, and lodging: Gas, food, and lodging can be found in Robbinsville, and lodges are located around Lake Santeetlah.

Nearest camping: Lake Santeetlah.

DeLorme map grid: Page 50, A2.

North Carolina Travel Map grid: B3.

For more information: Nantahala National Forest, U.S. Forest Service, (828) 257–4200; www.main.nc.us/graham/hiking/joycekil.html.

Appendix A: North Carolina Specialty Birds

This section presents information on the seasonal distribution of 122 North Carolina bird specialties. Specialties are considered to be those species that are frequently sought by birder-watchers. Species are arranged in their taxonomic, or phylogenic, order as commonly found in current editions of most North American and Eastern United States field guides for birds.

Snow Goose: Locally very common during winter at sites mostly in the northern coastal region. Large numbers at Mattamuskeet National Wildlife Refuge [NWR] (Site 5).

Ross's Goose: Rare winter visitor, usually in Snow Goose flocks at Pea Island NWR (Site 7) and Mattamuskeet NWR (Site 5).

Brant: Found in the winter at Cape Hatteras National Seashore (Site 8) and Ocracoke Island (Site 10). Usually present in several large flocks in Pamlico Sound near Ocracoke and Hatteras Inlets.

Tundra Swan: Locally common to very common during winter at several northern coast and northern Coastal Plain locations such as Mattamuskeet NWR (Site 5). Also present, often in good numbers, at Alligator River NWR (Site 6) and Pea Island NWR (Site 7).

Eurasian Wigeon: Rare but annual winter visitor to several Coastal Plain sites such as Mattamuskeet NWR (Site 5) and Pea Island NWR (Site 7). Easiest to see at North Pond, Pea Island, during fall and early winter.

Canvasback: Locally fairly common to common winter resident at several locations along the coast and in the Coastal Plain, such as Mattamuskeet NWR (Site 5) and western Pamlico Sound. Less common at several inland lakes and reservoirs.

Greater Scaup: Rare to uncommon winter visitor at lakes from the coast to the mountains, for example, Sunset Beach (Site 1), Falls Lake State Recreation Area (Site 19), Riverbend Park (Site 27), and Lake Junaluska in the Lakes of the Southern Mountains (Site 38).

Harlequin Duck: Rare in winter at several coastal sites, usually near bridges, piers, and jetties. Not found every year in the state.

Long-tailed Duck: Rare to locally uncommon winter visitor in the state. Good numbers tend to be found on Pamlico Sound most years. Often found in small numbers at a few coastal locations such as Fort Fisher State Recreation Area (Site 2), Pea Island NWR (Site 7), and Cape Hatteras National Seashore (Site 8). Very rare visitor to inland reservoirs during winter.

Hooded Merganser: Fairly common to common winter resident throughout the state.

Common Merganser: Rare breeder in parts of North Carolina. Rare to occasional winter visitor through the state, with most birds being found at inland sites such as Jordan Lake State Recreation Area (Site 16).

Ruffed Grouse: Permanent resident in the mountains, most often found at middle to higher elevations. Secretive nature of species masks its true abundance. Best method to see this bird involves driving mountain roads very early, before usual traffic hits the roads.

Red-throated Loon: Fairly common to common during the winter at most coastal sites, for example, Sunset Beach (Site 1), Fort Fisher State Recreation Area (Site 2), Pea Island NWR (Site 7), and Cape Hatteras National Seashore (Site 8). Large numbers are often found just off the beaches in the southern coastal areas.

Horned Grebe: Fairly common winter resident of coastal areas, for example, Sunset Beach (Site 1) and Cape Hatteras National Seashore (Site 8). Also fairly common to common inland on the reservoirs, for example, Jordan Lake State Recreation Area (Site 16), Greensboro Municipal Reservoirs (Site 25), and Salem Lake (Site 26), with a few in the western part of the state; see Lakes of the Southern Mountains (Site 38). Usually more common throughout during migration.

Red-necked Grebe: During most years is a rare but regular winter visitor in small numbers throughout the state. Some years, usually when the lakes to the north freeze, it can be locally uncommon for brief periods of time. During these times, usually late winter to early spring, it can be found along the coast and at inland reservoirs.

Black-capped Petrel: Uncommon to common, almost always out in the Gulf Stream from spring through late fall. Much less common during winter and early spring; see Gulf Stream Pelagic Birding (Site 9).

Bermuda Petrel: Very rare late spring to early summer and early fall visitor. Found annually since 1994, most likely due to some increase in its population and the increased number of trips searching for it; see Gulf Stream Pelagic Birding (Site 9).

Fea's Petrel: An annual, rare spring to fall visitor in very small numbers, usually out in the Gulf Stream. Most records come from the late spring to early summer period; see Gulf Stream Pelagic Birding (Site 9).

Herald Petrel: Annual visitor, with the best period of occurrence being from late spring to early fall. Also usually out in the Gulf Stream, this species has been found regularly in small numbers, especially on trips in late May and early June and in August; see Gulf Stream Pelagic Birding (Site 9).

Manx Shearwater: Found regularly in small numbers on winter and spring migration pelagic trips. Usually found inshore of the Gulf Stream in the cooler water; see Gulf Stream Pelagic Birding (Site 9).

Audubon's Shearwater: Common during the warmer months during Gulf Stream Pelagic Birding (Site 9). The best numbers are found from summer into early fall.

White-faced Storm-Petrel: Very rare, but probably annual summer to early fall visitor offshore. Usually found singly, offshore in areas north of Cape Hatteras. The peak period of occurrence seems to be late August through September. See Gulf Stream Pelagic Birding (Site 9).

Leach's Storm-Petrel: Uncommon to fairly common in spring and fall migration; see Gulf Stream Pelagic Birding (Site 9).

Band-rumped Storm-Petrel: Uncommon to fairly common during summer; see Gulf Stream Pelagic Birding (Site 9). Numbers of this species tend to peak during the summer.

White-tailed Tropicbird: An irregular rare summer visitor. Some years can be much easier to find than others. The best times tend to be late spring to late summer; see Gulf Stream Pelagic Birding (Site 9).

Masked Booby: Rare summer visitor offshore, with most sightings during early summer to early fall; see Gulf Stream Pelagic Birding (Site 9).

Brown Pelican: Commonly seen year-round along the coast and can be very common in the summer at areas near the several breeding sites. Numbers can be much reduced along the northern coast during times of extended cold weather.

Great Cormorant: Rare to uncommon visitor in winter at a few sites along the coast. Check areas with tall channel markers and pilings at inlets, sounds, rivers, and some areas with piers and pilings along the beaches; see Fort Fisher State Recreation Area (Site 2).

Anhinga: Common summer resident along the southern coastal area and at select Coastal Plain sites such as the area around the Roanoke River (Site 12). Most birds leave for the winter, but a few remain at some areas near the coast from Greenville Area (Site 13) south. Sunset Beach (Site 1) and Fort Fisher State Recreation Area (Site 2) and nearby Greenfield Lake are good bets. Also found at Alligator River National Wildlife Refuge (Site 6) on Whipping Creek Lake, which represents one of the northernmost breeding sites.

Least Bittern: Localized and uncommon summer resident, with most being found along the coast and some Coastal Plain sites. Rarely found in Piedmont and Mountains. Primarily found in freshwater and brackish marshes and tidal creeks; see Fort Fisher State Recreation Area (Site 2), Mattamuskeet National Wildlife Refuge (Site 5).

Snowy Egret: Uncommon to common year-round resident in coastal areas, although less common in winter; a regular postbreeding dispersant to inland areas.

Little Blue Heron: Uncommon to fairly common year-round along the coast. Winter populations are much reduced, especially in the northern coastal areas. It is also a regular post-breeding wanderer to inland areas of the state, with some even ranging to the mountains.

Reddish Egret: Localized rare post-breeding wanderer to select coastal locations, usually from late June through October. Often found at inlets at sites such as Sunset Beach (Site 1), Fort Fisher State Recreation Area (Site 2), and Ocracoke Island (Site 10).

White Ibis: Fairly common to common year-round resident along the coast, with fewer birds present in the northern areas during winter. During postbreeding is a regular but uncommon wanderer to inland portions of the state as far west as the mountains.

Glossy Ibis: Uncommon to fairly common summer resident along the coast in shallow water and marshes; much rarer in winter. Also some rarely found as inland wanderers during the warmer months; see Mattamuskeet NWR (Site 5), Pea Island NWR (Site 7), and Ocracoke Island (Site 10).

Wood Stork: Localized summer visitor to a few southern coastal and outer Coastal Plain areas, usually from June into October; also, a rare migrant and wanderer across the rest of the state. Easily the best location for finding the species is Sunset Beach (Site 1).

Swallow-tailed Kite: Rare but regular spring migrant in late April to June at coastal sites such as Cape Hatteras National Seashore (Site 8), Croatan National Forest (Site 4), and Green Swamp Preserve and Lake Waccamaw State Park (Site 3).

Mississippi Kite: Uncommon summer resident at several southern Piedmont and inner Coastal Plain areas. Breeding evidence found very locally a few sites. The best concentrations are along the Roanoke River (Site 12) and Howell Woods Environmental Learning Center (Site 14).

Bald Eagle: Locally uncommon at several coastal locations and throughout the Coastal Plain and Piedmont. Best opportunities for seeing are at Mattamuskeet NWR (Site 5), Jordan Lake State Recreation Area (Site 16), and Falls Lake State Recreation Area (Site 19).

Broad-winged Hawk: Locally uncommon summer resident in the Piedmont at Falls Lake State Recreation Area (Site 19), Occoneechee Mountain State Park (see Eno River State Park, Site 20), Charlotte-Mecklenburg Area (Site 24), and Riverbend Park (Site 27). Fairly common during summer throughout the mountains at the following sites: Amphibolite Mountains (Site 30), Max Patch Road and Environs (Site 37), Davidson River and Pink Beds (Site 40), and Heintooga Spur Road (Site 42).

Rough-legged Hawk: Rare and irregular winter visitor throughout the state. Lately has been regular at Alligator River NWR (Site 6).

Golden Eagle: Rare winter visitor throughout the state. Most reports come from Coastal Plain and Mountains locations, with Piedmont sightings being very unusual.

Peregrine Falcon: Winter resident along the coast from Fort Fisher State Recreation Area (Site 2) north to Pea Island NWR (Site 7). Summer resident, locally in the mountains, for example, Linville Gorge (Site 32), Davidson River (Site 40), and Devil's Courthouse (Site 41). Regular migrant throughout, with most numbers being found along the coast during the fall.

Yellow Rail: Very secretive winter resident in fields and freshwater to brackish marshes in the outer Coastal Plain and along the coast. Good sites for searching for this species include Mattamuskeet NWR (Site 5), Alligator River NWR (Site 6), and Cape Hatteras National Seashore (Site 8).

Black Rail: Year-round resident in freshwater to brackish marshes along the coast, with many birds withdrawing southward during the winter. Another extremely secretive species, most reports involve heard birds. Some good locations include the marshes along Pamlico Sound and along the central coast.

Purple Gallinule: Declining, locally rare summer resident in the southeastern Coastal Plain freshwater rice fields, marshes, and vegetated ponds. Some

are apparently still in the Sunset Beach (Site 1) mainland area.

Wilson's Plover: Uncommon summer resident along the coast on the upper beaches from Sunset Beach (Site 1) to Ocracoke Island (Site 10).

Piping Plover: Local with limited breeding populations being found at several sites along the coast, for example, Pea Island NWR (Site 7), Cape Hatteras National Seashore (Site 8), and Ocracoke Island (Site 10). Small numbers found along the coast, often at inlet areas throughout the winter and in migration.

American Oystercatcher: Fairly common along the coast throughout the year. Found year-round at Fort Fisher State Recreation Area (Site 2), Pea Island NWR (Site 7), and Cape Hatteras National Seashore (Site 8). Also found in the summer at Sunset Beach (Site 1) and on Ocracoke Island (Site 10).

Black-necked Stilt: Locally uncommon at several sites along the immediate coast during migration and summer. Best bets are Pea Island NWR (Site 7), Cape Hatteras National Seashore (Site 8), and Ocracoke Island (Site 10).

American Avocet: Year-round visitor to a select few coastal sites. Most birds are being found during migration and winter. Best site is Pea Island NWR (Site 7), with one or two flocks present from fall to spring. Very rare in migration at some inland sites such as Jordan Lake (Site 16).

Marbled Godwit: Uncommon to fairly common on the coast, particularly in fall and winter, at a few sites: Sunset Beach (Site 1), Fort Fisher State Recreation Area (Site 2), Pea Island NWR (Site 7), and Ocracoke Island (Site 10).

Purple Sandpiper: Locally uncommon to fairly common winter resident on jetties, groins, and pilings at Fort Fisher State Recreation Area (Site 2) and Pea Island NWR (Site 7).

Curlew Sandpiper: Rare late spring to fall visitor at a few coastal sites such as Pea Island NWR (Site 7) and Cape Hatteras National Seashore (Site 8).

Long-billed Dowitcher: Most common during winter and migration. Tends to be found in freshwater habitats, as opposed to saltwater areas frequented by Short-billed Dowitcher. See Fort Fisher State Recreation Area (Site 2) and Pea Island NWR (Site 7).

South Polar Skua: Rare late spring to early fall visitor, with most sightings coming during migration periods; see Gulf Stream Pelagic Birding (Site 9).

Long-tailed Jaeger: Rare spring and fall migrant; see Gulf Stream Pelagic Birding (Site 9).

Lesser Black-backed Gull: Locally uncommon at a few sites along the Outer Banks. Found to be less common but regular at other coastal locations; is a rare as inland visitor to some large reservoirs. Most are found at Cape Hatteras National Seashore (Site 8).

Gull-billed Tern: Local, uncommon summer resident along the immediate coast. Most easily found at sites such as Sunset Beach (Site 1), Fort Fisher State Recreation Area (Site 2), Pea Island NWR (Site 7), Cape Hatteras National Seashore (Site 8), and Ocracoke Island (Site 10).

Sandwich Tern: Fairly common to common summer resident usually associated with Royal Terns; see Sunset Beach (Site 1), Fort Fisher State Recreation Area (Site 2), Pea Island NWR (Site 7), Cape Hatteras National Seashore (Site 8), and Ocracoke Island (Site 10).

Roseate Tern: Rare summer visitor along the coast, with sightings usually coming from late spring to late summer. Best site is Cape Hatteras National Seashore (Site 8).

Least Tern: Summer resident that is locally fairly common from Sunset Beach (Site 1) north to Pea Island NWR (Site 7).

Bridled Tern: Uncommon to fairly common summer visitor offshore with largest numbers usually in late summer to early fall; see Gulf Stream Pelagic Birding (Site 9).

Sooty Tern: Uncommon to common summer visitor offshore, with biggest numbers in late summer to early fall; see Gulf Stream Pelagic Birding (Site 9). Also rare occasionally onshore at a few sites such as Fort Fisher State Recreation Area (Site 2), Cape Hatteras National Seashore (Site 8), and Ocracoke Island (Site 10).

Black Skimmer: Fairly common, particularly in summer at coastal locations from Sunset Beach (Site 1) to Pea Island NWR (Site 7); a few flocks winter locally at a few sites from the central coast to the southern coast.

Black-billed Cuckoo: Rare in summer at some Coastal Plain pocosin habitats such as those found at Alligator River NWR (Site 6); rare in migration throughout the state. Rare to uncommon summer resident in higher elevations of the mountains, for example, New River (Site 29), Linville Gorge (Site 32), and Heintooga Spur Road (Site 42).

Short-eared Owl: Locally rare winter resident, with most birds being found on the Coastal Plain and along the coast; see Fort Fisher State Recreation Area (Site 2), Alligator River NWR (Site 6), Pea Island NWR (Site 7), Cape Hatteras National Seashore (Site 8), and Greenville Area (Site 13).

Northern Saw-whet Owl: Year-round resident at high-elevation mountain sites such as Moses Cone and Julian Price Memorial Parks (Site 31), Roan Mountain (Site 33), Mount Mitchell State Park (Site 34), Devil's Courthouse and Black Balsam (Site 41), and Heintooga Spur Road (Site 42). A rarely observed but regular winter visitor in the eastern portions of the state; with most being found at the coast at sites such as Cape Hatteras National Seashore (Site 8).

Chuck-will's-widow: Fairly common to common summer resident from the Piedmont to the coast, with most

being found in the Coastal Plain. Increasingly local and rare toward the foothills; see Croatan National Forest (Site 4), Alligator River NWR (Site 6), Weymouth Woods Sandhills Nature Preserve (Site 15), Falls Lake State Recreation Area (Site 19), and Pee Dee NWR (Site 23).

Whip-poor-will: Fairly common to common summer resident across the state, with numbers increasing from the Coastal Plain to the western portions. Becomes increasingly local and uncommon toward the coast; see Croatan National Forest (Site 4), Alligator River NWR (Site 6), Jordan Lake State Recreation Area (Site 16), Falls Lake State Recreation Area (Site 19), Pee Dee NWR (Site 23), Linville Gorge (Site 32), and Davidson River (Site 40).

Red-headed Woodpecker: Uncommon to fairly common year-round resident from the coast to mountains up to 3,500 feet that tends to be quite local in its distribution throughout the state, favoring open woods with old, large trees or flooded swamps with standing dead timber.

Yellow-bellied Sapsucker: Locally rare summer resident in southern Appalachians at elevations above 3,000 feet; otherwise, an uncommon winter resident throughout the state.

Red-cockaded Woodpecker: Endangered, local year-round resident of pine savannas in the Sandhills and some Coastal Plain sites; see Green Swamp Preserve and Lake Waccamaw State Park (Site 3), Croatan National Forest

(Site 4), Alligator River NWR (Site 6), and Weymouth Woods Sandhills Nature Preserve (Site 15).

Olive-sided Flycatcher: Very rare fall and spring migrant across the state. Most sightings come from the Mountains in spring, with fewer reports coming from some Piedmont and coastal locations, often in the fall.

Alder Flycatcher: Breeds very locally in small numbers at high-elevation mountain balds with brushy thickets. Also a rare migrant across the rest of the state; see New River (Site 29), Moses Cone and Julian Price Memorial Parks (Site 31), Roan Mountain (Site 33), Mount Mitchell State Park (Site 34), and Devil's Courthouse and Black Balsam (Site 41).

Willow Flycatcher: Locally uncommon to fairly common breeding bird of the mountains and foothills that is usually found in thickets along streams in pastures and fields; a rare migrant throughout Piedmont and Coastal Plain. Found at New River (Site 29), Roan Mountain (Site 33), and Mount Mitchell State Park (Site 34).

Least Flycatcher: Locally uncommon breeding bird mainly above 3,000-foot elevation; see New River (Site 29), Amphibolite Mountains (Site 30), Linville Gorge (Site 32), Roan Mountain (Site 33), Max Patch Road (Site 37), and Heintooga Spur Road (Site 42). A rare migrant throughout the state.

Great Crested Flycatcher: Common summer resident throughout the state

that becomes increasingly common toward the coast.

Eastern Kingbird: Fairly common widespread summer resident that tends to be more common in the Piedmont, as opposed to Coastal Plain and Mountains.

Loggerhead Shrike: Uncommon year-round resident, mostly concentrated in the Piedmont and inner Coastal Plain, that becomes increasingly rare toward the foothills and the coast; see Greenville Area (Site 13), Howell Woods Environmental Learning Center (Site 14), Falls Lake State Recreation Area (Site 19), Charlotte-Mecklenburg Area (Site 24), and Riverbend Park (Site 27).

Warbling Vireo: Rare migrant throughout the state. A localized summer resident at a few sites in mountains that is easiest to find along the New River (Site 29). Also is irregularly very rare in some foothill and northern Piedmont sites during summer.

Common Raven: Locally uncommon year-round throughout the mountains. May occasionally be seen at lower elevations, but mainly occurs at elevations above 3,500 feet. Best bets are various sites along the Blue Ridge Parkway (Site 36) and Roan Mountain (site 33).

Horned Lark: Permanent resident at many large field areas, especially in the Piedmont and inner Coastal Plain. Mainly winter visitor at other areas of the state. Decreases in abundance westward to the mountains where it is very local and uncommon on some grassy mountain balds. See Alligator River NWR (Site 6) and Amphibolite Mountains (Site 30).

Cliff Swallow: Uncommon migrant throughout. Locally a common breeder at large lakes in the Piedmont; see Jordan Lake (Site 16), Falls Lake State Recreation Area (Site 19), Charlotte-Mecklenburg Area (Site 24), and Riverbend Park (Site 27).

Black-capped Chickadee: Small population largely limited to a very few high-elevation sites in and near the Great Smoky Mountains. Beware possible hybridization with Carolina Chickadee at lower to mid-elevations. Also see Roan Mountain (Site 33) and Heintooga Spur Road (Site 42).

Red-breasted Nuthatch: Fairly common resident in spruce fir zone but also occurs as breeding bird in spruce-hemlock areas at lower elevations. Present year-round at sites from Blue Ridge Parkway North (Site 28) and south to Heintooga Spur Road (Site 42). Is also an irregular winter resident throughout the state.

Brown-headed Nuthatch: Fairly common year-round resident that is widespread in the Coastal Plain and Piedmont. In the mountains, very local resident limited to small colonies mainly in the Asheville area; see "Nearby opportunities" in Lakes of the Southern Mountains (Site 38).

Brown Creeper: Uncommon to fairly common breeding bird in high-elevation spruce fir zone of the mountains; also ranges lower in elevation at times. A

fairly common winter resident throughout the state. Often overlooked in woodland habitat because of its retiring nature.

Winter Wren: Fairly common breeder at higher elevations in spruce fir forests. Moves to lower elevations in winter, where it is found throughout the state. See sites from Moses Cone and Julian Price Memorial Parks (Site 31) south to Joyce Kilmer Memorial Forest (Site 44).

Sedge Wren: Fairly common winter resident along the coast; see Mattamuskeet NWR (Site 5), Alligator River NWR (Site 6), Pea Island NWR (Site 7), and Ocracoke Island (Site 10). Also a few winter at some inland sites such as Pee Dee NWR (Site 23).

Veery: Fairly common to common breeding bird at elevations above 3,500 feet that is found at sites from Blue Ridge Parkway North (Site 28) to Joyce Kilmer Memorial Forest (Site 44); fairly common migrant throughout much of the state.

American Pipit: Rare winter resident in the mountains, becoming uncommon in the Piedmont and common in the Coastal Plain. Usually found in large, open, plowed fields; see Mattamuskeet NWR (Site 5), Alligator River NWR (Site 6), Pea Island NWR (Site 7), and Cape Hatteras National Seashore (Site 8). Also found in the Piedmont at locations such as the Charlotte-Mecklenburg Area (Site 24).

Blue-winged Warbler: Rare to uncommon migrant throughout that tends to be a rarer migrant along the coast; see Amphibolite Mountains (Site

30) and Jackson Park (Site 39). Also, reported as an occasional breeder at a few sites in the Mountains, such as New River (Site 29). Blue-winged and Golden-winged hybrids are consistently seen at Stecoah Gap (Site 43).

Golden-winged Warbler: Uncommon local breeding bird in the mountains, most often occurring in an elevation range of 3,000 to 4,800 feet, and a rare migrant across the state, especially toward the coast; see New River (Site 29), Amphibolite Mountains (Site 30), Roan Mountain (Site 33), Max Patch Road (Site 37), and Stecoah Gap (Site 43).

Yellow Warbler: Uncommon to fairly common summer resident in the mountains at low elevations and the upper Piedmont, mainly in areas along streams and ponds with willows; see New River (Site 29), Linville Gorge (Site 32), Max Patch Road (Site 37), and Davidson River (Site 40). Uncommon to fairly common migrant throughout the state.

Chestnut-sided Warbler: Common breeding bird at middle and higher elevations where there are open patches in the forest. Common along much of the Blue Ridge Parkway from Moses Cone and Julian Price Memorial Parks (Site 31) south to Heintooga Spur Road (Site 42). Also see Amphibolite Mountains (Site 30), Roan Mountain (Site 33), and Max Patch Road (Site 37). Uncommon to fairly common migrant in the Mountains and Piedmont.

Magnolia Warbler: Present during summer at a couple of high-elevation sites such as Roan Mountain (Site 33) and Mount Mitchell State Park (Site 34). Uncommon spring and common fall migrant across most of the state.

Black-throated Blue Warbler: A fairly common to common breeding bird at middle and higher elevations in the mountains. A fairly common to common migrant across the state, with increased numbers toward the Mountains.

Black-throated Green Warbler: Common breeding bird in high-elevation spruce fir zone but occurs, sometimes in large numbers, at all elevations, especially where there are hemlocks. Common along much of the Blue Ridge Parkway from Blue Ridge Parkway North (Site 28) south to Heintooga Spur Road (Site 42). Also see Max Patch Road (Site 37), Stecoah Gap (Site 43), and Joyce Kilmer Memorial Forest (Site 44). For the possibility of seeing at lower elevations, see Alligator River National Wildlife Refuge (Site 6).

Blackburnian Warbler: Fairly common but somewhat local summer resident at middle and higher elevations. Often common in spruce fir or hemlock. Common along much of the Blue Ridge Parkway from Moses Cone and Julian Price Memorial Parks (Site 31) south to Heintooga Spur Road (Site 42). Rare to uncommon migrant across the state, becomes rarer toward the coast.

Cerulean Warbler: Very local, uncommon summer resident in the mountains and along some portions of the

Roanoke River (Site 12). Fairly common at Blue Ridge Parkway from Craven Gap to Lane Pinnacle (Site 36) and Stecoah Gap (Site 43). Also present as breeding bird at Chimney Rock Park, a nearby site to Jackson Park (Site 39). A rare migrant across the state, with most occurring in the western areas.

American Redstart: Uncommon to fairly common summer resident from the Coastal Plain to low and middle elevations in the Mountains. Common migrant across the state.

Prothonotary Warbler: Common summer resident throughout the Coastal Plain and local in the Piedmont. Rare in the foothills and practically absent from low elevation areas in the Mountains. Uncommon to fairly common migrant across much of the same range.

Worm-eating Warbler: Uncommon breeder on dry slopes at low to middle elevations in the Mountains and some Piedmont areas. Also uncommon breeder in narrow zone in the outer Coastal Plain at sites such as the Green Swamp Preserve (Site 3), Croatan National Forest (Site 4), and Alligator River NWR (Site 6). Uncommon migrant across the state.

Swainson's Warbler: Uncommon and very local breeding bird mostly in the Coastal Plain and the Mountains. Coastal Plain sites are usually in moist forests, while the Mountains birds inhabit rhododendron and laurel thickets along streams. Very few birds in the middle to eastern Piedmont; see Green

Swamp Preserve (Site 3), Croatan National Forest (Site 4), Alligator River NWR (Site 6), Roanoke River (Site 12), Howell Woods (Site 14), Linville Gorge (Site 32), and Joyce Kilmer Memorial Forest (Site 44).

Kentucky Warbler: Fairly common summer resident from the inner Coastal Plain to the Mountains. Rare migrant in the outer Coastal Plain and along the immediate coast.

Hooded Warbler: A common summer resident in low- and middle-elevation forests from the coast to the mountains.

Canada Warbler: Fairly common breeding bird of higher elevations. Common along much of the Blue Ridge Parkway from Moses Cone and Julian Price Memorial Parks (Site 31) south to Heintooga Spur Road (Site 42). Also see New River (Site 29), Amphibolite Mountains (Site 30), Roan Mountain (Site 33), Max Patch Road (Site 37), and Joyce Kilmer Memorial Forest (Site 44). Rare coastal migrant that becomes more common as a migrant toward the western areas of the state.

Summer Tanager: Common summer resident of pine and mixed woods from the coast toward the mountains. Numbers decrease substantially from the western Piedmont westward.

Scarlet Tanager: Fairly common summer resident of hardwoods and mixed woods from the northern Coastal Plain to middle elevations of the Mountains. Numbers increase toward the mountains.

Bachman's Sparrow: Localized summer resident in certain Coastal Plain and Sandhills areas with open pine woods with grassy ground cover. Winter resident in some of the same areas, but often overlooked due to secretive nature. Good sites include the Green Swamp Preserve (Site 3), Croatan National Forest (Site 4), and Weymouth Woods Sandhills Nature Preserve (Site 15).

Vesper Sparrow: Mainly an uncommon migrant statewide and a locally rare to uncommon winter resident in the eastern Piedmont and Coastal Plain. Localized summer resident of open grassy balds in the Mountains at sites such as New River (Site 29), Amphibolite Mountains (Site 30), and Roan Mountain (Site 33).

Lark Sparrow: Uncommon fall migrant along the coast. Rare winter resident in the Coastal Plain and along the coast. Very local, rare summer resident at a few sites in the Sandhills.

Grasshopper Sparrow: Found during the summer at a limited number of sites from the coast to the mountains, with most being found in the Piedmont and inner Coastal Plain. Uncommon and very local bird of unkempt, grassy fields and sometimes hayfields; see Greenville Area (Site 13), Pee Dee NWR (Site 23), Charlotte-Mecklenburg Area (Site 24), and Stecoah Gap (Site 43). Uncommon migrant throughout and a rare winter resident at mainly Coastal Plain locations.

Henslow's Sparrow: Rare migrant and winter resident in the Coastal Plain. Very localized summer resident, mostly found at Voice of America sites in the Greenville Area (Site 13). This disjunct population is considered to be of high significance due to being one of the largest in the eastern part of the species' range.

Nelson's Sharp-tailed Sparrow: Winter resident in salt marshes along the coast at sites such as Sunset Beach (Site 1), Fort Fisher State Recreation Area (Site 2), Pea Island NWR (Site 7), and Cape Hatteras National Seashore (Site 8). Very rare migrant at inland freshwater marshes throughout the state.

Saltmarsh Sharp-tailed Sparrow: Winter resident in salt marshes along the coast at sites such as Sunset Beach (Site 1), Fort Fisher State Recreation Area (Site 2), Pea Island NWR (Site 7), and Cape Hatteras National Seashore (Site 8).

Seaside Sparrow: Fairly common to common permanent resident of coastal saltwater marshes. See Fort Fisher State Recreation Area (Site 2), Pea Island NWR (Site 7), and Cape Hatteras National Seashore (Site 8); summer only at Ocracoke Island (Site 10).

Rose-breasted Grosbeak: Common summer resident in the mountains at elevations above 3,500 feet. A common migrant in the Mountains that becomes fairly common in the Piedmont and uncommon at the coast.

Blue Grosbeak: Common summer resident from the coast toward the mountains, with considerably fewer birds in the western portions of the state. Found occasionally in the Mountains at Linville Gorge (Site 32) and Max Patch Road (Site 37).

Indigo Bunting: One of the most abundant breeding birds of open areas and forest openings. Common throughout all regions of the state during the summer.

Painted Bunting: Uncommon summer resident from along the central coast south to the South Carolina line. Found along the immediate coastal strip behind the beaches; see Sunset Beach (Site 1), Fort Fisher State Recreation Area (Site 2), and Croatan National Forest (Site 4). Also a very localized, rare winter resident, often at feeders, at some coastal sites such as Cape Hatteras National Seashore (Site 8).

Dickcissel: Rare to uncommon migrant statewide. Most are found at inland sites in spring and along the coast in fall. See Fort Fisher State Recreation Area (Site 2) and Pea Island NWR (Site 7). Localized, irregular summer resident or visitor in overgrown fields across the state. Very rare winter lingerer in the Coastal Plain and along the coast.

Bobolink: A common migrant in fields and marshes throughout the state, although it comes through in flocks and can be missed. Very rare, localized summer resident, at a few grassy fields in a couple of counties in the Mountains.

Baltimore Oriole: A rare to uncommon summer resident at several northern and central mountain areas. Also an irregular, sporadic summer visitor and breeder at mainly northern and western Piedmont areas. Occasional in winter in Piedmont and Coastal Plain. At other times is an uncommon spring migrant and fairly common fall migrant across the state; see New River (Site 29) and Linville Gorge and Surrounding Area (Site 32).

Red Crossbill: Permanent resident in the high-elevation spruce fir zone of the mountains. Otherwise, it is a rare, irregular winter visitor across the state. More common in the Black Mountains; see Mount Mitchell State Park (Site 34) and Big Ivy, Craggy Gardens, and Balsam Gap (Site 35). Also fairly reliable at Heintooga Spur Road (Site 42). Small flocks may show up at any time of year at Moses Cone and Julian Price Memorial Parks (Site 31), Linville Gorge and Surrounding Area (Site 32), and Roan Mountain (Site 33).

Pine Siskin: Occurs throughout the state in winter, usually at feeders, but is irregular in abundance and distribution. Fairly reliably found in the Black Mountains at Mount Mitchell State Park (Site 34), Big Ivy, Craggy Gardens, and Balsam Gap (Site 35), and Heintooga Spur Road (Site 42), but may also be found at Moses Cone and Julian Price Memorial Parks (Site 31) and Devil's Courthouse (Site 41). For the Piedmont see Weymouth Woods Sandhills Nature Preserve (Site 15), William B. Umstead State Park (Site 18), and Riverbend Park and Lower Lake Hickory (Site 27).

Appendix B: Official North Carolina State Bird List

Compiled by Harry LeGrand, chair of the North Carolina Bird Records Committee

The following list is North Carolina's accepted bird list as of August 2004. The list follows the A.O.U. (American Ornithologists Union) *Checklist of North American Birds,* 7th ed. (1998), plus supplements. Birds are listed in phylogenic order.

Official List (443 Species)

Fulvous Whistling-Duck
Greater White-fronted Goose
Snow Goose
Ross's Goose
Brant
Barnacle Goose
Canada Goose
Mute Swan
Trumpeter Swan
Tundra Swan
Wood Duck
Gadwall
Eurasian Wigeon
American Wigeon
American Black Duck
Mallard
Blue-winged Teal
Cinnamon Teal
Northern Shoveler
Northern Pintail
Green-winged Teal
Canvasback
Redhead
Ring-necked Duck
Greater Scaup
Lesser Scaup
King Eider
Common Eider
Harlequin Duck
Surf Scoter

White-winged Scoter
Black Scoter
Long-tailed Duck
Bufflehead
Common Goldeneye
Hooded Merganser
Common Merganser
Red-breasted Merganser
Ruddy Duck
Masked Duck
Ring-necked Pheasant
Ruffed Grouse
Wild Turkey
Northern Bobwhite
Red-throated Loon
Pacific Loon
Common Loon
Pied-billed Grebe
Horned Grebe
Red-necked Grebe
Eared Grebe
Western Grebe
Yellow-nosed Albatross
Northern Fulmar
Black-capped Petrel
Bermuda Petrel
Fea's Petrel
Herald Petrel
Bulwer's Petrel
Cory's Shearwater
Greater Shearwater

Sooty Shearwater
Manx Shearwater
Audubon's Shearwater
Wilson's Storm-Petrel
White-faced Storm-Petrel
Leach's Storm-Petrel
Swinhoe's Storm-Petrel
Band-rumped Storm-Petrel
White-tailed Tropicbird
Red-billed Tropicbird
Masked Booby
Brown Booby
Northern Gannet
American White Pelican
Brown Pelican
Double-crested Cormorant
Great Cormorant
Anhinga
Magnificent Frigatebird
American Bittern
Least Bittern
Great Blue Heron
Great Egret
Snowy Egret
Little Blue Heron
Tricolored Heron
Reddish Egret
Cattle Egret
Green Heron
Black-crowned Night-Heron
Yellow-crowned Night-Heron
White Ibis
Glossy Ibis
White-faced Ibis
Roseate Spoonbill
Wood Stork
Black Vulture
Turkey Vulture
Osprey
Swallow-tailed Kite
White-tailed Kite
Mississippi Kite

Bald Eagle
Northern Harrier
Sharp-shinned Hawk
Cooper's Hawk
Northern Goshawk
Red-shouldered Hawk
Broad-winged Hawk
Swainson's Hawk
Red-tailed Hawk
Rough-legged Hawk
Golden Eagle
American Kestrel
Merlin
Peregrine Falcon
Yellow Rail
Black Rail
Clapper Rail
King Rail
Virginia Rail
Sora
Purple Gallinule
Common Moorhen
American Coot
Limpkin
Sandhill Crane
Northern Lapwing
Black-bellied Plover
American Golden-Plover
Wilson's Plover
Semipalmated Plover
Piping Plover
Killdeer
American Oystercatcher
Black-necked Stilt
American Avocet
Greater Yellowlegs
Lesser Yellowlegs
Spotted Redshank
Solitary Sandpiper
Willet
Spotted Sandpiper
Upland Sandpiper

Whimbrel
Long-billed Curlew
Black-tailed Godwit
Hudsonian Godwit
Bar-tailed Godwit
Marbled Godwit
Ruddy Turnstone
Red Knot
Sanderling
Semipalmated Sandpiper
Western Sandpiper
Little Stint
Least Sandpiper
White-rumped Sandpiper
Baird's Sandpiper
Pectoral Sandpiper
Purple Sandpiper
Dunlin
Curlew Sandpiper
Stilt Sandpiper
Buff-breasted Sandpiper
Ruff
Short-billed Dowitcher
Long-billed Dowitcher
Wilson's Snipe
American Woodcock
Wilson's Phalarope
Red-necked Phalarope
Red Phalarope
Great Skua
South Polar Skua
Pomarine Jaeger
Parasitic Jaeger
Long-tailed Jaeger
Laughing Gull
Franklin's Gull
Little Gull
Black-headed Gull
Bonaparte's Gull
Mew Gull
Ring-billed Gull

California Gull
Herring Gull
Yellow-legged Gull
Thayer's Gull
Iceland Gull
Lesser Black-backed Gull
Glaucous Gull
Great Black-backed Gull
Sabine's Gull
Black-legged Kittiwake
Gull-billed Tern
Caspian Tern
Royal Tern
Sandwich Tern
Roseate Tern
Common Tern
Arctic Tern
Forster's Tern
Least Tern
Bridled Tern
Sooty Tern
Black Tern
Brown Noddy
Black Skimmer
Dovekie
Common Murre
Thick-billed Murre
Razorbill
Atlantic Puffin
Rock Pigeon
Band-tailed Pigeon
Eurasian Collared-Dove
White-winged Dove
Mourning Dove
Passenger Pigeon (now extinct)
Common Ground-Dove
Carolina Parakeet (now extinct)
Black-billed Cuckoo
Yellow-billed Cuckoo
Smooth-billed Ani
Barn Owl

Eastern Screech-Owl
Great Horned Owl
Snowy Owl
Burrowing Owl
Barred Owl
Long-eared Owl
Short-eared Owl
Northern Saw-whet Owl
Lesser Nighthawk
Common Nighthawk
Antillean Nighthawk
Chuck-will's-widow
Whip-poor-will
Chimney Swift
Green Violet-ear
Green-breasted Mango
Broad-billed Hummingbird
Ruby-throated Hummingbird
Black-chinned Hummingbird
Anna's Hummingbird
Calliope Hummingbird
Broad-tailed Hummingbird
Rufous Hummingbird
Allen's Hummingbird
Belted Kingfisher
Red-headed Woodpecker
Red-bellied Woodpecker
Yellow-bellied Sapsucker
Downy Woodpecker
Hairy Woodpecker
Red-cockaded Woodpecker
Northern Flicker
Pileated Woodpecker
Ivory-billed Woodpecker (probably
    extinct)
Olive-sided Flycatcher
Eastern Wood-Pewee
Yellow-bellied Flycatcher
Acadian Flycatcher
Alder Flycatcher
Willow Flycatcher
Least Flycatcher

Gray Flycatcher
Pacific-slope/Cordilleran Flycatcher
Eastern Phoebe
Say's Phoebe
Vermilion Flycatcher
Ash-throated Flycatcher
Great Crested Flycatcher
Tropical Kingbird
Western Kingbird
Eastern Kingbird
Gray Kingbird
Scissor-tailed Flycatcher
Fork-tailed Flycatcher
Loggerhead Shrike
Northern Shrike
White-eyed Vireo
Yellow-throated Vireo
Blue-headed Vireo
Warbling Vireo
Philadelphia Vireo
Red-eyed Vireo
Black-whiskered Vireo
Blue Jay
American Crow
Fish Crow
Common Raven
Horned Lark
Purple Martin
Tree Swallow
Northern Rough-winged Swallow
Bank Swallow
Cliff Swallow
Cave Swallow
Barn Swallow
Carolina Chickadee
Black-capped Chickadee
Tufted Titmouse
Red-breasted Nuthatch
White-breasted Nuthatch
Brown-headed Nuthatch
Brown Creeper
Carolina Wren

Bewick's Wren
House Wren
Winter Wren
Sedge Wren
Marsh Wren
Golden-crowned Kinglet
Ruby-crowned Kinglet
Blue-gray Gnatcatcher
Northern Wheatear
Eastern Bluebird
Veery
Gray-cheeked Thrush
Swainson's Thrush
Hermit Thrush
Wood Thrush
American Robin
Gray Catbird
Northern Mockingbird
Sage Thrasher
Brown Thrasher
European Starling
White Wagtail
Black-backed Wagtail
American Pipit
Sprague's Pipit
Cedar Waxwing
Bachman's Warbler (probably extinct)
Blue-winged Warbler
Golden-winged Warbler
Tennessee Warbler
Orange-crowned Warbler
Nashville Warbler
Northern Parula
Yellow Warbler
Chestnut-sided Warbler
Magnolia Warbler
Cape May Warbler
Black-throated Blue Warbler
Yellow-rumped Warbler
Black-throated Gray Warbler
Black-throated Green Warbler
Townsend's Warbler

Blackburnian Warbler
Yellow-throated Warbler
Pine Warbler
Kirtland's Warbler
Prairie Warbler
Palm Warbler
Bay-breasted Warbler
Blackpoll Warbler
Cerulean Warbler
Black-and-white Warbler
American Redstart
Prothonotary Warbler
Worm-eating Warbler
Swainson's Warbler
Ovenbird
Northern Waterthrush
Louisiana Waterthrush
Kentucky Warbler
Connecticut Warbler
Mourning Warbler
MacGillivray's Warbler
Common Yellowthroat
Hooded Warbler
Wilson's Warbler
Canada Warbler
Yellow-breasted Chat
Summer Tanager
Scarlet Tanager
Western Tanager
Green-tailed Towhee
Spotted Towhee
Eastern Towhee
Bachman's Sparrow
American Tree Sparrow
Chipping Sparrow
Clay-colored Sparrow
Field Sparrow
Vesper Sparrow
Lark Sparrow
Lark Bunting
Savannah Sparrow
Grasshopper Sparrow

Henslow's Sparrow
Le Conte's Sparrow
Nelson's Sharp-tailed Sparrow
Saltmarsh Sharp-tailed Sparrow
Seaside Sparrow
Fox Sparrow
Song Sparrow
Lincoln's Sparrow
Swamp Sparrow
White-throated Sparrow
Harris's Sparrow
White-crowned Sparrow
Dark-eyed Junco
Lapland Longspur
Smith's Longspur
Chestnut-collared Longspur
Snow Bunting
Northern Cardinal
Rose-breasted Grosbeak
Black-headed Grosbeak
Blue Grosbeak
Lazuli Bunting
Indigo Bunting
Painted Bunting
Dickcissel
Bobolink
Red-winged Blackbird
Eastern Meadowlark
Yellow-headed Blackbird
Rusty Blackbird
Brewer's Blackbird
Common Grackle
Boat-tailed Grackle
Shiny Cowbird
Brown-headed Cowbird
Orchard Oriole
Bullock's Oriole
Baltimore Oriole
Brambling
Pine Grosbeak
Purple Finch
House Finch

Red Crossbill
White-winged Crossbill
Common Redpoll
Pine Siskin
American Goldfinch
Evening Grosbeak
House Sparrow

Provisional List

(Species reports [17 species] reviewed
and accepted by Records Committee
as being valid but which have not met
the criteria for the Official List.)

Black-bellied Whistling-Duck
Garganey
Clark's Grebe
Black-browed Albatross
Gyrfalcon
Snowy Plover
Black-tailed Gull
Slaty-backed Gull
White-winged Tern
Black Guillemot
Long-billed Murrelet
Groove-billed Ani
Bell's Vireo
Mountain Bluebird
Bicknell's Thrush
Western Meadowlark
Lesser Goldfinch

2004 North Carolina Bird Records Committee

Keith E. Camburn
Samuel Cooper
Richard J. Davis
Eric V. Dean
Wayne K. Forsythe
Harry E. LeGrand Jr., Chair
Russ Tyndall

Appendix C: American Birding Association's Code of Birding Ethics

(Reprinted by permission of American Birding Association.)

1. Promote the welfare of birds and their environment.

    1(a) Support the protection of important bird habitat.

    1(b) To avoid stressing birds or exposing them to danger, exercise restraint and caution during observation, photography, sound recording, or filming. Limit the use of recordings and other methods of attracting birds, and never use such methods in heavily birded areas, or for attracting any species that is Threatened, Endangered, or of Special Concern, or is rare in your local area.

    Keep well back from nests and nesting colonies, roosts, display areas, and important feeding sites. In such sensitive areas, if there is a need for extended observation, photography, filming, or recording, try to use a blind or hide, and take advantage of natural cover. Use artificial light sparingly for filming or photography, especially for close-ups.

    1(c) Before advertising the presence of a rare bird, evaluate the potential for disturbance to the bird, its surroundings, and other people in the area, and proceed only if access can be controlled, disturbance minimized, and permission has been obtained from private landowners. The sites of rare nesting birds should be divulged only to the proper conservation authorities.

    1(d) Stay on roads, trails, and paths where they exist; otherwise keep habitat disturbance to a minimum.

2. Respect the law and the rights of others.

    2(a) Do not enter private property without the owner's explicit permission.

    2(b) Follow all laws, rules, and regulations governing use of roads and public areas, both at home and abroad.

    2(c) Practice common courtesy in contacts with other people. Your exemplary behavior will generate goodwill with birders and nonbirders alike.

3. Ensure that feeders, nest structures, and other artificial bird environments are safe.

    3(a) Keep dispensers, water, and food clean and free of decay or disease. It is important to feed birds continually during harsh weather.

    3(b) Maintain and clean nest structures regularly.

3(c) If you are attracting birds to an area, ensure the birds are not exposed to predation from cats and other domestic animals or dangers posed by artificial hazards.

4. Group birding, whether organized or impromptu, requires special care.

Each individual in the group, in addition to the obligations spelled out in Items #1 and #2, has responsibilities as a Group Member.

4(a) Respect the interests, rights, and skills of fellow birders, as well as people participating in other legitimate outdoor activities. Freely share your knowledge and experience, except where code 1(c) applies. Be especially helpful to beginning birders.

4(b) If you witness unethical birding behavior, assess the situation, and intervene if you think it prudent. When interceding, inform the person(s) of the inappropriate action, and attempt, within reason, to have it stopped. If the behavior continues, document it, and notify appropriate individuals or organizations.

Group Leader Responsibilities [amateur and professional trips and tours].

4(c) Be an exemplary ethical role model for the group. Teach through word and example.

4(d) Keep groups to a size that limits impact on the environment and does not interfere with others using the same area.

4(e) Ensure everyone in the group knows of and practices this code.

4(f) Learn and inform the group of any special circumstances applicable to the areas being visited (e.g., no tape recorders allowed).

4(g) Acknowledge that professional tour companies bear a special responsibility to place the welfare of birds and the benefits of public knowledge ahead of the company's commercial interests. Ideally, leaders should keep track of tour sightings, document unusual occurrences, and submit records to appropriate organizations.

Appendix D: North Carolina Birding, Bird Conservation Organizations, and Programs

The **Carolina Bird Club** is a nonprofit educational and scientific association serving the Carolinas. The association provides a range of resources to members, including a quarterly journal and newsletter which contains information about meetings, field trips, and club projects. The club also maintains a Web site, which includes rare bird reports, field trips, and an up-to-date official state bird list. The Web site can be accessed at www.carolinabirdclub.org.

The **North Carolina State Office of the National Audubon Society** is a nonprofit organization committed to the conservation and restoration of natural ecosystems, with a focus on birds as well as other wildlife. Information regarding conservation initiative, Audubon preserves, and Important Bird Areas for North Carolina may be found online at www.ncaudubon.org/nccas_home.html.

North Carolina Partners in Flight furthers bird conservation by involving government agencies, conservation organizations, private industry, the academic community, and citizens. The primary focus of the program is to coordinate and promote education, habitat conservation, and research efforts among its partners. Resources related to bird conservation efforts in North Carolina can be found at http://faculty.ncwc.edu/mbrooks/pif/index.html.

Appendix E: Rare Bird Alerts

The Carolina Bird Club operates the rare bird alert for North and South Carolina. Call (704) 332–2473 to hear the latest report or to leave a message. You can also e-mail a rare bird alert (RBA) to PiephoffT@aol.com or find a digest at http://list serve.arizona.edu/archives/birdeast.html.

Another resource for learning about North and South Carolina rare birds is the Internet e-mail discussion group "carolinabirds," operated by Will Cook. Learn more about the carolinabirds Listserv at http://www.duke.edu/~cwcook/cbirds.html.

Appendix F: Additional Resources for Birding in North Carolina

Other North Carolina Bird-Finding Guides

Bearden, Karen. 2002. *Birding in North Carolina State Parks.* Chapel Hill: Audubon North Carolina.

Bearden, Karen. 2000. *A Birdwatcher's Guide to the Triangle.* Raleigh: Wake Audubon Society.

Fussell, John F. 1994. *A Birder's Guide to Coastal North Carolina.* Chapel Hill: University of North Carolina Press.

Simpson, Marcus B. 1992. *Birds of the Blue Ridge Mountains.* Chapel Hill: University of North Carolina Press.

Guides to North Carolina's Birds

Potter, Eloise F., James F. Parnell, and Robert P. Teulings. 1980. *Birds of the Carolinas.* Chapel Hill: University of North Carolina Press. (Revised edition scheduled for release in 2005.)

Thompson, Bill III. 2004. *North Carolina Bird Watching: A Year-Round Guide.* Nashville: Cool Springs Press.

Bird Field Guides That Include the Eastern United States

Kaufman, Kenn. 2000. *Birds of North America.* New York: Houghton Mifflin.

National Geographic. 2002. *Field Guide to the Birds of North America,* 4th ed. Washington, D.C: National Geographic.

Peterson, Roger Tory. 2002. *Birds of Eastern and Central North America.* New York: Houghton Mifflin.

Sibley, David Allen. 2003. *The Sibley Field Guide to Birds of Eastern North America.* New York: Alfred A. Knopf.

Stokes, Donald W., and Lillian Q. Stokes. 1996. *Stokes Field Guide to Birds: Eastern Region.* New York: Little, Brown.

Informational Resources for North Carolina Natural History

Biggs, W. C., and J. P. Parnell. 1989. *State Parks of North Carolina.* Winston-Salem: John F. Blair Publisher.

Brock, J. P., and K. Kaufman. 2003. *Butterflies of North America.* New York: Houghton Mifflin Company.

Conant, R., and J. T. Collins. 1998. *Peterson Field Guides: Reptiles and Amphibians.* New York: Houghton Mifflin Company.

Frankenberg, Dirk. 1997. *The Nature of North Carolina's Southern Coast.* Chapel Hill: University of North Carolina Press.

Frankenberg, Dirk. 2000. *Exploring North Carolina's Natural Areas.* Chapel Hill: University of North Carolina Press.

Justice W. S., and C. Ritchie Bell. 1968. *Wildflowers of North Carolina.* Chapel Hill: University of North Carolina Press.

Martof, Bernard S., William M. Palmer, and Joseph R. Bailey. 1980. *Amphibians and Reptiles of the Carolinas and Virginia.* Chapel Hill: University of North Carolina Press.

Miller, James H., and Karly V. Miller. 1999. *Forest Plants of the Southeast and Their Wildlife Uses.* Champaign, IL: Southern Weed Society.

Nash, Steve. 1999. *Blue Ridge 2020.* Chapel Hill: University of North Carolina Press.

Rankin, Richard. 1996. *North Carolina Nature Writing.* Winston-Salem: John F. Blair Publisher.

Webster, William David, James F. Parnell, and Walter C. Briggs Jr. 1985. *Mammals of the Carolinas, Virginia, and Maryland.* Chapel Hill: University of North Carolina Press.

Weidensaul, Scott. *Mountains of the Heart.* 1994. Golden, CO: Fulcrum Publishing.

North Carolina Birding Software

Avendex. 2004 edition. Redshank Software.
www.redshanksoftware.com/index.html
Avendex is an application preprogrammed with over 30,000 bird sightings that have occurred in North and South Carolina over approximately the last fifty years.

Birds of North Carolina. Thayer Birding Software.
www.thayerbirding.com
Birds of North Carolina contains 298 species regularly seen, including color photos and songs.

Index

Page numbers in boldface refer to illustrations.

A

accommodations, 6

Alligator River National Wildlife Refuge, 41–45

Amphibolite Mountains and Elk Knob Game Land and State Natural Area, 127–31

Anhinga, 23, 41, 181

Avocet, American, 18, 46, 183

B

Balsam Gap, Big Ivy, and Craggy Gardens, 145–48

Beach habitat, 16, 18

bears, 7

Big Ivy, Craggy Gardens, and Balsam Gap, 145–48

binoculars, 4

bird guides, 4

Bittern, American, 18, 39, 48, 53, 60, 63; **Least,** 18, 36, 181

Blackbird, Red-winged, 44; **Rusty,** 39, 102, 117

Bluebird, Eastern, 34, 86

Blue Ridge Parkway, 170–73

Blue Ridge Parkway from Craven Gap to Lane Pinnacle, 149–51

Blue Ridge Parkway North, 121–23

Bobolink, 17, 191

Bobwhite, Northern, 44, 76

Booby, Masked, 55, 181

Brant, 50, 57, 179

Breeding Bird Survey (BBS), 160

Bufflehead, 25, 39, 53, 60, 113, 115, 117, 157

Bunting, Indigo, 17, 23, 32, 36, 41, 63, 71, 76, 79, 95, 97, 100, 103, 107, 111, 116, 127, 135, 145, 174, 191; **Painted,** 17, 23, 26, 32, **33,** 191; **Snow,** 141

C

Canvasback, 18, 23, 36, 111, 114, 179

Cape Hatteras National Seashore, 50–54

Catbird, Gray, 69, 86, 130, 134

Charlotte-Mecklenburg Area, 107–10

Chat, Yellow-breasted, 17, 18, 69, 99, 102, 106, 110, 113, 154

Cherohala Skyway and Joyce Kilmer Memorial Forest, 176–78

Chickadee, Black-capped, 17, 139, 170, 187

chiggers, 6

Christmas Bird Counts (CBC), 160

Chuck-will's-widow, 17, 23, 32, 41, 57, 74, 91, 103, 135, 185

climate, 10

clothing, 4

Coastal Plain physiographic region, 8

conservation, 1

Coot, American, 115, 157

Cormorant, Double-crested, 69; **Great,** 26, 46, 181

Craggy Gardens, Balsam Gap, and Big Ivy, 145–48

Craven Gap to Lane Pinnacle, Blue Ridge Parkway from, 149–51

Creeper, Brown, 17, 39, 63, 76, 86, 89, 96, 99, 110, 113, 117, 132, 135, 139, 142, 145, 163, 167, 170, 176, 187

Croatan National Forest, 32–35

Crossbill, Red, 17, 88, 132, 135, 139, 142, 145, 170, 191

Crow, Fish, 93

Cuckoo, Black-billed, 46, 124, 135, 159, 170, 185; **Yellow-billed,** 39, 44, 63, 69, 72, 89, 99, 138, 151, 154

D

Davidson River and Pink Beds, 163–66

Devil's Courthouse and Black Balsam, 167–69

Red-eyed, 34, 76, 86, 122,
  Warbling, 17, 124, 159, 18
  eyed, 17, 31, 39, 44, 63, 66
  throated, 72, 76, 86, 89, 1?
  151, 154, 162, 166, 175
Vulture, Black, 34; **Turkey,** ?

W

Warbler, Bay-breasted, 159
  and-white, 44, 63, 76, 12?
  151, 175; **Blackburnian,**
  135, 142, 145, 149, 152, 1?
  167, 170, 174, 188; **Black**
  Blue, 17, 32, 121, **122,** 1?
  135, 139, 145, 149, 152, 1?
  167, 170, 174, 176, 188; **B**
  throated Green, 17, 32,
  132, 135, 139, 142, 145, 1
  163, 167, 170, 174, 176, 1
  winged, 17, 159, **161,** 18
  Canada, 17, 127, 132, 13
  145, 152, 159, 163, 167, 1
  189; **Cerulean,** 17, 64, 1?
  159, 174, 188–89; **Chestr**
  17, 127, 132, 135, 139, 14
  159, 163, 167, 170, 174, 1
  Connecticut, 159; **Gol**
  winged, 17, 124, 127, 1?
  174, 188; **Hooded,** 17, 4
  79, 88, 91, 97, 100, 103,
  135, **136,** 139, 149, 152,
  170, 174, 176, 189; **Kent**
  64, 71, 74, 79, 88, 100, 1?
  139, 149, 159, 174, 176,
  Magnolia, 139, 142, 188
  141, 159; **Orange-crow**
  Palm, 69; **Pine,** 31, 86;
  42, 44, 48, 60, 63, 76, 99
  125; **Prothonotary,** 17,
  61, 68, 71, 79, 100, **101,**
  189; **Rose-breasted,** 17
  17, 29, 32, 41, 64, 71, 13
  189; **Worm-eating,** 17,

Mountains physiographic region, 9–10
Mount Mitchell State Park, 142–44

N

New River, 124–26
Nighthawk, Common, 76
Night-heron, Black-crowned, 39, 48,
  60; **Yellow-crowned,** 25, 48, 60
North Carolina Birding Trail, 38
North Carolina Partners in Flight, 1,
  129
Nuthatch, Brown-headed, 17, 23, 29,
  32, 36, 44, 57, 61, 71, 74, 79, 84, 88,
  91, 95, 97, 103, 107, 111, 114, **115,**
  116, 135, 187; **Red-breasted,** 17,
  88, 121, 127, 132, 139, 142, 145,
  147, 163, 167, 170, 187; **White-**
  breasted, 86, 122, 151

O

Ocracoke Island, 57–60
Oriole, Baltimore, 36, 71, 124, **125,**
  135, 159, 191; **Orchard,** 25, 39, 63,
  102, 110, 125, 135, 154
Osprey, 18, 31, 34, 39, 48, 63, 69, 93,
  107
Ovenbird, 34, 44, 63, 76, 86, 89, 99,
  122, 130, 139, 141, 148, 151, 154,
  166, 175, 178
Owl, Barred, 44, 66, 86, 151, 169;
  Great Horned, 44, 76; **Northern**
  Saw-whet, 17, 132, 139, 142, 167,
  170, 185; **Short-eared,** 41, 46, 68,
  185
Oystercatcher, American, 18, 23, 26,
  46, 50, 57, 183

P

parking, 6
Partners in Flight, 1, 129
Parula, Northern, 34, 44, 63, 66, 69,
  86, 102, 125
Pea Island National Wildlife Refuge,
  46–49
Pee Dee National Wildlife Refuge,
  103–6

Pelica
  181
Petrel,
  cap
  He
Phalar
Phoeb
Piedmc
Pine Fc
Pink B
Pintail
Pipit, ?
  107
Plover,
  Pip
  Ser
  23, ?
Pocosin
poisonc
Puffin,

R

Rail, B
  53, ?
  60; ?
Raven,
  135,
Razork
Redhea
Redsta
  100,
  170,
restaurar
Ritter P
  Hen
  84–?
Riverbe
  ory, ?
Roan M
Roanok

S

Salem L?
Sanderl
Sandpip
  184; ?

Dickcissel, 46, 191
Dovekie, 56
Dowitcher, Long-billed, 18, 25, 39,
  184; **Short-billed,** 18, 26, 46
Duck, American Black, 39, 48, 53, 66,
  125, 157; **Harlequin,** 18, 46, 179;
  Long-tailed, 18, 26, 27, 50, 179;
  Ring-necked, 39, 53, 69, 115, 157;
  Ruddy, 39, 157; **Wood,** 39, 44, 63,
  66, 96, 125, 134, 157
Duke Forest, 97–99
Dunlin, 39, 53, 60

E

Eagle, Bald, 18, 29, 32, 36, 41, 64, 68,
  79, 91, **92,** 103, 111, 116, 124, 182;
  Golden, 41, 127, 183
Early Successional habitat, 13–14, 17–18
Egret, Great, 28, 39, 48, 60, 69, 113;
  Reddish, 25, 182; **Snowy,** 18, 23,
  26, 36, 46, 50, 57, 155, 181–82
Elk Knob Game Land and State Natural
  Area and Amphibolite Mountains,
  127–31
Eno River State Park, 95–96
environments, 10–18
equipment, 4–5
ethics, birding, 7

F

Falcon, Peregrine, 26, 36, 46, 50, 57,
  135, 163, **164,** 167, 183
Falls Lake State Recreation Area, 91–94
Finch, Purple, 102
Flicker, Northern, 63
Flycatcher, Acadian, 17, 31, 44, 63, 66,
  69, 76, 86, 89, 96, 99, 102, 148, 151,
  178; **Alder,** 17, 124, 132, 139, 142,
  167, 186; **Great Crested,** 23, 32,
  57, 60, 61, 68, 74, 79, **80,** 97, 114,
  124, 152, 186; **Least,** 124, 127, 135,
  139, 152, 170, 186; **Olive-sided,**
  186; **Willow,** 18, 124, 139, 142, 186
Fort Fisher State Recreation Area, 26–28
Fraser Fir–Red Spruce Forest habitat,
  10–11, 17

Fulmar, Northern, 56

G

Gadwall, 39, 48, 53, 157
Gallinule, Purple, 18, 183
Gannet, Northern, 25, 53, 60
gear, 4–5
Gnatcatcher, Blue-gray, 69, 76, 86
Godwit, Hudsonian, 48; **Marbled,** 18,
  23, 26, 46, 57, 184
Goldeneye, Common, 157
Goldfinch, American, 63, 86
Goose, Ross's, 46, 179; **Snow,** 18, 36,
  37, 46, 50, 103, 105, 107, 179
Grebe, Eared, 113; **Horned,** 23, 46,
  50, 79, 91, 111, 112, 114, 155, 180,
  Pie-billed, 115, 157; **Red-necked,**
  46, 180
Greensboro Municipal Reservoirs,
  111–13
Green Swamp Preserve and Lake Wacca-
  maw State Park, 29–31
Greenville Area, 68–70
Grosbeak, Blue, 17, 23, 32, 36, 41, 61,
  74, 79, 95, **95,** 97, 100, 103, 107, 135,
  152, 190–91; **Rose-breasted,** 121,
  127, 135, 139, 145, 149, 152, 159,
  163, 167, 170, 174, 176, 190
Grouse, Ruffed, 17, 18, 116, 121, 127,
  135, 145, 149, 151, 152, 163, 167,
  170, 174, 180
Gulf Stream Pelagic Birding, 55–56
Gull, Bonaparte's, 83, 115; **Great**
  Black-backed, 48, 93; **Lesser**
  Black-backed, 18, 50, 184; **Little,**
  56

H

habitats, 10–18
Hardwood Forest habitat, 11–12, 17
Harrier, Northern, 44, 48, 60, 69
Hawk, Broad-winged, 17, 91, 95, 107,
  116, 127, 135, 139, 152, 163, 170,
  182, **Cooper's,** 44, 89, 130, 138, 173;
  Red-shouldered, 34, 44, 66, 162;
  Red-tailed, 34; **Rough-legged,** 41,

183; **Sharp-shinned,** 69, 89, 130, 138

Heintooga Spur Road and Nearby Parkway Locations, 170–73

Hemlock Bluffs Nature Preserve, Ritter Park, and Swift Creek Bluffs, 84–87

Heron, Great Blue, 34, 157; **Green,** 25, 34, 39, 69, 96, 113; **Little Blue,** 18, 23, 26, 46, 50, 57, 155, 182; **Tricolored,** 28, 48, 60

Howell Woods Environmental Learning Center, 71–73

Hummingbird, Ruby-throated, 39, 130

I

Ibis, Glossy, 18, 36, 46, 57, 182; **White,** 18, 23, 26, 32, 36, 46, 50, 57, 111, 155, 182

Important Bird Areas (IBAs), 109

insects, 6

J

Jackson Park, 159–62

Jaeger, Long-tailed, 55, 184; **Parasitic,** 56; **Pomarine,** 56

Jordan Lake State Recreation Area, 79–83

Joyce Kilmer Memorial Forest and Cherohala Skyway, 176–78

Julian Price and Moses Cone Memorial Parks, 132–34

Junco, Dark-eyed, 86, 122, 130, 141, 144, 148

K

Kestrel, American, 44

Kingbird, Eastern, 17, 23, 32, 36, 57, 61, 68, 79, 91, 100, 107, 114, 116, 152, 186; **Western,** 48

Kingfisher, Belted, 86, 157, 162

Kinglet, Golden, 44, 76; **Golden-crowned,** 86, 89, 134, 141, 144, 148, 166, 169, 178; **Ruby,** 86, 89; **Ruby-crowned,** 44, 76

Kite, Mississippi, 17, 29, 32, 64, **65,** 71,

182;

Kittiwa

Knot, F

L

Lakes of
155–

Lake Wa
Swar

Lane Pir
Crav

Lark, H

lightning

Linville
135–

lodging,

Loon, C
113,
50, 5

Lower L
Park,

M

maps, 4–

Marshlar

Martin,

Mason F
100–

Mattamu
36–3

Max Pato

Meadow

Merchan

Mergan:
Hooc
111,

breas
155

Merlin,

migration

Migration

Mixed C
12, 17

Moorhei

Moses Co
Parks,

184; **Semipalmated,** 39; **Soli** 69; **Spotted,** 69; **Western,** 39

Sapsucker, Yellow-bellied, 17, 76, 86, 89, 127, 132, 142, 149, 170, 171, 176, 185

Scaup, Greater, 18, 23, 91, 116, 155, 179; **Lesser,** 39, 115, 11

Scoter, Black, 25, 28, 53; **Surf,** 53, 60, 117; **White-winged,**

Screech-Owl, Barred, 63; **Eas** 34, 44, 63, 138; **Great Horr** 138

seasons, 3–4, 18

Shearwater, Audubon's, 55, 1 **Cory's,** 56; **Greater,** 56; **M** 180–81; **Sooty,** 55, 56

Shoveler, Northern, 39, 117,

Shrike, Loggerhead, 17, 68, 7 107, 116, 186

Siskin, Pine, 17, 74, 88, 116, 1 167, 170, 191

Skimmer, Black, 18, 23, 26, 4 185

Skua, Great, 56; **South Polai**

snakes, 6–7

Snipe, Wilson's, 39, 48, 63, 10

Sora, 48

Sparrow, Bachman's, 17, 29, 190; **Chipping,** 76; **Clay-** 110; **Field,** 63; **Fox,** 44, 76 **Grasshopper,** 17, 68, 103, 190; **Henslow's,** 17, 29, 68 **Lark,** 190; **Le Conte's,** 11 **Lincoln's,** 44, 125, 127, 13 **Nelson's Sharp-tailed,** 1 46, 190; **Saltmarsh Sharp** 18, 26, 46, 50, 190; **Savanr** 125; **Seaside,** 18, 26, 46, 5 **Swamp,** 44, 60; **Vesper,** 1 124, 127, **128,** 139, 159, 1 **crowned,** 125, 138; **Whit throated,** 76, 86

Stecoah Gap, 174–75

Stilt, Black-necked, 18, 46,

Stork, Wood, 23, 32, 182

Storm-Petrel, Band-rump

About the Editors

Marshall Brooks is a professor of education at North Carolina Wesleyan College. He conducts breeding bird surveys for the U.S. Geological Service, migration monitoring for the Gulf Coast Bird Observatory, participates in Cornell Laboratory of Ornithology's Feeder Watch Program, and is a licensed bander for the Institute for Bird Population's MAPS. He is Webmaster for North Carolina Partners in Flight and chair of their Outreach and Education Committee, which has received recognition at both the state and national levels.

Mark Johns has worked as the Partners in Flight Biologist for the North Carolina Wildlife Resources Commission since 1996. He has received awards for his work with North Carolina Partners in Flight from the North Carolina Wildlife Federation, the North Carolina Chapter of the Wildlife Society, the American Forest and Paper Association, and the National Partners in Flight Program. He is also the state coordinator for the Breeding Bird Survey. He holds degrees in wildlife and fisheries science and in zoology.

The Carolina Bird Club is the ornithological society of the Carolinas. The club was founded in 1937 and meets each spring, fall, and winter at different locations in the Carolinas. It offers monthly bonus field trips and publishes a quarterly ornithological journal, *The Chat,* and a bimonthly newsletter. More information is available at www.carolinabirdclub.org.

Coeditors Mark Johns and Marshall Brooks. PHOTO: KEVIN O'KANE

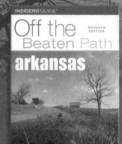

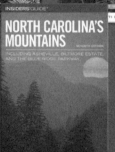